Fatal Prescription

A Doctor without Remorse

John Griffiths

hancock

house

ISBN 0-88839-369-5
Copyright © 1995 John Griffiths

Cataloging in Publication Data

Griffiths, John. 1944-
    Fatal prescription

    ISBN 0-88839-369-5

    1. Schlender, David--Trials, litigation,etc. 2.
    Charalambous, Josephakis--Trials, litigation, etc. 3.
    Trials (Murder)--British Columbia I. Title
    KE229.S34G74 1995   345.71'02523'09711
        C95-910746-0   KF224.S34G74 1995

Printed in the United States of America

Cover Design: Karen Whitman
Edited: Colin Lamont
Production: Myron Shutty, Nancy Kerr and Lorna Brown
Back Cover Center Photo: Peter Nielsen

Published simultaneously in Canada and the United States by

HANCOCK HOUSE PUBLISHERS LTD.
19313 Zero Avenue, Surrey, B.C. V4P 1M7
(604) 538-1114   Fax (604) 538-2262

HANCOCK HOUSE PUBLISHERS
1431 Harrison Avenue, Blaine, WA 98230-5005
1-800-948-1114   Fax (604) 538-2262

Contents

In Memory of Sian Simmonds

Prologue

The Fraser River springs to life pure and fresh below the glacial peaks of Mount Robson Provincial Park. Born on the British Columbia side of the Rocky Mountains, it flows falteringly for a short distance, before finding its direction and growing with youthful energy in its 850-mile southwesterly plunge to the sea. Joined by several tributaries during its turbulent journey to the Pacific Ocean, the young river squeezes through precipitous gorges and deep canyons in a frenzy of white water, its swirling rapids drowning the thunder of the Canadian transcontinental trains that snake their way impossibly atop the river's cliffs. Teeming with salmon, the Fraser courses as a lifeline through the barren sagebrush of semi-desert, slaking the thirsts of deer, bear and cougar, then rushes past once prosperous goldfields, finally escaping its mountain heritage as it approaches the mature rain forests of the southwest coast. The river is still innocent as it enters the Fraser Valley, meandering through the fertile farmlands of Langley, but before it can reach its estuary, the beautiful, pristine river has split into three arms to pass the heavily populated areas of the Lower Mainland, including Surrey, Coquitlam and Vancouver. And now it has become not only polluted—but muddy and murky indeed.

Preface

When I first met Shelley Charalambous and her three children at a secret, neutral destination in North America in early 1995, *Fatal Prescription* was ready to be published, and they were in hiding in the Royal Canadian Mounted Police witness protection program. Shelley had testified at her doctor husband's murder trial and was seeking a divorce from him on grounds that, among other things, he had abused her ever since seducing her as a fifteen-year-old patient. After years of terror in a loveless marriage, Shelley had begun to reestablish contact with her own family, from whom she had been cut off for almost ten years. Though still apparently struggling to overcome feelings of fear and guilt, she seemed to be an inherently decent and compassionate young woman, who was doing the best she could to pick up the pieces of her shattered life. I again extend my thanks to her, as well as to her sister Shawna MacKenzie, her ever faithful mother, Jacqueline Jongkind, and her stepfather Richard Jongkind, for their cooperation and candor in making this a better book than it otherwise would have been.

Truth is indeed stranger than fiction. No one could have imagined the events described in this story, and I'd like to thank the authorities and others for their generous cooperation and assistance in reconstructing certain of the unrecorded conversations and events as closely as possible to the way they actually happened. I especially thank the Simmonds family for their immeasurable kindness, which is an inspiration to all who meet them, and I express heartfelt condolences to them as they attempt to cope with the dreadful tragedy that has forever altered their lives.

This book would not have been possible without the assistance of the RCMP's General Investigation Section in Surrey, British Columbia, headed by Staff Sergeant Bob Briske. I express sincere thanks to him, as well as a huge debt of gratitude to Corporal Gary Straughan, the extremely capable file coordinator in this unusual and complex case.

Many other RCMP men and women took part in the investigation and all of them took the time to contribute their recollections with warmth and insight. Specifically, I'd like to thank in alphabetical order Gordon Black, Doug Comrie, Brian Fleming, John Gould, Nels Justason, Al Kautzman, Deanna Kohlsmith, Harry Pokorny, Wayne Rideout, Don Rinn, Tom Robertson, Bill Silvester and Mel Trekofski.

Integral to this story is the courage of a young woman named Angela Street, whose contribution deserves not only the thanks of the author but also that of the general public. For his thoughtful comments, I also extend thanks to Dave Sella, whose life was radically altered by the events described herein, and to Edna Neighbour and Sharon Frank. Thanks are also due to Dr. Tom Handley of the B.C. College of Physicians and Surgeons, who graciously agreed to be interviewed for this book despite the criticism faced by that organization.

And, last but not least, I would like to thank my own family, as well as friends including Brian Wensley, for their unwavering support throughout this project.

In this book, the names of some peripheral characters (denoted by an asterisk the first time their names appear) have been changed to protect their privacy.

Part One

Infamous Conduct

You do solemnly swear, each by whatever you hold most sacred, that you will be loyal to the Profession of Medicine and just and generous to its members....

Introduction, the Hippocratic Oath

1   Possessions

D r. Josephakis Charalambous put down the wine decanter, the flood-lit blue waters of his indoor swimming pool shimmering behind him through sliding glass doors off the living room as he prepared to entertain his guests. Prematurely gray in his early thirties, he was a short, swarthy man with thick glasses accentuating the darkness of his brown, almost black, startling eyes. He often wore a pouting expression on his somewhat thick, purplish lips, but he flashed a brief smile now as he filled the third glass with fruit juice.

Judging by the amount of time he was talking to her, he was more interested in his fifteen-year-old guest than her mother, but appeared proud that both his patients were impressed by the opulence of his home. With its pool and hot tub, the two-storey house was located on Foster Avenue in Coquitlam, a middle-class suburb a dozen miles east of Vancouver on Canada's mild southwest coast.

Seeing her family physician about to fill the third glass of wine, Jacqueline Jongkind had arched an eyebrow, but Charalambous had second-guessed her—and handed her daughter Shelley the soft drink instead. The tall, dignified cocktail waitress and her shapely teenage daughter had declined several previous invitations to come to the doctor's home, but this night of July 21, 1985, had brought an emergency. Jacqueline's second husband Richard Jongkind had been admitted to a nearby hospital, depressed over their marriage breakup.

Charalambous had departed the racetrack to meet all three of his patients at Royal Columbian Hospital in New Westminster. Telling them he didn't have privileges there, he had ascertained that Shelley's stepfather was in satisfactory condition, then proposed that Jacquie and Shelley follow him to the house to resume their discussions. "I'm hungry and tired," he explained, "and it's just a few blocks away."

He had got home before them, taking the cover off the pool and throwing on the underwater lights before letting them in. Charalambous confided to some that he'd always been afraid of water, but buying the house with the pool had forced him to learn how to swim. It had also enabled him to impress his karate students with parties at which he heated the entire pool to the temperature of the hot tub. Doing that cost a small fortune but his students were his fan club and, other than horseracing, karate was his passion. Besides, he never could stand being by himself. The doctor always had to have people around him.

Tonight, as usual, he was dressed in his trademark, casual open-necked shirt and slacks, his wavy gray hair a stylish collar length in back. At five-foot-four-and-a-half, he found most people taller than himself but, with his black belt in karate, he had the confidence of a much bigger man.

In high heels, Shelley Joel was a good head taller than him, but he seemed to enjoy her company regardless of their differences in height and age. Shelley had big brown eyes and her long shiny hair cascaded past strong shoulders and small breasts to slender waist, hips and legs of perfection. Her complexion was unblemished. She was no longer a virgin, the doctor knew, yet still a picture of sweet innocence.

Although he had privately denigrated women in the past, Charalambous thought Shelley Joel was pretty enough to be a model. Something about *his* appearance, however, made her secretly afraid of him. Perhaps it was the fact that his white eyelashes appeared sparse or non-existent, or maybe it was just that he looked so old.

Until recently, Shelley had imagined her doctor to be a kind, fatherly man but she had since learned that he was childless and had never been married. He had recently split up with his girlfriend. Shelley wasn't sure he was coming on to her. She didn't find him attractive, but she was flattered to be receiving all this attention from a professional man such as him.

It had all begun when Charalambous had delivered Jacqueline's fourth child in 1983, after he'd bought the existing medical practise of

Dr. John See-Ming Lam at 9808 King George Highway, across the Fraser River in Surrey.

Located southeast of Vancouver, Surrey traditionally had been an inexpensive bedroom suburb, but high real estate prices had brought changes. With a quarter million people from all parts of the world, it had become the second most populous municipality in the region. It was perceived to have a high crime rate, but in fact the per capita statistics proved it no worse than most other places.

Many of Dr. Lam's patients were saddened when their family physician moved to Vancouver to specialize in pediatrics, but his popular receptionist Edna Neighbour stayed on to help Charalambous with the transition. Up until then, Charalambous had been interning at Royal Columbian Hospital and doing locums. With help from his mother, he had been able to buy the already thriving practise and get a head start in the medical business.

Edna, an experienced receptionist, was a slender, middle-aged woman who looked people straight in the eye and practised what she preached. If Lam, a devout Christian, had known what Charalambous was really like, she reflected, he would never have sold him the practise. Changing employers, she reckoned, had been "like going from day to night" and soon she had felt badly that she had personally encouraged many of Lam's valued patients to stay on.

One of them, Chris Simmonds, possessed a black belt in judo and regarded Charalambous as a fellow martial artist. The doctor who had been treating the rest of his family had been about to retire, so Chris had been pleased to introduce his wife and children to the new practise. Katie Simmonds was a cute, bossy little girl, aged eleven, and Sian Simmonds was a chubby and gawky nine-year-old with glasses. "They were both very nice little girls," said Edna. "Always very polite even when they came in without their parents."

The practise was located on the second floor of the King George Professional Building, a brown, stucco building two blocks north of Surrey Memorial Hospital. Despite its open courtyard, some people found it a foreboding structure, but the pharmacy on the ground floor had always been a good drawing card and the highway exposure didn't hurt business either. As well as doctors' offices, the building also was home to several dentists, physiotherapists and lawyers.

Edna showed Charalambous his new facilities. There was a large waiting room with a reception area containing a desk and files. Behind this was a small coffee room and the doctor's own private office. On one side of the hall was a storage cupboard containing old inactive files, pharmaceutical samples, sterilization equipment and a fridge with allergy serums. There were three examining rooms.

Charalambous had his big, red cherrywood desk delivered and placed on it his telephone, a blotter and some plastic mail trays. The desk had been a graduation gift from his family. He brought in some inexpensive shelves for his medical books. Then he adorned his office with a jade plant that seldom needed watering. Beige drapes covered the wall to wall window. Later, he would put up a picture of his racehorses.

Edna's relationship with her new boss had become strained almost from the start. Charalambous had wanted his receptionist to serve coffee to him, rather than just make it as she'd done for Dr. Lam. He also thought she was getting too much money and quibbled about the extra week of paid vacation that she had been receiving from her previous employer.

"You haven't been working here long enough," Charalambous told her. "I've been talking to my accountant and he thinks you're overpaid."

"Well, if you think I'm such an inadequate staff member," Edna had fired back, "you can just find yourself somebody else."

The next day she had refused to come to work, and Charalambous phoned her at home. "There's no need for this," he said. "Some of the patients are asking about you. I want you to come back but I don't want to be blackmailed into giving you a raise."

"There are a few things you need to get straight," Edna retorted. "I don't blackmail and I am not going to serve you coffee. I put the coffee on in the morning. If you want a cup, help yourself."

After agreeing to Edna's terms, including the three weeks' vacation, Charalambous embarked on improving the relationship with his employees. During secretaries' week, he took Edna and a part-time receptionist to the nearby Ding Ho restaurant for a Chinese lunch.

Edna knew it was important for her boss to have good help. A medical practise had to be managed properly and the appointment diary had to be kept full. Medicine was big business. Cancelled appointments had to be replaced. Charalambous kept his eyes clearly focussed on the appointment book. Regardless of any other shortcomings, he *was* a hard worker. He had sacrificed much of his youth learning about medicine and now, after years of study, he was finally about to reap the rewards.

In just two years in medical practise, he'd bought the house in Coquitlam. "It was the builder's own home," he told people proudly. "I paid it off in one year."

Although he was very much into physical fitness, Edna observed that Charalambous did have one nagging medical problem—he suffered from allergies. If he were upset or angry, his sniffling would be quite noticeable.

Edna also noticed that Charalambous had some other strange quirks. Often, he would stay up nights and invite karate students to his house for what he would describe as "an evening of fun." He didn't smoke and, as far as Edna knew, he didn't use drugs either. "That," she said, "would have been like taking contaminants into his body."

Charalambous had laughed, in fact, that one of his parties had been raided by the police. "Certain substances found in the house were seized," Edna recalled. "He thought it hilarious that laboratory analysis of the 'drugs' proved they were nothing more than antacids." The receptionist could see that Charalambous disliked authority, but she didn't realize he hated the police with a passion. The doctor said he'd had some bad experiences with the police, but he didn't elaborate.

Edna also discovered that the doctor was an extremely heavy gambler. He loved horseracing—it was the sport of kings—but he also splurged on poker and other forms of gambling. Often, when the lottery was over $2 million, he'd buy as many as $2,000 worth of tickets. Arriving one day at his medical practise after a night of particularly heavy casino losses—reportedly in the vicinity of $6,000—the doctor looked to his associate as though he had been "dragged through a knot hole."

Upon divorcing her first husband Doug Joel after a ten-year marriage, Jacqueline Jongkind had received custody of their daughters Shelley and Shawna, and subsequently had two more children, both boys, by her marriage to the tall, young sales manager Richard Jongkind.

Richard had seen Dr. Charalambous for sports injuries, but also sought marriage advice because Jacqueline felt he was spending too much time drinking with his football friends. Later, however, Rick Jongkind was shocked by the doctor's private attitude when he chanced upon Charalambous ogling the dancers at a local strip bar. "Women are nothing but shit," he recalled the doctor telling him, "to be used and thrown away."

In any event, the doctor's marriage counseling attempts failed and Jacqueline and her husband split up on two separate occasions. Feeling depressed, Richard made an appointment to see Charalambous but found the doctor was only interested in talking about Shelley.

Each time he tried to discuss his own problems, Richard was thwarted as the doctor continually changed the subject to that of his stepdaughter. "I felt then that he was obsessed with her," Richard said. "I was also mad that he ignored my medical problem. That was the last time I saw him as a patient."

While she and her husband were separated, Jacqueline went back to work as a waitress at a neighborhood pub. During this time, Shelley willingly looked after her younger brothers, but resented being cast back to the role of a child when her mother and stepfather became reunited between separations.

Shelley had always been a model child, but their arguments became so frequent that Jacqueline knew something far more serious was troubling her. Finally, in late 1984, Shelley confided to her mother that two years before, when she was only twelve, she had been raped by a male boarder.

Dr. Charalambous, learning of this from Jacquie, agreed that Shelley should get counseling but seemed affronted by Jacquie's suggestion that her daughter should see a specialist. "I'm perfectly able to do that," he told her. "She can come and talk to me."

Charalambous raised the matter during Shelley's next visit to his office, but the girl adamantly refused to talk about it. Undaunted, the doctor invited her to his house to serve food and drinks at a party for his karate students. "It would be good for you to get out and meet some new people," he suggested.

Shelley told the doctor she had to work that night at a restaurant busing tables, and declined the invitation even when he offered to pick her up and reimburse her for lost wages. Later, however, she was surprised one evening when the doctor just happened to drop by her place of work for a pizza.

Although she shunned the attention, Shelley was required to see Charalambous again when her mother caught her in her bedroom with a boyfriend and insisted she get a prescription for birth control. Finding out shortly afterwards that Shelley and her boyfriend had split up, the

15

doctor began inviting her out for coffee and lunch. "Mom," asked a confused Shelley, "why does he keep calling me?"

Charalambous had assured Jacqueline that his interest in her daughter was purely professional. "He probably just wants to steer you into a more fitness-oriented group of friends," Jacqueline replied.

But Jacqueline began to have doubts when Charalambous started phoning almost daily, asking about Shelley and inviting Jacqueline to his home to discuss the family's problems over a drink and a barbecued steak. No sooner had she declined the invitation, it seemed, when he phoned back inviting both her and Shelley to join him for dinner at the racetrack.

"Why are you so interested in my daughter?" Jacqueline demanded.

"Does that bother you?" asked the doctor.

"Yes," said Jacqueline. "It does. For one thing, you are her doctor. You're in your thirties and she's only fifteen. She's far too young to be seeing a person of your age. You've got nothing in common."

"I'm not that much older than her," argued Charalambous. "Where I come from, girls get married younger than that. By the time they're Shelley's age, they've already got kids."

"This is Canada!" fumed Jacquie. "The culture here is very different."

Jacqueline had been annoyed that, while she was at work, the doctor had continued to phone Shelley, but tonight all three of them, at last, had got together at his home after Richard had ended up in the hospital. "Thanks for the wine," Jacqueline said, finally beckoning her daughter. "It's time we were going. It's getting late."

Following them outside, Charalambous showed Jacquie and Shelley his two Nissan ZX sports cars in the driveway, insisting that Shelley sit in the driver's seat of the Special Edition to observe the stereo controls on the wheel.

"It's like the cockpit of a plane!" exclaimed the girl, awed by the switches and dashlights. "I can't wait until I'm sixteen so I can get my driver's license."

"You should start coming for rides with me so I can teach you how to drive," Charalambous beamed.

As Jacqueline drove home with her daughter, she felt there was a good chance that she and her husband would get back together once he was discharged from the hospital. Jacqueline had far deeper doubts, however, about the interest that Charalambous was showing in her daughter. "It's getting very uncomfortable," she told Shelley. "He seems to be enamored with you. We're going to have to get a new doctor."

2 Chip off the Old Block

If Jacqueline Jongkind had known more about the doctor's background, she presumably would have found it ludicrous that he'd cited
Hellenic marriage customs as justification for his attraction to her
daughter. For although he *was* born of Greek heritage in Cyprus—fa-
bled Mediterranean birthplace of the love goddess Aphrodite—Dr.
Charalambous had lived in Canada all of his adult life.

And his own villager mother Petrou didn't tie the knot until she was
almost twenty-two, marrying Eleodoros Charalambous twelve days before Christmas, 1949, in a Church of Cyprus ceremony in the ancient
seaport of Famagusta.

Born there on April 5, 1952, Josephakis was their second child—
after older sister Susan—but as the first grandson in the Greek Cypriot
family he was the object of great expectations. Raised in a home with
no fridge and dirt floors, he was occasionally spoiled by his Uncle
Joseph as his parents worked hard to save money to emigrate.

Joe loved his diminutive, dark-haired mother, who had come from
the village of Avgorou, but his father, a self-taught watchmaker from
the seaside resort of Varosha, was a selfish and domineering man whom
he feared and despised.

The Cyprus in which Josephakis grew up was a dangerous place,
littered with violence and hostility as rival factions fought to replace the
British administration. Joe, however, was proud of his heritage. Having
learned of venerable Greek icons such as the medical man Hippocrates,

he wandered alone for hours at a time amid the citrus fruit bazaars, thinking one day he'd rise above the crowd to become a doctor himself.

After Charalambos Charalambous, the youngest child, was born five years later, Eleodoros moved to Canada to establish his watch repair business before sending for his family. Though a girlfriend tried to persuade him to leave them behind, Petrou and the children ultimately joined him in 1960, just as the exiled Archbishop Makarios was returning to Nicosia to proclaim Cypriot independence.

Joe was eight years old. He remembered leaving a beautiful, hot land where it seldom rained, but the timing seemed to have been propitious. In 1974, when Makarios was overthrown by Greek unionists, the Turkish army invaded the northern third of the island, driving Greek inhabitants from their homes and turning Famagusta and other communities into virtual ghost towns.

Eleodoros and his family were now living safely in Canada, but the bitterness they'd left behind on the divided island was never far below the surface. In the young family, by Joe's own admission, he was brought up amid a "lot of emotional loose talk" about threats, violence and killing.

The family settled on Francis Street in north Burnaby, a nondescript, middle-class, urban neighborhood on the edge of Vancouver. It was much more stable than their homeland—but some of Joe's young contemporaries were known to break the peace, and one of them was involved in a wild jailbreak and shootout with the police while Joe was still in school.

The Charalambouses remained a traditional, patriarchal family, but daughter Susan aspired to be an actress and eventually escaped their clutches to enrol in theater classes in Los Angeles. The youngest child, nicknamed Harry, grew up to be much bigger than his brother, but Joe always was considerably more dynamic than either of his siblings and teased them mercilessly, especially about their relationships with friends of the opposite sex.

Even when they were kids, according to their friends, Joe was always very motivated. Fingers constantly drumming, he would apply himself to his studies, then pick beans after school to earn money. Friends also noticed he always had to be in control. When his brother Harry received a set of toy soldiers, Joe had to get a bigger set of his own. Members of the family enjoyed playing board games, but Joe always had to win and dictate what they'd do next.

Frequently, neighbors heard yelling and screaming coming from the house, and Joe watched at various times as his father abused his brother and sister, once flushing one of their heads in the toilet bowl. Generally, Joe thought the abuse was directed at them, seldom him, but he did recall his father once humiliating him in front of one of his girlfriends.

Eleodoros and Petrou Charalambous never did lose their strong dialect, but they did become somewhat more North American by informally changing their names from Eleodoros and Petrou to Elliot and Betty. Soon, though, Eleodoros seemed to experiment with as many names as there were Greek islands. Apart from his given name, he was sometimes known as Harry, Elliot or Andreas.

Charalambous senior cut a confident figure in a suit and tie, but it was becoming increasingly apparent that he was more interested in his freedom than in his responsibilities to his family. Despite his dark, receding hairline, he was a handsome, clean-shaven man with well-proportioned features—but his smile barely concealed his underlying arrogance.

Often he would disappear for days at a time, returning only when he needed more money to fuel his indulgences. Without reference to his family, he'd eat all the food in the fridge before heading out once more on yet another binge of drinking, womanizing and gambling.

Although disrespectful of his father, Josephakis emulated his outward self-confidence. Like Eleodoros, he also appreciated a fine watch movement and he, too, remembered with fondness the ancient ruins, citrus groves and azure waters of his arid Cypriot homeland. He longed to go back some day, if only for a holiday.

Joe was considered suave by his contemporaries, especially girls, many of whom found him energetic and charming. To the amazement of local boys, he always seemed to win out over them by getting dates with the best looking girls in the neighborhood.

"Blondes were always his thing," said a childhood acquaintance. "He ended up with the best looking blonde in Alpha Secondary School. I remember he threatened some girl's family because she broke off with him," the acquaintance added. "He never could handle rejection."

The childhood acquaintance remembered that the doctor's mother and sister would do almost anything for him, but that many neighborhood boys didn't like Charalambous and avoided him. "He thought he was superior," the acquaintance said. "He had a mean, angry side.

Strange as it seems, even then he thought becoming a doctor would get him the most desirable women." This was borne out in comments beside his graduation photo in the 1971 Alpha Secondary School yearbook. "The Greek is interested in skiing, motorcycles, and most of all, girls," said the caption. "Joe will go to UBC to take up medicine."

Charalambous had wanted to be a doctor for as long as he could remember. It would enable him to escape, said acquaintances, from what he perceived to be an unbefitting, peasant background. When one of his professors called him "boy," he was furious. He had long felt his tastes were more those of the Renaissance, and he wanted to be accepted. He admitted that he resented his parents for not giving him music lessons, saying he would liked to have played the guitar.

But although he wrote poetry and was fascinated by ancient mythology, his artistic tastes leaned more toward the mundane. He appreciated some classical music but more often listened to fifties' rock. His favorite movies were action and martial arts.

Joe had begun to study karate before he left school. He spoke softly with the intonations of a Chicago gangster and was about to turn the tables on everyone who'd bullied him in the past. Now that he was accomplished in martial arts, he and sister Susan finally stood up to Eleodoros Charalambous, and banished their father from his own house.

Thereafter, Eleodoros existed pathetically alone, living and sleeping in the back of his ramshackle watchmaker's shop on West Broadway. Although Susan and Joe no longer needed his support, he was supposed to pay $75 a month for Harry, then fourteen years old. The payments, however, were irregular, and continued to be sporadic, especially later when they were increased to $100 per month.

Eleodoros was a broken man. To make ends meet, Joe's mother worked as a seamstress, mending garments at her home, and later working as a housekeeper at the International Plaza Hotel in North Vancouver. She could scarcely wait to end all ties with her abusive husband and filed for divorce in 1974, on grounds that they had been living apart for more than three years.

Her husband's address was now at a cheap, rooming house hotel—the Invermay—on Vancouver's skid row. Prior to the separation, she claimed, her husband's conduct had been such as to completely destroy the marital relationship, and there were no effective efforts that could be made towards reconciliation.

After the *decree nisi* was signed in April 1975, Betty Charalambous continued devoting herself to the rest of her family. Joe was her favorite son and he helped supplement the family income by working as a bus boy at the Blue Boy Hotel on the southern fringes of Vancouver.

Now that he was *de facto* head of the family, his diminutive mother decided to do whatever was necessary to help Joe with his career aspirations—even if it meant mortgaging the house. "My son Joseph the doctor," Mrs. Charalambous would say later with pride. Other people, though, saw the similarities to Eleodoros.

In addition to his drinking, Eleodoros was a chain smoker, and he finally ended up with respiratory problems in Vancouver General Hospital, where he died a frail, lonely man, far from his homeland, leaving little behind other than bitter memories and a collection of pocket watches.

Though he proclaimed no respect for Eleodoros, Joe was annoyed that Susan and Harry had scattered his father's ashes without consulting him. There was also nothing worse, he said, than seeing a once proud man end up a pauper.

Joe was a chip off the old block, but he avoided his father's addictions to liquor and cigarettes. He drank only moderately and shunned drugs—drinking gallons of Coke. He was, however, compulsive about work and play, love and money. "He shut himself away for hours on end," said one of his acquaintances. "He was a regular bookworm."

Joe's interest in karate had been more than a passing fad, and now he got his brother Harry interested, too. Charalambous was fascinated by the thousand-year-old Oriental martial art, learning its special breathing techniques, and how to deliver potentially lethal blows with speed, timing and surprise. If he toughened his hands by driving them repeatedly into containers of sand, he could break boards or bricks with his bare hands and he could visualize driving his hand right through somebody's head.

Soon, Charalambous began teaching karate. Showing students the most vulnerable parts of the body—face, neck, solar plexus, spine, groin and kidneys—may have seemed a strange pursuit for a medical student, but karate's emphasis was after all on self-defense.

About this time, a young friend named Mario Como was killed in a car crash on the winding Barnet Highway after offering to stand in for one of Joe's karate classes. Students comforting an apparently distraught karate instructor found his response typically fatalistic. "He was such a decent guy," Joe speculated. "It should have been me."

Female students from that era said Charalambous had a lot of charisma but most women found him "very dominating and controlling."

For someone aspiring to be a doctor, they added, he was also surprisingly down to earth in his choice of associates. Rather than a fellow medical student, his best friend was a burly motorcyclist named Brian Gerald West, whom he'd met through karate. According to Charalambous, West was "solid" and the friendship was such that either of them would always come through if the other were in need.

He had met West while teaching karate at Madison and Hastings Street in Burnaby in 1972, when West had come in to watch one of his twice weekly classes. "When he first came in he looked intimidating," Charalambous admitted. "He looked like a biker type guy but I approached him anyway.

"I didn't think he would join but he did. He said that he had been in jail—I think he got out in 1970—I don't know how many years but it was the result of an assault in his teens, I think."

Of twenty-five or thirty students, Charalambous recalled, West became one of the half-dozen regulars attending two or three times a week over the next two years.

"In the karate situation he was definitely not a violent man," Charalambous maintained. "I sparred with him on many occasions. Most of the students were younger and lighter and not as proficient as he was, and he seemed to pull his punches when he was sparring with them."

Charalambous described his own karate accomplishments in a one-page article about the history of Butokukan karate in Canada: "*Sensei* Joe Charalambous began his study of Butokukan karate in 1969," said the article. "While some of his fellow students broke away to study other methods, Charalambous traveled to Bellingham once or twice a week, receiving his black belt in 1974. His brother followed suit in 1977, while *Sensei* Joe, head instructor in Canada, opened a *dojo* in Coquitlam and later two more, in Port Coquitlam and Maple Ridge."

Some exponents of the art denigrated his skills, however, saying Charalambous was awarded his black belt for no reason other than the fact that the head honcho of his Butokukan school, Bob Hill from Bremerton, Washington, needed a disciple in Greater Vancouver. "Up to that point," said one of his students, "he was just a mediocre brown belt."

Another of his female students was even less complimentary. "He couldn't fight his way out of a wet paper bag," she taunted.

Charalambous operated one of his first karate schools in the basement of the Willingdon Heights United Church in Burnaby. "He was usually late paying his rent," church treasurer Stan Bailey recalled. "We always had to go after him for that."

Although his far-sightedness meant Charalambous had to wear his thick glasses even in the gym, he went on to become a fifth degree black belt and his black *gi* set him apart from the white tunics of his students.

Many of the students were young women and typically it was the more attractive ones who were interested in learning self defense. As the *sensei*, the dark-haired young man with the mustache was owed a high degree of respect; and some of the students remember how he relished power, not only over his young female students but over some of their mothers, too. If they found him attractive, that was fine, but they were expendable. Charalambous and his career came first.

Regardless, in his capacity as a martial arts instructor, Joe Charalambous was respected as a role model and a leader; and the karate schools were quite profitable. "He mostly held the classes in public locations, such as school gymnasiums, to keep down expenses," said a former associate.

At the University of B.C., many of the medical students thought Charalambous was arrogant—but he was equally critical of them and resented a lot of them too. Feeling they were prejudiced against his ethnic background, he preferred to devote his spare time to karate.

Karate judge Jon Funk remembered first meeting him in 1977, when Charalambous put on a tournament in the War Memorial Gym at the university. "He put on some big, well-attended tournaments," said Funk. "He seemed a reasonable sort of guy at first but he started to change when he became a physician.

"He kind of grew into being self-centered and pretentious. He'd say he had a $20,000 week. It struck me as odd—being in a helping profession thinking about people's lives in terms of dollar bills."

Funk made no secret he was angry that Charalambous once went behind his back in an effort to date his ex-wife. "In 1981 or 1982 I was separating from my first wife, Christine. Joe found out about it from me.

He phoned her up and asked her out. She and I both thought it was a pretty scummy thing to do."

Funk related how Charalambous once got permission from a rival Tae Kwan Do academy to sign up some students for a small karate tournament. "He used the information he got to ask one of the young teenage students out for a date," Funk recalled. "The owner of the academy was quite incensed that he used personal information to target this young girl."

Although Funk didn't know it at the time, Charalambous had already had several altercations with the law. On June 30, 1978, the young medical student was placed on probation for one year after being convicted in Vancouver of common assault. Court heard that he had punched a woman in the face at her house on Prince Albert Street on December 12, 1977. He had met and had a drink with her two weeks earlier, and the woman had resisted his efforts to see her again. She received facial injuries.

Charalambous was still on probation on January 28, 1979, when the Vancouver police were called at one o'clock in the morning to an apartment he was renting on West Tenth Avenue. When two men had attempted to take his TV—in payment for a hooker he'd allegedly shortchanged—Charalambous had run into his bedroom, firing a warning shot. A second shot from the .22-caliber rifle had struck one of the men in the hand.

Upon learning of the incident, shocked medical students urged the dean of medicine to expel him. They were told nothing could be done, however, because it was self-defense and no charges had been laid. "We felt he was not a suitable candidate to be a physician," one of the students said later. "It's amazing that the medical school didn't expel him."

And that was not all. On August 17, 1979, a Vancouver police officer was driving his marked car at 2:30 A.M. when a prostitute stepped off the sidewalk to flag him down. The distraught woman said she'd been performing fellatio in a male customer's car when the man had suddenly turned on her, hitting her in the head and pulling her hair. She gave the policeman the car's license number. The officer checked it out. The car was registered to Joseph Charalambous.

But nothing further was done about the complaint and Charalambous graduated from the University of British Columbia in 1981, subsequently interning at Royal Columbian Hospital in New Westminster, where he bragged that he slept with a different nurse every night of the week. After his name was entered in the medical register on July 7, 1982, he was ready to prove something he'd always suspected, and to capitalize on at least one of the reasons he'd gone into medicine.

"Everybody wants to screw a doctor," Charalambous said.

3   Sian Simmonds

Other than the fact that Sian Simmonds had strikingly blonde hair, she and Shelley Joel shared at least three similarities. Both were born in New Westminster, historic first capital of British Columbia, both grew up, tall, south of the Fraser River in the same municipality of Surrey—and both eventually would become patients of considerably more than passing interest to Dr. Josephakis Charalambous.

Although Shelley went to school with one of Sian's cousins, she didn't know Sian Simmonds until she met her much later through the Charalambous medical practise. By then, the Jongkind family had moved to Coquitlam, while the Simmonds sisters had moved with their parents to the pastoral suburb of Langley.

Three years older than Sian, Shelley was born at New Westminster's Royal Columbian Hospital on January 29, 1970, at a time when karate student Charalambous had just one more year of high school before going to the University of British Columbia to learn about medicine.

But while Sian Simmonds never had more than typical childhood ailments, Shelley often had to go back to hospital with recurring bouts of asthma, and was stricken with insecurity on account of the frequent separations from her family.

When it came to dealing with other children, Shelley was extremely protective of her little sister Shawna, but was so painfully shy that she could scarcely look adults in the eye. She imagined she could always

27

count on the presence of her father, Doug Joel, a supervisor with the British Columbia Telephone Company, but her parents had married very young and were finding they had little in common. When she was six years old, Shelley begged her dad to stay. "I bet you all the money I've got in my piggy bank that you'll never leave," she implored.

Shelley and Shawna were devastated when their parents did split up, praying for a reconciliation but finally giving up when Doug and Jacqueline Joel followed through with their divorce in 1980.

Although they continued to see their father, both girls remained with their mother, who was married again in 1982 to Richard Jongkind. Soon, the girls got to play with two new half brothers whom they adored, and a third son was born later.

Unlike the Joel sisters, Sian and Katie Simmonds never experienced parental breakup—but tragedy struck often in the Simmonds family, both before and soon after Sian's birth.

Sian Simmonds had a happy childhood, protected by loving parents and her older sister Katie. As teenagers in Langley's Willoughby Hill area, the girls were as close as two sisters could be, and Sian's future seemed full of promise.

Katie Simmonds was eighteen months older than her sister, and remembered other kids teasing Sian at elementary school because she wore glasses and was a bit chubby. "Every lunch, she looked for me to play with because some of the other children didn't want to play with her," Katie recalled. "Mom and Dad told us that we would always have one another, so it never mattered to us.

"When Sian went to high school, she seemed to change overnight, no glasses and no more teasing. She was a beauty, tall, blonde, blue-eyed...the envy of every girl in the school. We were known to all of our friends as the Simmonds sisters. We were proud of the fact we were such good friends.

"I always loved Sian so much."

Sian's parents, Chris Simmonds and his wife Susan, were born in southwest England, in the picturesque Gloucestershire district known as the Forest of Dean. Bordering on South Wales to the west, and the River Severn to the east, the forest had been noted since antiquity for its abundance of conifers, hardwoods, and mineral resources.

By tradition, people born in the forest were granted free mineral rights, and some of them did take advantage of the abundant coal deposits that were to be found throughout the district. Some other traditions, too, had remained unchanged through the centuries. In their broad west country dialect, a good number of the inhabitants still addressed each other with old English pronouns such as "thee" and "thou." Few among the populace were rich, but there was stability and the roots grew deep.

Chris Simmonds was the eldest of five children, born forty-six years ago in his grandmother's house in the picturesque village of Nailbridge, a hamlet so small it didn't even have a pub. Nearby, however, was the Royal Forest Church, where his mother taught Sunday school. Next in the family was his brother Dave, who represented England as a middleweight boxer in the 1970 Commonwealth Games. The youngest were Brian, Gillian and John.

The children were devastated one night in 1960 to learn that their father, Percy Simmonds, a merchant seaman and former physical training instructor, had been killed in a fiery gas barge explosion on the Bristol Channel. After searching through fog to save his unconscious skipper from the inferno, Percy drowned in the fast flowing currents. He was thirty-four years old and the family had been in the midst of moving from their country cottage to a new house in Gloucester. Chris was only thirteen and remembered the sadness. "Dad never did get to move into that house with us," he recalled, adding his mother had to run a tight ship after that to raise five children on a widow's pension.

But the city was abuzz with commerce and, after leaving school, Chris became an apprentice fitter/turner, assembling parts for industrial machinery. Through a schoolmate when Chris was fifteen, he had already met Susan Davis, a petite girl one year younger, with long hair, a proud posture, and a mischievous smile.

Living on the outskirts of town, they went for walks together in the park. "Would you like to watch the cricket match?" Chris asked one day, as cumulus clouds gave way to midsummer sunshine. "Sure," Sue replied. She wasn't crazy about the English summer sport, but Chris was an endearing young man and she welcomed the opportunity to enjoy the fresh breezes that blew in from the Bristol Channel on a lazy, idyllic afternoon.

Chris was twenty when they got married, Sue was still nineteen. For Sue, her new companion was her first really serious boyfriend. Born at the hospital in Cinderford, she was the second youngest of seven girls. Her four oldest sisters—Barbara, Shirley, Rita and Pat—were born in

London, but the family had been evacuated to the remote Gloucestershire forest to escape the wartime blitz. Then came Carol, Sue—and Sian, the youngest sister and baby of the family.

"We lived in an old cottage with stone walls three-feet thick," Sue recalled. "It had belonged to my Dad's family for well over a hundred years. I shared a bedroom with three of my sisters." After leaving the two-room village school, Sue went to work in a shirt factory in Gloucester. The future seemed bright but tragedy was about to strike her side of the family too.

Chris and Susan Simmonds were married in November, 1966, at the village church in Matson, on the outskirts of Gloucester. After paying for their own wedding, they had little cash left for a honeymoon, but managed to save enough during the following year to make the down payment on a new house.

When the British pound was suddenly devalued, the young couple abandoned their plans, deciding instead to emigrate. Sue's sister Pat was already living in Melbourne, Australia, and within a couple of weeks, her sister Rita would be leaving for Perth. But Chris had thought about Canada since school days, especially British Columbia, and at the eleventh hour the couple decided on their new destination.

In October, 1968, they sold their furniture and flew to Vancouver. Chris Simmonds went looking for a job but most of the employers weren't hiring and others felt he was too young to have the necessary experience.

Dressed in a three-piece suit with his umbrella and briefcase, Simmonds persisted. Finally, Frank Knudson at Local 712 of the Iron Workers' Union saw that the young man had good qualifications and lots of determination, and lined him up with a job. "The only thing you're missing," Knudson chuckled, "is a bowler hat."

Outside working hours, Chris Simmonds was keenly interested in martial arts, and by the time he arrived from England, he already had his black belt in judo. Having now found work, one of the first things he did in the growing metropolis of Vancouver was to look for a judo club. "Any sport at that level gives you a high degree of self-discipline," he said. "Judo was all I thought about. It was my life."

Joining a club in New Westminster, he went on to represent British Columbia as a middleweight contender in the national championships, but his interest in judo was almost brought to a sudden end by a serious accident at work. That first Christmas in Canada, Chris had been laid off but had found a new job as a maintenance mechanic with the Dominion Bridge Company. He hadn't been working there long when a hoist fell from the roof, breaking his right arm and crushing several fingers in both hands.

After three months of therapy, he rejoined the provincial judo team. Then he trained with weights until he felt he was stronger than he had been before the accident. Though his fingers never did heal completely straight, the only person to beat him after that was Canadian champion Hank Mukai.

The young couple had arrived in Canada with three suitcases and less than $1,500 but things were about to improve. In 1971, the couple bought their first house. It was a modest but brand new two-storey home on Peterson Hill in Surrey. "I wouldn't want to live there now," Chris recalled. "SkyTrain runs right by it." But the house was fine at the time and in June of 1971, Katie was born in Saint Mary's Hospital, New Westminster.

It was the beginning of a happy family life. For the next two years, Chris worked as a millwright with the Weiser lock company in Burnaby. "At that time, I was quite a good letter writer," he recalled. "I wrote to everybody back home expounding on the virtues of Canada and in particular, of British Columbia."

Chris' brother Dave was the first of many relatives to follow in his footsteps. Dave brought his boxing skills with him and won a provincial Golden Gloves award. Eventually, Chris's sister and both his other brothers also emigrated to Canada, but Dave later surprised everyone by announcing he was returning to England. Back home, Dave went into the taxi business in Gloucester, but soon Chris and Sue were also joined in Canada by Sue's sister Carol, mother Kate and youngest sister, Sian.

Expecting their second baby just after Christmas, 1972, Chris and Sue were on their way to pay yuletide greetings to relatives. Sian Davis was in the car with them, still a newcomer to Canada with an English accent as broad as the wide open countryside. She was just four weeks short of her sixteenth birthday.

"Guess what Sian," Chris Simmonds told his wife's sister, "if the baby's born on your birthday, we'll name her after you."

Sian Davis was a beautiful girl and was delighted by the gesture. But it seemed unlikely. The baby was due well before her birthday. Sue had decided to return to St. Mary's Hospital for her second child. When the baby did arrive, it was another girl, pink, healthy, a pound heavier than Katie had been—and two weeks late arriving. It was January 28, 1973, her aunt's sixteenth birthday.

As promised, Chris and Sue named their new baby Sian. It was a pretty Welsh name reflecting part of her heritage. It turned out to be an ominous choice. Less than two months later, the new baby's Aunt Sian was killed in a car crash.

Mourned desperately by her friends and family, Sian Davis had been in her boyfriend's vehicle near the 200 Street Langley exit on the Trans-Canada Highway. It was never clear exactly what happened. No charges were laid but it was suspected that a truck had forced their car off the road. Sian Davis and her boyfriend were thrown clear. Her boyfriend escaped but Sian died when the car ran over her head.

It was doubtful that the new baby could sense the full extent of the sadness in her mother's heart. Sue was a devoted mother. Like Katie, Sian was a good baby and soon was sleeping through the night without any fuss.

On Sian's first birthday, her Dad started a new job at Canada Safeway, where he remained working as the children grew up. In 1977, the family bought an idyllic, partially treed property in the rural Willoughby Hill area of Langley. The five-acre property was conveniently close to the Trans-Canada Highway, but far enough south of the busy freeway so as not to be disturbed by the traffic.

Three years later, Chris and Sue moved with the girls into a trailer on the property while they built a luxurious split-level home with three bedrooms, a den as well as the family room and two fireplaces. Tragedy seemed far behind.

When he and Sue first came to Canada, Chris didn't even own a car, and after footslogging for a job it was not only his enthusiasm that had been dampened. For his first day at work, Chris had borrowed a bicycle and pedalled to work in the westcoast rain. The bike had a flat tire, so the next day he got a ride with some friends, only to get wet again as the car dropped him off and splashed through a puddle.

The family had lived modestly for several years but, finally, with a new house and acreage, they were realizing the rewards of their hard work. Despite working full time in government liquor stores, Sue remained meticulous as a homemaker and always kept the house gleaming.

After selling half the land, Chris and Sue bought a recreational property on Saltspring Island, landscaped the rest of the grounds surrounding their Langley home, and spent many happy hours with their children in the well-manicured garden.

Sue made all the dresses for the children. "The first time Chris went hunting," she recalled, "I knitted them special outfits that had orange and white hats with pigtails.

"I always made hats to go with all their outfits," she smiled.

Describing costumes she'd made for Halloween, she remembered Sian as a rabbit and Katie as *Alice in Wonderland.* "They didn't win a prize," Sue recalled. "The teacher said they'd rented them."

Neither of the sisters got too many treats during the year but Katie remembers Christmas stockings four- to five-feet long. "We always got what we wanted but we had to wait till then," Katie recalled. "One Christmas, I remember writing to Santa wanting a doll with blonde hair like Sian's, and she wanted a doll with brown hair like mine. But I got the one with brown hair so we traded.

"We were in school plays and Brownies together. For a while, Sian wore a patch to correct a lazy eye and some of the kids teased her about it. But we always stuck up for each other.

"Sian liked to play volleyball and basketball and she learned to ski. She wore a navy blue ski suit. When we skied together, we always wore matching pink hoods. She learned piano and played 'Send in the Clowns.' She could read music and play just about anything like that.

"We enjoyed growing up in the country but, when we got to be teenagers, we both got cars and liked to party and let our hair down."

Turning back to childhood, Katie remembered visiting Disneyland when she and Sian were preschoolers, holding hands as the two of them rode together on the Pirates of the Caribbean and other rides. "I knew she was my best friend but I never realized just how dependent on her I really was," said Katie. "If there's one thing I'd really like to say it would be how much I loved and admired Sian. I had other friends but she would be the one I would call most often and was the most interesting."

About the same time, the Joel sisters also visited Disneyland, where "Shell," five, and "Shawn," four, were likewise thrilled as they took in the same sights and sounds and went on many of the same rides. During the long car trip home, Helen Reddy sang their favorite song on the radio, and over and over again the little Joel sisters attempted "Delta Dawn" until their parents could stand it no longer.

Eventually, their mother Jacqueline turned to hush her children in the back seat and pretended to frown. Neither she nor anyone else in the family knew yet exactly how happy these times were.

4 Playing the Field

D r. Charalambous maneuvered his silver ZX sports car through the east gate at Exhibition Park.

By 1984, being a doctor for two years had enabled him to realize one of his dreams. At the Vancouver racetrack, the orange sticker on his windshield meant he could drive straight through Gate 9 and park in the horseman's lot reserved for owners, trainers, and grooms.

With any luck, he'd be just in time to see Mac's Reserve in the mile and one-sixteenth. He'd bought the three-year-old bay filly at Alsadie Farms, earlier in the year. She still hadn't broken her maiden but she showed promise and maybe tonight would be the night.

Last time, before the parade to the post, he had no sooner been enjoying a drink in the Paddock Lounge, albeit from a plastic tumbler, when he'd been called away to deliver a baby. Despite the prestige, being a doctor sometimes had its drawbacks, such as patients picking inconvenient times to go into labor.

But Charalambous didn't know whether or not she had smelled the beer on his breath. His present concern was to thread his way through the frenzy of punters to place his last-minute bet. Some of them had heard about the heavy-betting doctor and his strange combination wagers, but he seemed unconcerned by the gathering notoriety. This was the place to be. The money, the excitement, the color of the silks. The glamor of the track. The sport of kings. Mac's Reserve ran seventh in a field of nine, finishing ten-and-three-quarter-lengths behind the winner on a fast track. It was disappointing but, if he himself could ride, Charalambous would be sitting tall in the saddle.

Not only had he bought the dark brown filly and proudly mounted her picture in his office, his karate schools were doing well, and he hadn't yet begun dallying with Shelley Joel. He'd smoothed things over with Edna after the argument about the coffee, and he was still accepting new patients.

The practise was growing and Charalambous was riding a wave of popularity. Members of the Greek community had begun calling to inquire if the new doctor spoke their language, and to them he came across as the loyal, doting son. "I'll have to brush up on it with Momma," he said.

Sian and Katie Simmonds had seemed to like him too, as had most of the patients. Sometimes, he seemed a bit overly affectionate, but there was no reason to be suspicious of his motives. He seemed a nice friendly man and he was their family doctor.

For some time, however, Charalambous had voiced discontent with the fact that the women he was dating were the same age as him. When one of them turned thirty, acquaintances heard him say, "I could trade you in for two fifteen-year-olds."

Edna had noticed how he treated one petite, dark-haired girlfriend. He had her constantly running errands for him, either purchasing mono-grammed T-shirts at the local mall or picking up karate trophies for him in Bellingham, thirty miles across the U.S. border in Washington State.

Although he liked his mother's Greek cooking, Charalambous was known to be a finicky eater. He wasn't a health food nut—to the contrary he liked to slather his food with salt and sour cream—but acquaintances heard how he'd scraped one girlfriend's first and only culinary effort into the garbage, telling her: "If that's the best you can do, we're going to eat out."

But that was about six years ago, when he was still a student. Now that he was a doctor, he had pretty much made it clear to everybody that he'd outgrown his previous girlfriends. They were no longer his type. Younger and taller women with long blonde hair would be more suit-able as mother potential for his future children.

In October, 1984, his dream seemed to be coming true: at a hair-dressing school just a few blocks from his office, a beautiful fair-haired teenager named Angela Street had suddenly collapsed in inexplicable pain and was in urgent need of a doctor.

Eighteen-year-old Angela had only just moved to Surrey to train for her new career and hadn't yet contacted a family physician in the area. As she writhed on the floor, her colleagues quickly scanned the listings for doctors in the yellow pages, trying to find one nearby. Doctors with names beginning with an A weren't taking any new patients but, when they got down to C, Charalambous's office said she could come in right away.

Angela learned that her pain was caused by simple indigestion. Though in agony, she was still embarrassed as she was instructed to pull down her nylons and panties in front of Dr. Charalambous, and to bend over his examining table with lifted dress for a shot of Demerol. Before she left, the doctor asked Angela if she were married, and suggested she return for a follow-up visit the following month.

When Charalambous wheeled up beside her in a chair on casters during that next appointment, Angela thought he was unnecessarily moving his hand up and down her thigh. After that, she didn't see him until February, 1985, when she sought medical attention at Surrey Memorial Hospital. As the doctor on call, Charalambous surprised her by confiding he'd just broken up with his girlfriend. "Are there any young, good-looking girls at your hairdressing school?" he asked.

Angela had deflected the question but saw Charalambous again a week later while she and a friend lunched at Church's Fried Chicken near his office on King George Highway. "That's the guy I've been telling you about who's been coming in and staring at the student hairdressers," said her friend. "Oh, really," replied Angela, "that's my doctor."

Although she intended to select another doctor, Angela made one last visit to Charalambous in May, 1985. Edna handed her a wrapped gown. "No, I don't want to get undressed." Angela said. "It's only an infection. I just want a prescription." Although the receptionist persisted, the young patient was equally adamant. "It's okay," she said. "I'll tell the doctor myself."

When Charalambous entered the examination room, Angela thought he appeared surprised that she'd disregarded the receptionist's instructions, possibly angry that she was requesting a prescription prior to an examination. He flung the gown at her like a frisbee, she thought, as he left the room.

Angela did as she was told, but was thinking about getting dressed again and leaving when Charalambous came back in with a smile. "Are you always this shy?" he asked, running a speculum under the hot water tap.

Before she could answer, Angela felt the doctor's fingers inside her. Strange, she thought, that he would wash a speculum, then not bother to use it. Charalambous began telling Angela about karate and all the moves. As the doctor continued his examination, it seemed to Angela that he was sighing, moaning and breathing heavily.

"Is your husband fooling around behind your back?" she recalled him asking.

Often, when Angela was nervous, she would giggle hysterically. The examination and the questions had made her laugh out loud, too loudly apparently for the doctor's liking. Both doctor and patient knew that walls between examination rooms, from a privacy standpoint, tended to be somewhat thin. "Be quiet!" the doctor ordered her.

Charalambous continued to have problems with his women, believing his blonde, live-in girlfriend Cathy was going through his desk and pilfering while he was at work. After allegedly hitting her, he gave her Demerol and Percocet for the pain. Finally, he tried blackmailing her not to break off with him—and followed through on his threats to tell her parents about her sex life after she dumped him anyway.

The doctor then allegedly stormed over to her parents' house in Surrey, kicking and breaking the front door when they refused to let him in. After the landlord threatened to report him to medical authorities, Charalambous reluctantly agreed to pay for the damage, but hurled some frightening invective in the process. "I hope I see you in the hospital emergency room some day," the landlord was told. "I will look after you."

In January 1985, while prowling the red-light district in downtown Vancouver, Charalambous picked up a pretty, seventeen-year-old girl to take back to his home in Coquitlam. But he became angry, she reported, when her efforts at fellatio failed to please him. "He started throwing me around the room and splattered me against the wall," the frightened hooker told the police. "I satisfied him after that but then I warned the other girls to watch out for him."

The street girls arranged to publish a description of Charalambous and his car license number on their "bad tricks" list, telling prostitutes' advocate Marie Errington that he thought he could do anything to them and nobody would believe them because they were only whores and he was a doctor.

By July, things weren't going so well. Angela Street had ignored his overtures, and she hadn't fixed him up with any of her girlfriends. He'd finally gotten around to impressing Shelley Joel with his sports car, but could he get her away from her mother? It might be taking a risk but, if he could figure out a way, he'd go for it. He was, after all, a gambler.

Nine days after Shelley and her mother had visited his house, the doctor decided he'd try his luck with one other woman, a friend of his sister flying in from Los Angeles. It was July 30, 1985, and Charalambous had arranged to meet his sister's friend at Vancouver International Airport. Hurrying into the terminal building, he scanned the U.S. arrivals board. Barbara had left L.A. on the Western Airlines dinner flight at 6:45. The two-and one-half-hour flight was on time. She should be here any moment.

The doctor was looking forward to meeting her. Barbara, if he remembered correctly, was an extremely pretty woman, five feet seven, with a sweet feminine voice and long dark curly hair. She kept in top shape with a regimen of exercise and health food. She had grown up in Surrey but had moved with Joe's sister to California, where both women aspired to be actresses.

It had been nine years since he'd met Barbara the first time. She hadn't been interested in him then, but that was when he was a medical student. It might be different now he was in practise. Everybody wants to screw a doctor, he reminded himself.

Barbara walked through the gate marked U.S. Arrivals and looked for the man who was supposed to pick her up. She didn't recognize Charalambous at first. He'd turned prematurely gray since the last time they'd met. Finally, she noticed the casually dressed man ogling her and realized it was her old acquaintance.

Barbara had accepted an invitation to stay overnight with Joe's mother in Burnaby, intending to pay a surprise visit to her own family the following day. The doctor had graciously arranged to pick up Barbara at the airport, and now he helped her with her suitcase and a trunk.

"Good to see you," Barbara said. "How's life as a doctor?"

"Good," said Charalambous, looking her up and down. "You look healthy. You must be working out."

"I feel healthy," confirmed Barbara. "I go to the gym every day."

At Charalambous' request, she explained her daily routine with weights, aerobics, and swimming. Suddenly, Charalambous affected doctorly concern: "That's too much," he said. "You should slow down."

Barbara had first got to know Charalambous in 1976 after she had met his sister at an acting audition in Vancouver. Susan Charalambous had just started working as a teacher but both women had been interested in pursuing acting careers. Barbara had found Susan to be a positive, upbeat person and the two of them had shared a hotel room after they'd enrolled together at the Lee Strasberg Theater Institute in Los Angeles.

Before they'd left, Susan Charalambous had invited her to meet her mother and other members of the family. Back then, Joe had been a dark-haired young medical student. When Barbara had first walked in, he had dropped the paper he'd been reading and his mouth had fallen open. Barbara had heard he was a womanizer so she wasn't completely surprised.

Barbara also remembered that Charalambous had a nasty temper. Susan had disagreed with him about some article in the newspaper and Joe had become quite irate. "This is the way it is," he'd shouted as he stormed out of the room.

On a subsequent visit to the Charalambous home, Joe had persuaded Barbara to accompany him to the play *Talking Dirty* at the Queen Elizabeth Theater in Vancouver. She'd been reluctant to go with him at first, but had then allowed him to convince her that the play had been getting rave reviews.

Barbara had let him know she hadn't wanted to stay out late and he had agreed. He had picked her up and taken her to a restaurant beforehand. It was then, she recalled, that he had started talking dirty himself, as though in anticipation of the play. "I guess you know about the 'Chicken Ranch' near Las Vegas?" she recalled him telling her. "A guy there can be a connoisseur and choose from a whole lineup of girls."

Barbara had hinted she found the conversation unpleasant. "You know," she remembered Joe had continued, only partially changing the subject, "it'd really turn me off when I become a doctor if I had to examine unattractive women."

When the time had come to pay the bill, Barbara had been embarrassed that her escort had tried to impress her by pulling out a wad of cash from his wallet.

Afterwards, Barbara had felt, the medical student's grasp of the play had been similar to what she might have expected from a high school student. Charalambous, she recalled, had driven her home and had slipped his hand under her skirt as she'd got out of the car. She had thought him immature and ill-mannered and, when he'd called the next day, she had motioned to her father to tell him she wasn't home.

Now, these several years later, Barbara was still living near Los Angeles, although she hadn't been able to find full-time work as an actress. She sat back in the passenger seat as Joe put her luggage in the trunk and started up his car.

"I don't know if it's really a good idea for you to stay at my mother's place," Joe told her. "There are a lot of people at the house because Harry just got married."

"Oh well, that's okay, then," said Barbara. "If we can find a phone I can just call my Dad and go there after all."

"Yeah, okay," said Charalambous, "but you can stay at my house if you like. I bought a new house in Coquitlam with a swimming pool."

Barbara declined and phoned her father, but he wasn't able to pick her up right away. Since the doctor was being so gracious and helpful, she told Joe she liked swimming, and she would accept his invitation provided he realized that she already had a boyfriend and was spoken for.

Joe took Barbara to his Tudor-style home and proudly showed her the indoor pool. Apparently, he'd made a deal on the house after the previous owner had lost it through financial difficulties. Barbara was tired after her trip from California so Joe showed her one of the upstairs bedrooms, furnished with a foam rubber futon on the floor.

Barbara had trouble falling asleep but had just nodded off when there was a knock on the door. "Is there anything you need?" asked Joe. Slightly annoyed that he had woken her up, Barbara called out her reply. "No," she said. "Thanks all the same."

Now, Barbara couldn't get back to sleep so she decided to go downstairs for a swim. Perhaps some exercise would make her tired, she thought, but she was unable to get into the pool area. Wearing a white bikini, she knocked on Joe's bedroom door to get his help. "I can't open the glass doors," she explained.

"Okay," Joe told her. "If you're going for a swim I'll go with you too."

In the pool, Charalambous had swum up beside her. "Tell me

Barbara," he asked, "was there ever a time in your life when you were really very frightened?"

"Yes," Barbara replied, sniffing chlorine up her nose. "One time I was leaving a restaurant with a friend in L.A. when I was robbed. I was forced to kneel at gunpoint and hand over my purse."

Suddenly, Barbara felt disconcerted, and it wasn't just the memory of having been robbed. Charalambous seemed to be staring at her with a look of inner satisfaction. "How about if we take off our swimsuits?" he suggested. Brushing him off, Barbara declined the offer and the two of them returned to their rooms.

The next morning, the doctor drove Barbara across the river to her father's house, where she stayed for the next two days. Then she returned to Coquitlam, having arranged with Joe to join him and his mother for dinner after a day at the races.

It was Saturday, August 3, 1985, and Joe had explained that Mac's Reserve wouldn't be running till Monday. It was too bad Barbara couldn't see her. Mac's Reserve had broken her maiden in 1985 with two firsts, three seconds, and one third for total winnings of $6,765.

Barbara sat in the lounge area with Joe and his friends, enjoying a glass of juice and ice cream, when suddenly she felt bad vibes. The three men were speaking in Greek and all of them, she thought, seemed to be looking at her in a strange way.

Joe gave her the impression he was a successful gambler and the money flowed freely but, on the way home, Barbara let him know she had felt uncomfortable. The doctor seemed to want to make up for it. "How about if we pick up some things at the health food store?" he suggested.

Barbara was beginning to have second thoughts about dinner with Joe and his mother, especially when she had to brush off his hands as they neared his home in Coquitlam. "I thought you had a girlfriend," she said firmly. "I'm your sister's best friend. I thought we had defined our relationship."

Charalambous suddenly showed a lot of intensity. "You've been raped before, haven't you Barbara?" he said.

Barbara was upset. She had told Susan Charalambous that she had been raped when she was fourteen, and now she felt her friend had betrayed her confidence. "I'm tired," she told Charalambous when they got back to his house. "I need to lie down and take a nap."

It had been a hot day at the races and Barbara washed her cotton blouse in the upstairs bathroom, intending to hang it up to dry while she napped. But someone was coming up the stairs and intercepted her as she hurried in her bra and skirt to her bedroom, stopping her before she could fully close the door.

Barbara was terrified as she suddenly found herself being thrown about the room like a rag doll. Following a blitz of karate violence, she found herself being dragged into the master bedroom, thrown on the floor by an assailant who was now pulling down her elastic waist skirt and panties.

Wriggling onto her stomach, the hysterical woman was pinned down as the assailant sat on her back facing her heels, slapping her repeatedly on her exposed buttocks with the palm of his hand. Barbara sobbed and begged her assailant to stop, but found her pleas were only prompting him to strike her all the more. She realized now he was intending to hurt her. He appeared angry and filled with hate. As she resigned herself to the beating, Barbara felt she was his punching bag.

The half-naked woman found herself being flipped onto her back, her assailant kneeling with full weight on her chest, a thumb and forefinger pinching her, another thumb thrust in her mouth, roughly, almost breaking one of her teeth. Barbara understood now what it was all about. She was the captive. He was the jailer and he was showing no mercy.

Thinking he would kill her, Barbara tried a ruse. "Please," she asked. "Let me get my Bible from my suitcase." It was actually Susan's Bible but her captor allowed her to fetch it. As she held it against her chest, Barbara was surprised that the distraction appeared to work. Her captor allowed her to go into the ensuite. Trembling, lightheaded and dizzy, she threw up.

Barbara didn't know if her assailant had been satisfied by the encounter. He'd kept his clothes on the whole time. Downstairs, she was surprised that she was allowed to call her father. "Dad please help me!" she screamed into the phone. "He tried to rape me."

Charalambous picked up an extension phone. "Your daughter is very ill," he told Barbara's father. "She's schizophrenic, catatonic, and should be institutionalized and given shock therapy."

As Barbara squeezed quickly into a dress from her suitcase, she noticed a plaque in the living room that read, "Trust me, I'm a doctor."

"Trust!" Barbara yelled. Eyes flaming, she yanked the plaque from the wall and hurled it on the floor. Then she grabbed a nearby karate trophy and made as though she was going to throw it through his television set. "Please don't destroy the TV," Charalambous pleaded.

Nervously glancing behind her, Barbara noticed a bag full of syringes, in the living room. Was Charalambous in the drug trade or might he jab her with one of the needles as though to tranquillize a wild cat?

Barbara was terrified as Charalambous held out some pills and urged her to take them but, as he got closer, she suddenly kicked him as hard as she could in the groin. Wearing open-toed sandals, she knew she'd got him where it counted. The doctor turned white but was still in control. He didn't even flinch.

Outside, Barbara waited on the doorstep with her suitcase. She saw Charalambous watching her from a second-storey window. Now that her father was on his way, the doctor appeared sheepish and cowardly, she thought. Finally, her father arrived. "I think I've heard enough!" he said curtly to the doctor. "Come on Barbara, let's go."

After having two doctors examine her for scrapes and bruises, Barbara reported the incident to the Royal Canadian Mounted Police in Coquitlam, attending at the detachment on August 19, 1985, for an interview.

As Constable Tom Robertson, a dark-haired young man with a mustache, listened to her story, he realized that it should be followed up, and he met with Barbara and her father over the next two days.

Checking computer records, the policeman was surprised to learn about Charalambous's run-ins with the Vancouver City Police. He decided he wanted to know more about this Dr. Charalambous, and picked up the phone to call the College of Physicians and Surgeons of British Columbia.

Robertson was put through to college investigator Daryl Beere. For many years, the college had hired only investigators with police training and Beere, a serious, slightly balding man, fit the bill nicely, having only recently retired from the RCMP customs and excise section after twenty-seven years' service.

"Yes," Beere confirmed, after looking up Charalambous in the college files. "He's a Canadian citizen, born in Cyprus, graduated in 1981, registered 1982, no previous complaints."

"Thanks," said Robertson, "I'll keep you posted."

Shortly afterwards, the policeman found other women who'd also alleged problems with Dr. Charalambous, and a clear picture began to emerge as one interview led to another. Other than Barbara, however, none of the women was willing to come forward as a witness. Either they wanted to get on with their lives or were afraid of reprisals.

"From what my investigation was revealing, it indicated to me we definitely had a problem," the policeman recalled.

5   A Bad Case of Asthma

You will lead your lives and practise your art in uprightness and honor....

It was the worst attack of asthma that her mother could ever remember, Shelley gasping desperately for breath in the car as Jacqueline and her husband sped frantically through the night to Surrey Memorial Hospital.

Earlier that August 7 evening, when Rick had come home, both he and Jacqueline had cherished the thought of permanent reconciliation. Shelley, however—although she was fond of her stepfather—had been upset. Once again, she would lose her role as surrogate mother.

At the hospital, Shelley was virtually comatose. Richard and Jacqueline were assured by the doctor on call that she would be all right but she would have to stay overnight in intensive care.

Since the family hadn't yet found a new doctor, Jacqueline spoke by phone the next morning with Dr. Charalambous. The doctor said he had been notified that Shelley was in the hospital and he would be seeing her during his morning rounds.

As expected, Shelley's condition improved over the next three days, but Jacqueline was surprised, visiting after work, to find her daughter's bedside table covered with gifts of magazines and chocolates. "That's from Dr. Charalambous," Shelley smiled innocently.

Jacqueline frowned. "That's not right," she said, concerned by the continuing familiarity. "Doctors don't do things like that. If he brings you anything else, just tell him there's no need for this."

At home that night, Jacqueline found it difficult to put the gifts out of her mind. She was relieved, however, that Shelley had seemed much better, and she picked her daughter up the next day after Charalambous said she could be discharged.

Upon their return home, Shelley told her mother that the doctor wanted also to see her the following day. "Dr. Charalambous starts his holidays tomorrow," she said. "He wants to come pick me up for lunch and take me to the races...."

Jacqueline had been preparing dinner. She lowered the elements on the stove before she turned around. "What?" she asked rhetorically. "Shelley, this man is supposed to be your doctor. You are not to go out with him and that's final. You can tell him what I said."

Although she didn't have a home phone at the time, Jacqueline received a desperate call at work the following day from her younger daughter. Shawna had run next door to use a neighbor's phone. "Mom!" she cried, "Dr. Charalambous is at the house having coffee. He's going to take Shelley out to lunch and a movie."

"Tell her absolutely she's not to go!" said Jacqueline.

But when Jacqueline got home from work, she found that Shelley and the doctor had defied her. Jacqueline made dinner for the rest of the family, fuming as she waited for Shelley to return home. Finally, her older daughter breezed in at 11:30 P.M., happy and excited. In her purse, she had $350 which she claimed she'd won at the races. "Joe put the bets on for me," she said.

Jacqueline insisted that her daughter was to return the money the next day, but her model child was becoming increasingly defiant. "I'm a grown woman," Shelley protested. "I don't have to listen to someone telling me where and when I'm allowed to go on dates. He just wants to see me during his holidays anyway."

Concerned not to alienate her daughter entirely, Jacqueline accepted the explanation and offered a compromise. If it were just a "summer fling," Shelley could go out with the doctor during the day and could attend his karate classes twice a week. But it would have to stop when Shelley went back to school. Peer pressure, Jacqueline hoped, would then dissuade Shelley from wanting to date someone more than twice her age.

Jacqueline was about to find out, however, that events were quickly to escalate from bad to worse. Charalambous was brazenly uncooperative with her wishes. Aware that Shelley had been grounded for a week for coming home very late, the doctor took her out next day anyway and phoned Jacquie at work.

"How dare you," said Jacquie. "I told you she's grounded and not allowed out."

"In my country, they have no such thing as grounding a person," Charalambous said, glibly. "Do you own this person? Do you have her in prison? You can't do that to her while you're at work. You're not being fair to her."

"I think that's my decision to make," retorted Jacquie. "Not yours. I want Shelley home by four o'clock when I get home from work."

"No," said the doctor. "She's going to help me buy some new clothes and then we're going out for dinner. You don't want me walking around in old rags, do you?"

"What you wear is no concern of mine," said Jacquie. "I think you should be concerned you might be endangering your license, going out with an underage patient."

"There's nothing you can do about it," Charalambous said.

As he planted a new medical theory in his fertile, young companion, the doctor had other than mere intellectual concerns in mind. If a man didn't have sex at least every other day, he told Shelley, the build up of seminal fluid might cause him to have a stroke.

Back at his home in Coquitlam, the doctor invited Shelley to join him in his hot tub. She had not brought a bathing suit with her, but she took off her jeans and slipped in across from him. Taking off his glasses, Joe inched closer, admiring the outline of her breasts as they pushed upward against her wet T-shirt, but the nubile teenager backed away as his hand slipped inside her nylon panties. There had been no embrace or tender kiss. "Ahh, come on," persisted Joe. "If you don't have sex with me, I'll find a new girlfriend." Feeling guilty that he'd spent a lot of money on her, the teenager gave in. Bracing her firm young body against the ledge, she removed her panties beneath the swirling waters—allowing him to feel her tender young skin as she was mounted for the first time by the man who until a few days ago had been her family doctor. Though she felt nothing herself as he moaned and sighed,

48

she knew she had satisfied him. "It's time to get dressed," he told her immediately afterwards.

Hearing the doctor's car pull up at 11:30 P.M., Richard Jongkind stormed outside to order Shelley into the house. "Just what in the hell are you doing here!?" he said, confronting Charalambous in the driveway.

"What are you talking about?" said the doctor coolly.

"When we tell Shelley she's grounded, that's exactly what it means," Jongkind shouted. "We're not going to have you countermanding our orders!"

"Most people would pay me to take out their daughter," said Charalambous. "I'm introducing her to new friends. I'm helping her with her education and self-respect."

"Why are you seeing her?" Rick persisted. "What can you possibly have in common with her? Why can't you go out with someone your own age?"

"She's very mature," said the doctor. "She's lonely. She needs to get out. She needs to experience fun things. I'm giving her the chance to go to the racetrack and meet people and go out for nice dinners and build up her self-confidence."

"She's just getting over a rough relationship," said Rick. "Her boyfriend didn't treat her very well. I don't see how getting involved in a relationship with you is going to help matters. It's just going to make things worse."

Inside the house, Shelley was irate and hysterical. "He might hurt Rick," she warned defiantly. "He's a karate expert."

Jacqueline looked questioningly at her daughter. "Has he been having sex with you?" she asked.

"We're not into that," Shelley lied. "We're going to wait a while and see how things go. He's going to make me a model and maybe an actress. He has a sister in L.A."

The dating didn't stop when school started. On September 9, Jacqueline was in her nightgown when she got into a heated argument with her daughter for coming in after her 10:00 P.M. schoolnight curfew. "You always try to make me feel so guilty," Shelley screamed. "I don't need this. I can make $200 to $300 a night at the racetrack."

As Shelley stormed out of the house, Rick Jongkind jumped in his car and went looking for her. He spotted Shelley in a nearby phone booth and was about to take her home when Charalambous drove up. Shelley jumped into the doctor's car.

In his company car, her stepfather followed the Nissan ZX, then cut in front and came to a stop. As Richard Jongkind walked over to talk to the doctor, Charalambous pulled his vehicle around him and drove away. Jongkind gave chase but abandoned his pursuit as Charalambous sped through two red lights.

Richard Jongkind went to the Coquitlam RCMP station to make a statement concerning the evening's events.

When Jacqueline woke up next morning, Shelley was still not home. She phoned the doctor's house when she got to work. "Yes, she's here," Charalambous confirmed. "She's sleeping. Just leave her be."

"Let me speak to her," Jacqueline demanded.

"No," said Charalambous. "She's tired. She's emotionally drained. Shelley's not returning home. She's decided to stay here with me."

"What?" Jacqueline asked incredulously.

"She wants to be independent," replied the doctor. "I'll take good care of her. She's welcome to stay here as long as she wants."

Jacqueline suddenly sounded less soft and feminine. "Are you prepared to risk your license over this?" she asked.

"It's not nice to threaten people," said the doctor. "Bad things could happen to people who threaten people."

"Are you threatening me, then?" Jacqueline asked.

"No."

"I'm not threatening you either," Jacqueline continued. "But, if Shelley doesn't return home, I might just report this matter to the College of Physicians and Surgeons."

"There's nothing you can do to endanger my license," Charalambous rejoined. "You don't have enough money to do that."

Jacqueline slammed down the phone. She never wanted to speak to this man again but, the following Sunday, she could stand it no longer. She drove over to the doctor's house and knocked on the door. Charalambous answered, Shelley peering over his shoulder. Both he and her daughter had apparently just finished showering as their hair was wet. "I'm going out for coffee," Charalambous said. "You two have a talk."

Though Jacqueline pleaded and reasoned with her daughter for the next hour, Shelley refused to come home, and both were crying when

Charalambous returned. "You've never been supportive of Shelley," the doctor castigated.

"That's not true," protested Jacqueline.

"Yes it is," said Charalambous. "You haven't been a proper mother. You haven't given her a stable environment. If you had, she'd never have left."

The shouting match escalated. Jacqueline departed in tears. This is a nightmare, she reflected. A one-man cult has abducted my daughter and nobody seems able to do anything about it. Shelley's father seems to think I'm overreacting. Edna Neighbour doesn't seem to be aware of it. Rick's been to the police—but they don't seem to be able to do anything either.

By September 20, however, the police did do something. That day, Jacqueline learned that a Los Angeles woman named Barbara had also complained about Charalambous, and that Constable Tom Robertson had gone to the doctor's house to charge him with sexual assault.

Robertson had learned through his colleagues that the doctor was living with a teenage patient, and had arranged for one of them to take her back to the Coquitlam RCMP station if they found her at the house.

Crying, Shelley had phoned Jacqueline's neighbor from the doctor's house to report that Joe had been taken away in handcuffs. Shelley thought her mother was behind the arrest because the police were saying they'd only release her into her mother's custody.

Jacqueline, accompanied by her husband, arrived at the Coquitlam RCMP station to inform Shelley she'd known nothing about it. She had to wait, however, while police continued to interview Charalambous and her daughter in separate rooms. Meanwhile, Jacquie decided to make a mother's appeal to Betty Charalambous, who was also waiting with her family, while the police finished taking her son's photograph and fingerprints. "Joe's a good boy," said the doctor's mother, her family warning Jacqueline not to pester her.

By coincidence, Constable Don Adam, who had picked up Shelley, found that Jacqueline was also his tenant. He'd leased his rental house to Rick and Jacqueline some time ago, but hadn't connected them with Shelley because of their different last names.

The constable talked briefly with them while Shelley was detained for questioning for the next four hours. Apart from Barbara's case, the police were exploring whether they could get enough evidence to charge

Charalambous with having sex with a minor. "Are you on any birth control?" Shelley was asked, as her mother waited outside.

"Yes," Shelley responded nervously, "the pill."

"When did you go on the pill?" the interviewer asked.

"About one month ago," said Shelley, "but I've been on it before."

"Was this in anticipation of having sex with Joe?"

"Yes."

The next question contemplated breach of trust. "Were the contraceptive pills given to you by him?"

Shelley was scared. She began a misleading reply, but then corrected herself. "No, I had them from before," she said. "He has now given me some more. Actually, Joe had prescribed the pills for me in January of 1985 when he was just my doctor.... Once I broke off with my boyfriend I went off the pills and still had some left."

Further questioning, however, led police to believe that Shelley would not be willing to testify against the doctor in court. As they released the teenager to her mother's custody, police told Shelley they would bring in child welfare authorities if they found her with the doctor again. The best course of action, Jacquie was advised, would be to lay an official complaint with the College of Physicians and Surgeons.

Back home, Shawna was delighted by the return of her older sister. She had always looked up to Shelley and worshipped the ground that she walked on. To her mother, Shelley seemed tearful and contrite. As they hugged, Shelley admitted it had been wrong for her to stay with the doctor. At one point, she related, Charalambous had warned her: "Never tell anyone about what is said or done in my house."

During the next week, the Jongkinds found a new family doctor—a woman—and, on September 24, Jacqueline and her husband followed up on the RCMP's suggestion of making an official complaint to the College of Physicians and Surgeons. "We didn't know where else to turn," Rick explained later. "We wanted to know if we were correct in our disdain for this conduct by a doctor, or whether it was appropriate in the college's eyes. The reason for the complaint was to disclose our feelings that Dr. Charalambous had, as our family doctor, acted despicably."

Dr. C.R. Arnold, the elderly registrar of the British Columbia College of Physicians and Surgeons, which was established in 1886 to protect the public interest, put down his glasses and gazed out the window for a moment as he absorbed the contents of the letter. The

52

registrar had seen a lot of complaints in his time but the Jongkinds' allegations of such brazen behavior by a fellow physician clearly upset him. "If this is true," he told Jacqueline and her husband, "I agree with you, it's absolutely outrageous."

The registrar picked up his extension phone to call Daryl Beere. Although busy with some 500 complaints a year, Arnold wanted the college investigator to begin his inquiries immediately. About 10 percent of complaints to the college concerned sexual misconduct (most being allegations of incompetence) but this complaint was one of the worst that Arnold could ever remember, involving any of the province's 9,000 doctors.

As Dr. Arnold called in the ex-Mountie, however, he was painfully aware—even if the allegations were true—that Charalambous would continue to practise at least until Beere could complete his investigation and the college could hold a hearing. Under the Medical Practitioners Act as it then stood, a physician's license could not be revoked prior to a hearing, unless the doctor was either mentally unstable or patients were at risk of malpractice.

Thus, while the self-regulating college ultimately did have the right to discipline and even remove fellow doctors, legal and other considerations often meant lengthy delays. Beere did, however, begin his investigation almost immediately on September 28, and the Jongkinds met about the same time with the friendly, bespectacled lawyer David Martin, the college's outside legal counsel, who impressed them with understanding and patience.

Soon afterwards, however, Jacqueline became suspicious that Shelley—rather than going out with schoolfriends as she'd said—had begun seeing the doctor again. She confirmed her suspicions one night by waiting in the carport to observe Charalambous dropping her daughter off. Following an argument the next day, the teenager went "out for a walk" and didn't come back.

For the balance of the year, Shelley lived with Jacqueline's sister in Vancouver while continuing to give the doctor oral sex after school. Angry that she'd signed a statement at the police station, the doctor had ripped her dress and her schoolbooks, but Shelley didn't tell anyone about that. In January, she said, when she turned sixteen, the doctor had promised that she could drive one of his cars to modeling courses, which he would pay for....

Jacqueline again spoke to officials at the college, who advised her that the investigation had produced sufficient evidence to refer the matter to the first available inquiry committee. Meanwhile, though, it seemed to Jacqueline that her daughter was slipping ever further away. Charalambous had called at her sister's house in January 1986 and had told Shelley to get her things. Shelley had gone with him. She was living once more with the doctor—and this time it seemed for good.

6   Vigil

Jacqueline Jongkind was a woman obsessed. Even her own mother said so—but she would ignore them all. Every maternal instinct in her body told her that she was right. Provided she lived long enough, no intimidation or threat could ever match the flame that she'd keep alight for her eldest child.

Well after midnight, finding herself unable to sleep, Jacqueline got dressed and drove to Vancouver's Mount Pleasant hooker district. She had observed the street girls along Broadway as she'd headed home each night from her new job as a downtown secretary. She wanted to know more about their bad tricks list.

Parking her car, Jacqueline observed a blonde, leggy girl she'd seen before, standing under a streetlight, always on the same dilapidated corner. Overcoming her reservations, Jacqueline approached nervously as the hooker puffed impatiently on a cigarette.

Perhaps thinking her an undercover cop, the street girl eyed Jacqueline with suspicion. The girl was wearing a bomber jacket but shivered in a short skirt in the cold night air. Balanced precariously on four-inch stilettos, she was almost as tall as Jacqueline herself.

But quickly, the mutual wariness evaporated as Jacqueline explained the circumstances of her daughter's plight. "She's only fifteen," said Jacquie. "I'm very afraid for her. I know she's being beaten."

Despite her own circumstances, the street girl listened with incredulity. "Sure, I've heard of him," she sneered. "He thinks he's such a hotshot just because he's a doctor. I'd like to help you. We'll nail him if we can."

Shelley's mother thanked the girl, arranging to meet her again as she got back in her car. She stopped to talk with two more street girls on her way home. If the police couldn't do anything yet, Jacqueline was hoping to produce more and more evidence until they could. She'd been abruptly cut off the night before when she'd phoned her daughter on her sixteenth birthday—and she was ready to fight back. "Tell your mother to fuck off," she'd heard Joe screaming in the background. "Don't let her push you around. Hang up on her."

Determined now to get all the evidence she could, Jacqueline Jongkind listened while Barbara from Los Angeles testified at her preliminary hearing in Coquitlam. After the judge ruled there was sufficient evidence that Charalambous should stand trial, the two women compared notes and agreed to stand by each other until justice could be done. Soon, they were meeting with some of Charalambous's previous girlfriends, and passing on each new piece of information to the police.

Jacqueline remained cut off from her eldest daughter for the next two months, but Shawna did see Shelley from time to time at Hastings Junior High School, where her sister arrived each day by cab. Shelley said she'd soon have her driver's license, and promised they could then go out for drives together on their lunch break. "I saw your sister at Lougheed Mall on the weekend with your dad," a schoolfriend told Shawna one day. "That's not my dad," said Shawna disgustedly after her friend elaborated. "That's her boyfriend."

Shelley did get the use of the black Nissan in the spring, and took Shawna out for rides as promised, their long hair sometimes flying in the wind with the T-roof off. Shelley remained protective, and Shawna still idolized her. Sometimes too, they'd still mimic the lyrics on the radio, just as they'd done when they were little girls, but Shawna could see now that her sister was living in a different world. Shelley's expensive leather purse, open on the console between them, was crammed with the most expensive make-up she'd ever seen.

By phone, Jacqueline at last got through to the house on Foster Avenue while Joe was at work one day—and Shelley for once didn't hang up on her. "If this is what you've chosen for your life, okay," said Jacqueline. "Just know that I love you and will always be here if you need me." Shelley now had mobility however and, after that phone call, began sneaking over to her mother's house each day to take Shawna with her to school. "You make the best blueberry muffins in the whole world," Shelley told her mother.

Jacqueline hoped desperately that Shelley would move back home, but her daughter seemed programmed by forces out of her reach. The school counselor told Jacqueline one day that her daughter would be transferring to a school nearer the doctor's house. The counselor reported that Shelley seemed unhappy about the situation, but suggested the family could do little other than to give her their love. "I can't understand it," the counselor told Jacquie. "It's as though she's been brainwashed."

Then in May, as if things weren't already bad enough, Jacqueline found they were suddenly about to turn even worse.

Shelley told her sister that she could no longer drop by each day to drive her to school. Furthermore, Shelley would have to stop talking to her. The doctor had forbidden Shelley from speaking to anyone until "all these trials are done with." Shawna *might* be allowed to speak with her if she were no longer living at home. In the meantime, Shelley handed back the ring that her mother had given to her as a belated sixteenth-birthday present.

Jacqueline managed to get through on the phone to Shelley later that day. "What have I done now?" she asked.

"I can't see any of you any more," Shelley replied coldly.

"What brought this on?"

"I can't say," Shelley said, refusing to elaborate. "It's all started all over again."

Angry and frustrated, Jacqueline picked up the phone to report these developments to college lawyer David Martin, who assured her that everything possible was being done to speed up the date of the college hearing. The next day, Shawna, who was now fifteen, boldly called at the Foster Avenue house, after anonymously phoning the doctor's office to ensure he was at work, but Shelley appeared nervous and aloof.

Shawna and her stepfather Richard Jongkind began to feel now that Jacqueline had too little time for them. Special events such as family birthdays no longer meant what they should. In a family torn apart, Jacqueline refused to go out with them on such occasions in case Shelley might phone. "You've got other children too," Rick told her.

Finally, in July, the tension became so thick that Shawna moved out to live with her father. Although she feared she was now losing her second daughter too, Jacqueline knew the real reason was that Shawna hoped to reestablish her relationship with Shelley. Subsequently, she was proved correct when Charalambous intercepted one of Shawna's calls. He was screaming so angrily about the evils of her mother that Shawna had an asthma attack and dropped her schoolbooks. "It's very simple," the doctor told her. "You've got a mother and you've got a sister. You make the choice."

Jacqueline chanced upon Shelley one more time that summer at Coquitlam Center. "I do love you, Mom," she said, backing away. "But it's too complicated. I can't see you. I'm being watched."

The school counselor was right. Shelley was being brainwashed. Repeatedly, the doctor told Shelley that her mother was evil and manipulative and she was ruining his life. "She's a pathological liar," Charalambous said continually. "I forbid you to speak to her."

Shelley didn't want to displease him. "I would have talked to her," she admitted later, "but I didn't want to run the risk of getting beaten. He would have intercepted the calls.... I didn't like sneaking around. I like to keep things up front.

"Often, when she called, Joe was sitting right there. I had to hang up on her. He would have been very displeased. I couldn't risk the abuse. He was so overbearing and domineering.

"The difficulties I had with my mother were difficulties that many teenagers have. I would never have cut her off in that way. In cutting her off, I also cut off my infant brothers, aged three and five. I never would have done that. It was a little bit drastic. What fifteen-year-old doesn't want contact with her own mother?"

Meanwhile, the doctor insisted that Shelley be at his shoulder while he pursued his passions for horseracing, karate and gambling. He proudly introduced her to his friends, but warned her to add a year to her age and to tell fellow doctors that she was seventeen.

At a card game at his mother's house, he introduced her to a bearded tattooed biker named Brian West, whom he described as his best friend. For years, the doctor explained, he and West had been like brothers— ever since the short, burly biker had wandered into one of his karate classes in 1972 appreciative of the fact that Charalambous had treated him "like an ordinary guy." In addition to his karate skills, West was a trained boxer. Charalambous explained he had once helped him get a job with a contractor friend and that West had also worked at a shipyard in North Vancouver. But he had hurt his back and was getting benefits from the Workers' Compensation Board.

When Charalambous wasn't at work, he proudly took his new girlfriend everywhere. They were an odd-looking couple: the short graying, bespectacled man with the tender young concubine on his arm, but the doctor drew envious glances, from stewards at the racetrack, as well as some of the male karate students in the church basement. Jon Funk, the karate tournament judge, was astonished, however, that the church didn't expel Charalambous, and that his patients still stuck by him. Even the doctor's own brother, Funk noted, publicly disassociated himself from the doctor and wanted no part of it.

The threats to Jacqueline Jongkind continued. It might be safer if she dropped the charges, but they were now out of her hands—reposed with a college that seemed to be taking for ever while her daughter was slipping away, irretrievably, with each passing day. Then, one morning as she prepared to go out after breakfast, Jacqueline received a terrifying phone call. "Don't take your kids with you today," growled an unknown male caller, "'cause you won't be coming back."

With trembling hands, Jacqueline slammed down the receiver, immediately picking it up again to phone her husband at work. Richard Jongkind rushed home, adrenaline flowing. He bundled everyone in his car and took them to his mother's house.

If Charalambous felt Jacqueline could be dissuaded, however, he had a rude awakening on August 1, 1986, almost a year after the Jongkinds had made their official complaint, when he received a double-registered letter from college lawyer David Martin advising him of the college's intention to proceed with a hearing.

According to the letter, he had breached his professional relationship with the Jongkind family by having Shelley move in with him. Not only was she a patient, she was still legally an infant. Charalambous focused on the letter with dismay. It was the worst case scenario. The college had taken the complaint seriously after all. "You cohabited and had sexual intercourse with her," the letter concluded. "In relation to the foregoing facts, you have been guilty of infamous or unprofessional conduct."

It was obvious to Shelley the doctor realized now that the complaint might ruin his career, but he was buoyed by the more encouraging news on August 7, 1986, that prosecutors had decided to stay the sexual assault charge against him. A review of Barbara's evidence, they said, had pointed to certain inconsistencies.

When she had returned to Los Angeles, Barbara's friendship with Susan had come to an abrupt end. Susan Charalambous had accused Barbara of pushing her down a flight of stairs and had sent her brother an impromptu tape recording in which Barbara had acted the role of a neurotic woman.

Back in Vancouver, prosecutors concurred with Charalambous' lawyer Richard Peck that the tape, so far as Barbara was concerned, demonstrated emotional instability. Coupled with the alleged inconsistencies, they agreed, the charge should be stayed.

Barbara felt betrayed by the system. "He's going to do this again," she warned. The "inconsistencies" were easily explained, she told Jacquie, one of them being a mistaken assumption on the part of the lawyers pertaining to telephone records. "He's like a rabid dog running around on the loose," Barbara said.

As promised, Constable Robertson phoned the College of Physicians and Surgeons to inform Daryl Beere of the latest developments, letting the college investigator know that the charge had been stayed—all hopes now resting on the college hearing.

Barbara felt she had reached a dead end, but could still warn others. She made up several dozen flyers, sending copies to neighbors of Charalambous in the King George Professional Building. "Warning!" said her flyers. "Dr. Joseph Charalambous is a rapist. Police report sixteen victims. Silence is the protection of the rapist. Exposure of the rapist is protection of others."

Sympathetic women's groups also placed copies of the poster—including a reproduction of Charalambous's business card—on bulletin boards at Surrey Memorial Hospital and at St. Paul's Hospital in Vancouver.

Barbara intended to complain to the British Columbia attorney-general, but dropped the matter after getting into financial difficulties. She sent Shelley a copy of her poster and phoned to warn her about the doctor. "She just hung up the phone," Barbara recalled. "She didn't believe me."

Barbara's father believed her, though. Perhaps it was something he'd detected in the doctor's eyes. Or maybe the lack of something. A lot of people felt that way. When they made eye contact with Charalambous, there seemed to be nothing there.

7   Edna Calls it Quits

Edna Neighbour was furious.

The receptionist was a straight-shooting woman and she wasn't used to this type of thing. It had seemed innocuous enough earlier in the week when Charalambous had asked her to cancel today's appointments, but now it was beginning to dawn on her the reason why.

Before moving to the British Columbia coast, Edna had grown up in a strict Christian farming community in Saskatchewan; and the present circumstances were not something she expected, as the hard working, middle-aged receptionist of a family medical practise.

Edna had closed the office on Thursday, November 27 as requested, but had come in to do some paper work and answer the phone. Apart from the empty waiting room, however, something else was different too. As her boss fumbled with his keys to enter via the glass door, she could see that Charalambous was actually wearing a tie.

Instead of his trademark, casual open-necked shirt and slacks, he was also wearing a dark blue suit. "Hi Edna," he called to his receptionist, as he walked past the empty chairs. "I thought I'd better drop by to let you know what's happening."

Edna scowled as she put down the phone. She had been irked by some of the doctor's ways in the past but now, after a morning of answering phone calls from concerned patients, she was hopping mad.

"Thanks for leaving me holding the bag," she glowered. "Just what the hell is going on."

The receptionist couldn't help but think how different everything had become since she'd worked for Dr. Lam. Despite a chill in the relationship with her new boss right from the beginning, she had stayed on to work for Charalambous, against her better judgment, after he'd bought the practise in 1982.

She hadn't thought much about it earlier in the week when Charalambous had asked her to rebook today's appointments but, if there was one thing about Edna, it was her propensity for routine. Before leaving for work each morning, she always scanned the newspaper, and today she had been astonished to read that her boss was going to court. According to the paper, Dr. Charalambous was seeking to quash a proposed hearing by the College of Physicians and Surgeons into allegations that he was living with one of his teenage patients. Such a hearing, he'd reportedly maintained, would violate his Charter rights to liberty and security.

Edna digested the news. If the Charalambous medical practise was floundering under such circumstances, she as first mate wasn't about to go down with the ship. "Well I'll be damned," Edna thought. "No wonder the rotten bugger wanted me to cancel his appointments."

No sooner had Edna arrived at the office and turned off the answering machine when she began receiving phone calls from concerned patients. "I read the same article as you did," a perplexed receptionist said. "I honestly don't know anything more about it than you do." Edna repeated the same reply at least thirty times. By the time Charalambous called her at noon, she was fuming.

"Did you read the paper?" the doctor inquired on the phone.

"Yes," replied Edna, "and so did quite a few of your patients."

"What have you been telling them?" Charalambous asked.

"I told them I didn't know what it was all about. I suggested they ask you."

"I'm on my way to the office," said the doctor. "I'll explain it to you when I get there."

Edna sat and waited. It had better be a pretty good explanation, she thought. When he finally arrived in his best courtroom attire, Charalambous seemed to be smirking. He asked his receptionist to take down a prepared statement to be read to his patients. "I don't want you saying anything to jeopardize my practise," he cautioned.

"I am not going to lie for you," Edna replied. Dressed in her nurse's uniform, she fixed Charalambous with a frosty stare as he came round her side of the reception desk. In response, the doctor squinted from behind his ever-present glasses, showing no sign of embarrassment or emotion.

It was amazing, thought Edna. According to the paper, the patient had just turned fifteen.

"You know of course who the girl is?" Charalambous said.

"No, I have no idea," Edna replied.

"It's Shelley," said the doctor.

"Shelley Joel!" Edna retorted. "You must be joking! That's absolutely disgusting."

As far as Edna was concerned, Shelley was just a child. She had started coming to the practise four years ago as a twelve-year-old. Vaguely, Edna recalled that Jacqueline Jongkind had seemed upset when she phoned to change doctors last fall: something about her daughter going to the doctor's house. But Edna hadn't known what it was about, and Charalambous had brushed it off as a misunderstanding. It was clear enough now though. The doctor—like the villain in Nabokov's *Lolita*—had been living for the past year with a teenage girl, who also happened to have been one of his patients.

"I don't know why you're so surprised about Shelley and me," Charalambous said.

Edna was astonished. "Are you kidding?" she snapped. "For God's sake, man, you're in your thirties. She's just a child."

"Age means nothing," the doctor said. "You're just being old-fashioned and narrow-minded."

"What two consenting adults do is their business," said Edna. "When it's an adult and a child, it's everybody's business."

"I was seeing Shelley with her parents' permission," Charalambous protested. "I can offer her a much better way of life than she can ever hope to have with anyone else." Not only could the doctor take Shelley around the world and buy her nice clothes, he also owned two Japanese cars—and he could give one of them to Shelley.

Edna exploded. "You stupid ass!" she said. "She's not even old enough to drive."

Charalambous was standing on Edna's side of the reception area. He wasn't used to having people give him a piece of their mind. He was caught off guard.

"Well she is now," he stammered.

Edna shook her head. "Where are you coming from?" she asked. "What on earth are you thinking about? Haven't you thought about how this is going to reflect on you and your family?"

Charalambous drew to his full five-foot-five in shoes. "I can do as I please," he told his receptionist. "When I see something I want, I go for it. I don't care who gets in my way. I have enough money to buy the best lawyer in town."

"For heaven's sake man, you're pathetic."

"Oh Edna, be realistic."

The receptionist looked at the doctor with despair. "I really don't think I want to work for you any more," she concluded.

"What's this got to do with you?" asked Charalambous.

"Don't you realize what you've done?" retorted Edna. "I certainly don't respect you. You should be ashamed of yourself."

"You'd better think about what you're doing," said the doctor. "You need me."

"I don't need you at all," said Edna. "I'll give you my decision tomorrow."

Edna tossed and turned sleeplessly through the night. She had known many of the patients for such a long time, but her employer had left her no choice. She returned to the office the following morning to help him find a replacement, but handed in her resignation. "You can't be serious," Charalambous said. "You're destroying my practise."

"You're destroying yourself," Edna replied. "Don't blame anybody but yourself. This is just the start of your downhill slide."

Furious, Charalambous withheld Edna's last cheque and her holiday pay, forcing his slender, dark-haired former receptionist to go to the labor board. In the meantime, he replaced her with his Saturday receptionist, Sharon Frank. The doctor offered Sharon more money than he had been paying Edna, and the fair-haired single mother accepted. It was closer to home than her previous weekday job and would save her from having to commute.

Charalambous told everyone it had all been a tempest in a teapot. Most patients continued to find him charming and polite, but some of them began to look upon him as being selective and aloof. "Before speaking," one of them said, "he would sit back, squint with a rather penetrating stare, and wait for you to speak first. He wasn't very conversational. His manner made me feel uncomfortable."

The doctor also seemed to have some strange friends. One day a tough looking man visited the office. "Who was that?" people inquired of the fearsome-looking visitor. "You really don't want to know," Charalambous smirked. "You don't want to know what he does for a living either. He does night work."

After work, Charalambous took Shelley to the White Spot for dinner. Having had to tend her younger brothers, Shelley welcomed not having to cook and wash dishes. Throughout the time she lived with him, she never did own a proper set of pots and pans. At times, though, the young woman felt trapped. She had only a Grade 10 education, and yet she was living with a man who had a number of undergraduate degrees, as well as a medical degree. He was domineering and overpowering. Having sex with him would usually prevent problems for a while but, no matter how much she tried to please him, he was always stressed out.

"I was a possession," Shelley said later. "I was a symbol. There was no companionship, no emotion. For a start, Joe doesn't know what love is." By October 30, 1986, however, Shelley was becoming ever more deeply mired. On that day, her mother received a phone call from the school counselor. Shelley had come to class wearing a large diamond engagement ring.

Then, less than a week before Christmas, Jacqueline awoke to flames licking the carport directly beneath the bedroom of her two-month-old son. The fire had mysteriously begun in her parked yellow Toyota while she and Rick slept.

As always, the Toyota was locked, but at four o'clock in the morning, Jacqueline had been awakened by the car's horn. "I must be dreaming," she thought. "The horn hasn't worked ever since I owned the car." As she drifted back to sleep, Jacqueline heard the horn again. This time, she got up and rushed out to investigate. The house was already beginning to fill with smoke as she ran back inside. At the top of the stairs, she could see her husband with their two oldest children. "Rick!" she screamed. "The baby!"

Jacqueline waited at the foot of the stairs as her husband rushed into the nursery. After plucking the infant from its crib, he threw the baby boy down the stairs into his mother's outstretched arms. Everyone had made it safely outside.

Firemen arrived in time to save the house, but the car was a write-off. Someone, it seemed, had put newspapers in the front of the vehicle and set them on fire. The carport ceiling had turned black. Constable Adam's house had been on the verge of going up in smoke.

Had someone pressed the car horn to awaken Jacquie? Or had the horn sounded because of a short circuit as electrical wiring melted in the fire? The police questioned Dr. Charalambous about the fire as he arrived home with two unused airline tickets to Hawaii. He and Shelley had been turned back at the airport. The authorities had apparently been alerted that his girlfriend did not have her parents' permission to leave the country. Angry that he'd lost money by having to cancel his trip, Charalambous was unable to help the police with their inquiries.

One month later, Jacqueline Jongkind went outside to use her husband's company Oldsmobile, which he had parked on the street. The paint was peeling off and the bare metal was buckling as if under the force of some ugly alien power. "It was all bubbling up," Jacqueline told her husband later. "It was really ugly." Somebody, it transpired, had thrown acid on the car while it was parked outside. Neither the police nor the insurance corporation were able to solve that mystery either.

In the meantime, a report of the Jongkinds' complaint to the college appeared in a December issue of the *Surrey Leader*. Nearing full term with her first pregnancy, Angela Street was not surprised to read that her former doctor was being investigated by the College of Physicians and Surgeons. Feeling vindicated after reading the article, Angela sat down to write to the college, saying she had also been defiled as a Charalambous patient, and would be willing to come forward to help the complainant.

At the college, Daryl Beere immediately recognized the significance of the complaint, arranging to meet with Angela a few days after she returned home in January with her new baby. Though he could feel the bitter cold as he walked up to the semidetached house on January 15, 1987, Beere preferred to visit complainants in person. Seeing how they lived enabled him to form a better assessment of their character.

While Angela's baby slept, Beere cupped his hands at the kitchen table, gratefully accepting a mug of hot coffee. The complainant, for all he knew, could have been a model. Angela didn't flaunt her appeal but she was slim, with long shiny hair and striking, green eyes. The investigator, she thought, seemed a bit aloof, although sympathetic. "This man is absolutely evil," Beere told her. "You don't even know the beginning of it."

Before leaving, Beere asked Angela for the dates of her visits to Charalambous' office; and he corrected her notion that the complaint to the college had come from the patient. "It's the mother who's made the complaint," he explained. "The girl is saying, 'No, no, no, it isn't abuse.'"

Beere may have perceived that as a problem, but soon after the interview he and other college officials received some encouraging news from the British Columbia Supreme Court. The judge had rejected the doctor's argument that a college hearing would violate his constitutional rights. After almost a year and a half of wrangling, the stage, now at last, was set for the inquiry to begin. "I want to see his license totally revoked in Canada," Jacqueline Jongkind told reporters.

8   The Hearing

The prevailing cold had given way to typical Vancouver weather, and the rain that began falling overnight continued on the dark, overcast morning of February 11, 1987, the teenager watching apprehensively as the imperious-looking officials jostled with their umbrellas in the foyer of the college building at 1807 West Tenth Avenue.

Briefly exchanging pleasantries as they entered, the adjudicators wasted no time removing their raincoats to take their places at the boardroom table. As the recording secretary prepared to take notes, Dr. Charalambous looked dapper in a dark suit, wondering if the partial clearing forecast for later would apply to him as much as to the weather conditions.

Shelley Joel glanced nervously at the doctors assembled in the college boardroom, recognizing only one of them. Since moving in with Josephakis Charalambous M.D. more than a year ago, she'd been physically beaten by him several times. But the short, gray-haired man sitting with his lawyer at one end of the huge boardroom table was at least someone she knew. The other doctors, the recording secretary and the college lawyer, all sitting in their overstuffed pink swivel chairs, appeared even more formidable by comparison, and she could scarcely look them in the eye.

Besides, she'd vowed to stick by the doctor at least this far. Even she had begun to doubt her mother, and Shelley had promised she wouldn't leave him facing the college inquisitors alone. It wouldn't be fair, in Shelley's opinion, to "leave him hanging there" without any support. Like the doctor, she had never believed things would actually go this far. Now, if it would save his practise, she'd tell the college that she loved Dr. Charalambous, while her mother had caused needless trouble and was nothing but a manipulative liar.

In truth, Shelley felt as though she was up against a wall. She ached to be home with her family. She desperately missed Shawna and her brothers, but things had gone way too far. It was much too late now to think of going back. Charalambous had carefully stage managed her story with her over and over again. "Tell them you want to finish high school and take sociology," he'd instructed. "How can I tell them that?" Shelley had replied, "...I don't even know what sociology is."

Despite having lost his court injunction, however, the doctor had almost convinced Shelley that he had done nothing wrong. Inquiry committee members might view things differently, but they wouldn't be the ones to pass sentence. The panel would merely ascertain the facts of the case and report to the college council whether or not the complaint had been proven.

Blinking under the bright lights, Charalambous nervously stroked his chin and adjusted his glasses as he took his place at the table, but presumably he was relieved the college hearings were at least held behind closed doors. (According to the college, this was to protect the privacy of patients—but college critics felt the lack of public scrutiny afforded unwarranted protection for guilty doctors.)

College lawyer David Martin prepared to open the case, while, as expected, the lawyer for Charalambous was the somber, intimidating Richard Peck, dressed in striped trousers and a strangely mismatching, crumpled blue jacket. Whether he knew it or not, Peck projected a frightening air, his unusual eyes apparently gazing off in two directions at the same time.

Peck, nonetheless, was considered among the top lawyers in the city, often representing doctors through his connections with the Canadian Medical Protective Association. One of his clients had been the notorious Dr. Glen Gold Stewart, a Smithers surgeon who'd finally committed suicide in prison after murdering two people and drowning his baby daughter in a bathtub full of water. "A brilliant man," the lawyer recalled.

Charalambous, meanwhile, suppressed his anger as he watched the committee members take their places at the head of the boardroom table.

Privately, he'd told Shelley that the college was "out to get him"—prejudiced, he felt, against his ethnic origins and jealous of his above-average income.

Joined by Vancouver lawyer Len Doust, the inquiry committee consisted of Dr. I. B. Thomson, as chairman, Dr. W. F. Bie and Dr. A. Nyhof.

The first witness, Daryl Beere, tendered Shelley's medical chart, along with billings that Charalambous had submitted to the government health plan for his services to the Jongkind family. There were no questions for Beere from the panel, and none from Peck in cross-examination.

It was time for Jacqueline Jongkind to tell the committee how Charalambous had first defied her parental control, then used his knowledge of the family's intimate affairs to seduce her daughter. Since then, Jacqueline complained, the doctor had prohibited Shelley from having any further contact with her family.

Jacqueline was apprehensive. The doctor had threatened to make her look like an unfit mother, but she was steadfast in her testimony, explaining she had been "appalled" by the doctor's conduct. "Dr. Charalambous betrayed my confidence," she concluded. "He betrayed my trust. My relationship with my daughter has been substantially damaged."

The next witness was Richard Jongkind. He testified having called on Charalambous to discuss his own medical problems only to hear the doctor turn the discussions around to Shelley. "He seemed to be obsessed with talking about her rather than my problems," Jacqueline's husband said.

Shelley's stepfather had left the doctor's office feeling angry and confused. Later, he added, he was shocked and disgusted when he learned the full extent of matters. "I can't imagine...someone of that age and having that type of a profession, being interested in a young girl, I just can't understand that.... In comparing her to other children her age, Shelley looked more mature, acted more mature, but emotionally she was no more mature."

Cross examined by Richard Peck, the witness insisted Shelley had a very loving and caring mother.

The next witness was church minister Marion Lowe, Jacqueline's mother, who testified that Charalambous called her at home wanting to speak to Shelley so often that she (Mrs. Lowe) asked the doctor if there

70

was something wrong. "Dr. Charalambous responded by saying he wanted to talk to her about her medicine.... She has this asthma so bad and he's trying to change medicine to see which one was best for her."

Her evidence was followed by that of Jacqueline's sister Gloria Gale, who testified that Shelley had lived with her for a month before moving in with the doctor. While Shelley was staying with her that previous Christmas, said the witness, the doctor showered her niece with expensive jewelery and clothing.

By the time she began her testimony, Shelley was so nervous she wondered if the committee members could see how badly she was shaking and the fact that her green, silk blouse was already soaked with perspiration.

Shelley admitted right away that she was living with the doctor as husband and wife in a common-law relationship. Originally, she said, the doctor had asked her if she had her mother's permission to go out with him, and she'd told him that she did. She'd had dinner with him at the racetrack but had never gambled.

Charalambous, she maintained, had ceased to be her doctor before she'd begun living with him. She'd had no reoccurrence of asthma since that time. Neither since she'd moved in with him had he given her any drugs. Currently, she added, she did not have a doctor.

In response to inquiry committee questions, Shelley stuck by her story that she loved Dr. Charalambous and planned to marry him. Her school marks, she added, had improved since she'd moved in with him. "Previously," she claimed, "I spent too much of my time taking care of the other children."

Shelley testified her mother was always going out with different men and having them stay overnight at the family home. "We were always fighting," she alleged. "We could never get along. I didn't like the fact that she was always lying to me and trying to get involved in my personal relationships...."

By comparison, she testified, life with Dr. Charalambous was a model of peace and stability. If she were unable to live with him, she maintained, she would not return to her mother's home in any event. She denied that Charalambous had ordered her to cut her mother off. "He always encouraged me to try to get along with my family," the witness maintained.

Shelley hoped her evidence would be enough. She'd seen firsthand how the doctor could react if he were angry. (In order to buy some

71

stocks, he'd once got his mother to remortgage her house, only to berate her afterwards that she'd dallied too long to cash in. Later, Shelley had seen him throw his mother's coffee table against the fireplace in her living room. His mother had denied his request to remortgage her house so that he could open a Greek restaurant. He respected his mother as long as she did what he wanted. But he could also be very cruel to her, and he didn't speak to her after that for several months.)

Richard Peck now called his only witness on behalf of Dr. Charalambous. But the doctor's former receptionist was still angry that she'd had to go to the labor board to get her holiday pay when she had quit.

Edna Neighbour had not wanted to testify and had already told Peck, "I have nothing nice to say." But Peck had decided to subpoena her as a witness anyway. Before entering the room, Edna had been advised by Peck to answer questions with a simple "yes" or "no" and not to offer any of her opinions.

Once on the witness stand, Edna was asked to confirm that she had been in charge of office billing for Dr. Charalambous and that indeed it was her handwriting on bills that had been submitted to the medical insurance plan for the Jongkind family.

But the receptionist was unable to recall the date that Jacqueline Jongkind had phoned asking her to recommend a new family physician. Unaware of any problems, Edna had assumed Jacqueline's inquiry stemmed from a proposed change of residence. The inquiry had been made, the receptionist thought, some time before Shelley's August 8th to 11th hospitalization for asthma.

Dr. Charalambous was then called to give his evidence. Answering questions from his lawyer, he said he listened "from behind" to Shelley's chest when he visited her in hospital on August 11 and told her she could be discharged. He knew she had been living with different members of her family and asked "just for interest" where she would be moving to next.

When Shelley told him she was going to live with her mother in Coquitlam, he asked the girl to check with Jacqueline if she could join him some time for lunch or a soft drink. He said Shelley had phoned the next morning to confirm she had asked permission and "it was okay" if he met her for lunch. "It was my impression that I wasn't the family doctor any more," he said.

Despite her age, he found Shelley very attractive, physically mature

72

and intelligent. She was good company and they enjoyed doing a lot of things together. She was a bit "strong-willed" but was emotionally very mature, almost maternal.

He said he had encouraged Shelley to see her family but exhorted her to stay in during the week to do her homework. When she reached eighteen, he said, they planned to find a jurisdiction outside the province that would allow them to get married.

Charalambous acknowledged it was as their doctor that he had learned about the Jongkind family background. He believed the family was "disorganized" and in economic turmoil, but claimed he'd encouraged Shelley's mother and stepfather to maintain the family unit and develop greater trust.

He confirmed that he had prescribed birth control pills for Shelley early in 1985, but added he'd been living with another girl until the summer and didn't think about dating Mrs. Jongkind's daughter until he discharged Shelley from hospital on August 11. "I think I developed an interest in her then," he stated.

Charalambous was subsequently cross-examined by college lawyer David Martin. "Do you agree that on August 11 you treated Shelley Joel and you also made some overture to her about seeing you later?" inquired Martin.

"I asked her if she wanted to call me, that she could, and we could get together," Charalambous confirmed.

"All right," continued Martin. "That is what I will call the overture, accept that, okay? Now, with those facts, what do you say to my question, do you think that is proper conduct for a doctor?"

"I think it was clear to both Shelley and me...and her mother...that she wasn't my patient."

"She was that day?"

"That was a special instance she came there," said Charalambous, "...that she came to that hospital."

"Okay doctor," said Martin. "You agree there is a doctor/patient relationship existing on August 11?"

"Yes."

"Right," Martin continued. "Okay. She was your patient that day."

"Yes," Charalambous conceded.

"You think that is right?" asked Martin. "You think that is proper conduct for a doctor to make an offer to a patient on the day you are treating them?"

73

"It was the day I discharged her actually," Charalambous countered.

"Well, did you treat her that day?" Martin repeated.

"I didn't treat her that day," replied Charalambous. "She was already better."

"Doctor, did you bill the Medical Services Plan...for the visit that day?"

"Yes, I did."

"You provided—I am using the word *treatment* because I am a layman. If you quarrel with that word, let me know, all right? You attended her as a doctor and you did something which in your mind justified billing the medical plan?"

"Yes."

"That day, okay?"

"Yes."

"All right, I don't think you've answered my question yet. Do you think that is proper conduct?"

"I think you can make arrangements, yes."

"You wouldn't be concerned about the closeness in time of a professional to a social relationship....?"

"I was concerned about that."

"I see.... What did you do about that concern, doctor? You went and dated her, didn't you?"

"We went out, yes. She called me."

"You didn't do anything about your concerns then. You went ahead?"

"No," said Charalambous. "I talked to her and made sure she had permission from her mother. We already went over that."

"All right," said Martin. "Well, I am just not clear on that point. From the role you see yourself in as a doctor, do you think it is the mother's approval that is what governs your conduct—or do you think it is what your conduct ought to be yourself?"

"No," Charalambous replied, ambiguously. "I don't think the mother's approval will necessarily govern your conduct."

Members of the committee wanted to know if Charalambous was aware he could have been charged with having sex with a minor, but for the fact (known to him as her doctor) that Shelley was no longer a virgin by the time she began dating him.

"Yes, I knew that," Charalambous said.

"And the fact that she had been sexually active relieved you of this?" the doctor was asked.

Charalambous stuttered. "I didn't really...I didn't think about that, actually in Shelley, in my relationship with Shelley...."

But, the panel member persisted: "The problem I have is that the reason you know she had been previously sexually active was the fact that you were her physician—and you had privileged and confidential information."

Charalambous attempted a reply: "...I didn't think of it in those terms, that I would, you know, that a...I wasn't taking her out because she had been sexually active.... I was taking her out because there was some attraction and that wasn't, you know, that wasn't in my decision making process."

The questioner still persisted: "Well, do you not think from a physician's point of view that there is something ethically or morally wrong in engaging in intercourse with a fifteen-year-old girl, when you previously knew that she had been sexually active because of confidential information that occurs in the doctor/patient relationship?"

"You could view it that way," said Charalambous. "But I think in our particular instance it would be unfair."

"...You were aware of this but you didn't think about it. Do you think that you were a little careless at times about your attitude towards the ethical responsibilities of a physician?"

"Well," Charalambous replied, "this is the only time that I have gone out with a girl that was fifteen years old at the time."

"Yes. There are many other areas in which a physician has ethical responsibilities besides this one though."

"Yes," agreed Charalambous. "I don't think I've been careless in other areas."

"Just in this one?"

"Yes," the doctor conceded.

Charalambous was asked if he had considered how it might appear to fellow professionals that he was living with a fifteen-year-old former patient. "Did you direct your mind to how that might appear?" he was asked.

"Yes," said Charalambous. "I was uncomfortable with that."

"Did you realize that that was something that might not—let me put it this way—might not look very professional?"

"Yes. I considered that, yes."

"To both your peers...and to the public as well, I suppose?"

"Yes, I was concerned about that, but I think the relationship was a good relationship—and it still is a good relationship—and I think that I was still concerned about that. But it was just that things worked out so well for us, and certainly we never envisaged that things would go to this point where we would be up before the college...."

The hearings had taken four days. The proceedings were finally adjourned on February 18, pending a verdict. Afterwards, one of those who had been present said: "He was the most thoroughly reprehensible character I've ever seen come before the college."

Meanwhile, however, Shelley learned that Charalambous had been pleased with her performance. "He was satisfied with what I said," she recalled later. "He had wanted them to recognize that I seemed much older than I was." The weather had also turned out as predicted. As Charalambous headed away, the rain stopped and the sun poked through the clouds. Could it have been the break for which the doctor had been hoping?

While college officials concentrated on the hearing, the complaint of Angela Street had become virtually forgotten. Daryl Beere had forwarded his findings to college legal counsel on February 3—with the observation that Angela and her husband seemed to have developed cold feet.

At almost the same time as the Jongkind hearing was ending, college lawyers were telling Beere that nothing could be done about Angela Street's complaint pending clarification of the young woman's intentions. But when Beere contacted her again on March 5, Angela confirmed she would proceed with the complaint after all. Her husband, she added, was supportive of her decision and Beere notified college legal counsel the same day.

The investigator called Angela back on March 13, to advise her that the college lawyer wanted her to come in for an appointment. Angela agreed that she would call the lawyer's secretary to arrange a time. Though Beere telephoned three days later to remind her of this, the teenage mother felt the college was placing too much of the onus on her, and used the opportunity presented, by what she considered too much red tape, quietly to let the matter drop.

It was a decision that meant the file of Angela Street and the College of Physicians and Surgeons had come to a close. It would not be reopened for more than six years. By then, for another pretty young woman—about the same age as Angela was now—it would be too late.

9 "Honeymoon" in Vegas

The doctor finished a plate of meat and cheese and gulped down a Coke. He was sitting in the dining room overlooking his indoor pool. "We've got to get married right away," he told Shelley. "The college would look ridiculous charging me with living with my own wife."

It was a few days after the college hearing and Charalambous was in a hurry. He'd just returned home from his office and, as usual, had no more than forty-five minutes to eat before leaving to teach his karate class.

Shelley had learned always to have his meat plate ready in the fridge, along with his plate of raw vegetables—and she knew better than to make the mistake of getting him anything other than his favorite cola.

She poured him another one into his favorite mug as she listened to his proposal. He'd first broached but shelved the marriage option last year after failing to get her mother's approval. Now that it was time to act, Shelley suddenly felt trapped. The proposition complicated everything.

Charalambous saw the frightened look in her eyes. "Look," he insisted, "you've got no choice. You owe it to me. It's the only way."

Shelley listened apprehensively as Charalambous explained how they could forge her birth certificate to say she was nineteen rather than seventeen. In most jurisdictions, that would make her an adult, no longer requiring parental approval for her actions. "We'll get married in Las Vegas," he said.

A few days later, the not-so-happily betrothed were on their way to the airport. Shelley had always dreamed of a romantic wedding, with Shawna as one of the bridesmaids. Now, however, she felt isolated as she sat beside a tense, much older man whom she secretly found repugnant. His hands and feet stopped fidgeting just long enough for him to ask her a question.

"Did you remember the key for the suitcases?" he inquired.

Shelley thought for a moment, then realized the suitcase keys were something she'd forgotten. "No, I left them in the house," she stammered.

The doctor was furious, berating Shelley as they secured the cases with packing tape at the airport counter. As she and the doctor became airborne, the harangue continued and, by the time the plane touched down in Vegas two and a half hours later, an embarrassed and humiliated Shelley was on the verge of tears.

After checking into their hotel, the doctor insisted Shelley accompany him downstairs to the casino, where she had to stand close enough that everyone knew she was with him. Shelley watched for several hours, bored as she waited for her escort to finish playing baccarat and roulette.

The next morning heralded the big day, March 19, 1987. Wearing high heels, Shelley towered over the diminutive doctor as the patently mismatched couple stood awkwardly in line waiting to apply for their marriage license.

Shelley felt sure everyone was looking at them, and her nerves were on edge in case someone might challenge her forged birth certificate. The doctor had relaminated it after entering the new birth date, but the type faces no longer matched and it wasn't a particularly good job.

No one seemed to notice or care, however. Given a checklist at the wedding chapel, the couple declined music, flowers and pictures, with the exception of one photograph. As the female minister recited the vows, Shelley giggled nervously. She knew it was a charade and she found the whole ceremony pseudocomical. Afterwards, the bride and groom went for breakfast.

Over two orders of eggs benedict, Shelley told her new husband she'd rather spend the morning shopping than gambling, and she hadn't even finished her meal when Joe impatiently pushed away his plate and got up from the table. "See you at the hotel," he told her. "I'm going back to the casino."

Bored and lonely on her wedding day, Shelley walked around the hotel by herself. She could barely wait until her four-day "honeymoon" would come to an end, but now she was truly trapped. Cut off from her own family, going home would be meaningless too.

When she returned to the marital home, Shelley described her trip to fellow karate students. At first, they thought she was joking when she told them that she'd become the doctor's wife, but their smiles quickly evaporated as the truth sank in.

Jacqueline Jongkind sent flowers to the couple when she learned about the marriage through her ex-husband two weeks later, but others in the family could see that she was devastated. "It'll never last," Jacqueline told them. "Shelley always wanted a fairy-tale wedding. They've done this only because he needed her to get out of a mess."

Charalambous, meanwhile, put the original and the forged copies of Shelley's birth certificates in a kitchen cupboard and forgot about them. Upon returning to work, the doctor was pleasantly surprised that most of his patients were sticking by him despite the scandal. Medical patients, he learned, don't like to change doctors.

The doctor explained to Chris Simmonds and others that he was "in love" with his wife, and that marriage to a younger woman was simply a Greek tradition. Unaware of the details, Chris Simmonds saw no reason to doubt someone of presumably good character. Along with virtually all the other patients, the Simmonds family continued to visit the Charalambous practise.

Meanwhile, right on cue, Shelley became pregnant with her first baby. Jacqueline Jongkind, however, wouldn't be allowed to see her grandchild unless she would retract her allegations. "Joe blamed my mother for all his problems," Shelley said later. "She was screwing up his life."

Charalambous remembered things differently from Shelley. "What I tried to do was get her and her mother to talk to each other and work things out," the doctor claimed. He admitted, however, that his efforts at family mediation had failed.

While Jacqueline remained cut off, Shelley proudly showed her new baby girl Allison* to staff and patients at the medical practise, sometimes asking Sharon Frank, the full-time receptionist, to babysit while she applied for modeling jobs.

Charalambous thought it cute that the baby would fit in his favorite crystal punch bowl. "My punch bowl baby," he called her, but in truth he was an authoritarian father and the baby cried a lot. The doctor lost no sleep cutting Jacqueline Jongkind out of the family, yet insisted that a sometimes hesitant Shelley should take the baby more often to see his mother. Betty Charalambous welcomed Shelley into the family, but later confided to some people that her daughter-in-law seemed to be a bit of a gold digger.

Soon after the birth of their first child, Shelley began working for the doctor as his weekend receptionist—sometimes performing her duties in high, spiked heels and an alluring dress with a bow in the back. Given the title of office manager, she was responsible for hiring replacement staff and ordering equipment for the practise. Some of the patients were taken aback by Shelley's tender age and were reluctant to answer her questions as to the nature of their medical problems.

Others in the building, however, were clearly mesmerized by her. Speaking in hushed tones—so as not to be overheard during lunch at a nearby Greek restaurant—a lawyer, who used to rent space in the same three-storey office complex, offered his impression. "What a knockout broad!" he recalled.

Evidently, Charalambous did not share the embarrassment of some of his patients. Emerging one day from an examination room, he ogled his provocatively dressed, young wife and exclaimed: "Oh, Shelley, I like that. That looks great!"

Before her daughter was born, Shelley had at least gone out with her husband to play cards or to watch the races at Exhibition Park. Afterwards, however, her husband had taken to going out by himself. Often, she recalled, he played poker in the back of Greek and Italian restaurants after they closed down.

"He always told me he was with his Greek buddies," said Shelley, though right from the start she knew better than to expect fidelity. No sooner had she married him, it seemed, than tales of his dalliances with downtown hookers had begun filtering back to her from some of her friends.

Shelley continued to feel trapped, as though sinking ever deeper into an abyss, but there appeared no way that she and her daughter could escape. In the event of marriage breakdown, Charalambous had always maintained he would be the one to have custody of his children. He wouldn't give them up like other fathers. "It would never happen," he said. "We Greeks don't do things that way."

Shelley did, however, enjoy meeting the patients—including the Simmonds sisters. The practise was becoming ever more successful, her husband earning over 50 percent more than the average British Columbia physician. At last, however, Shelley and the doctor received word that the College of Physicians and Surgeons was ready to hand down its decision—and the future once more was very much in doubt.

10   Infamous Conduct

L ooking nervously over her shoulder, Shelley lifted a corner of the baby's blanket, allowing Jacqueline Jongkind a chance glimpse of her new grandchild. The teenage mother had been nursing the infant in a waiting room at the College of Physicians and Surgeons, while a preoccupied Dr. Charalambous headed upstairs for the college boardroom to learn his fate.

By March 25, 1988, more than twelve months had elapsed since the inquiry committee hearing. But at last the college, which attributed the delay to legal considerations, was ready to hear final submissions before rendering its verdict.

"Ohh, could I hold the baby?" Jacquie pleaded.

Shelley hesitated. "Sure," she relented, but as Jacqueline cradled the child, the two women heard someone coming down the hall. "Quick!" said Shelley, terror in her voice. "Give her back to me!"

The footsteps, however, only belonged to a security guard, advising Jacqueline that the council was ready to hear her submission in the boardroom.

Crying, Shelley had phoned her mother at home the previous week to say that Jacquie could visit her and the baby if only she'd put in a good word for the doctor prior to the verdict. Rick and Jacqueline Jongkind had talked it over—and in desperation had agreed to do what they could.

Subsequently, they had gone over their proposed statement with

Richard Peck, who struck them as friendly and sympathetic. "I'm a family man too," the lawyer commiserated, suggesting they make only one or two changes for the sake of clarity.

The couple were now granted permission to read their statement, but the college had already received a report from the inquiry committee upholding their complaint. The committee had taken a dim view of the fact that Charalambous had disparaged the Jongkinds' possible recourse to the college.

Finding that the doctor had shown contempt for the Jongkinds' parental authority and that he had "exacerbated" the family's problems, the committee was generally critical of Charalambous, but appeared to stop short of outright condemnation. "...At least in one dimension, that of her schooling, Shelley has settled down to a pattern of improvement," the committee reported. "Her grades have improved and there are therefore clearly some benefits from her relationship with Dr. Charalambous that flow directly to Shelley Joel herself."

As he rose to his feet to address the college, Rick Jongkind also intended to be conciliatory, but broke down midway through his prepared statement. Picking up from where her husband had left off, Jacqueline urged the council to spare Charalambous from losing his license. "If we'd known he was truly in love with Shelley and not just toying with our emotions, we wouldn't have objected," said Jacqueline. "Now that they're married, we don't want him to lose his practise."

As she left the boardroom, Jacqueline was sure the council members had been skeptical. Her appeal, however, together with a committee finding that the affair appeared to have been based on genuine attraction, perhaps contributed to softening the outcome. The complaint of Angela Street might have made a difference, but it had been filed away and forgotten. Instead of revoking his license entirely, the council voted to suspend Charalambous from practise for six months.

Though he had been found guilty of infamous conduct, Charalambous would, after all, have a second chance. After his suspension, his name would be entered on a temporary register with the proviso that, in future, he would have to practise medicine "in a manner that is beyond reproach in all respects." He would have to take an acceptable course in medical ethics and pay a fine of $10,000. He was also ordered to pay $20,000 in costs.

After the verdict, Jacqueline told media representatives that her opinion of Charalambous had not changed. She stated, however, that she didn't want to damage her daughter's future. "She's not the fifteen-year-old she was when this started. She's seventeen now. That's young to be married, but that's her choice. It's out of love for our daughter that we don't want to get involved now. We're willing to accept him into our family if that's what she wants."

Though pressed at the time by newspaper reporters for a statement, Charalambous refused to discuss the matter. "I prefer not to comment," he said shyly. "We really don't want any publicity. I'm hoping all this will blow over."

Back at the house on Foster Avenue, Shelley found her husband was reasonably satisfied with her efforts, but that he wanted to speak further with Jacqueline Jongkind. He invited her to his house that evening, seeking further concessions to help him get the verdict over-turned. Jacqueline attended with her husband, but the conversation was stilted and restrained as Shelley, the gracious hostess, brought them two bottles of Perrier from the fridge. Quickly, it became apparent the doctor wished to speak with Jacqueline alone in another room. Reluctantly, she agreed, leaving Rick to speak with Shelley in the living room.

"Thanks for the flowers," Charalambous began. "It was too little too late, but it was a nice gesture." Fetching the baby from her bedroom, the doctor placed the child out of Jacqueline's reach, but explained she could have normal relations with her granddaughter if only she would retract her lies. Jacqueline denied his contention that, among other things, she'd been behind the distribution of the posters at the hospital. Apart from her last-minute statement to the college, she felt, she didn't think there was anything more she could do. As Jacqueline and her husband prepared to leave, Charalambous was apparently dissatisfied. Behind Rick's back, he took Jacqueline by the arm in his doorway. "I'm not through with you yet!" he hissed.

The doctor also was reportedly angry when he met Rick Jongkind one day outside a Coquitlam credit union. "This whole thing has cost me about $80,000," he told Jacqueline's husband. "Nobody screws me for that amount of money and gets away with it."

Under the Medical Practitioners Act, Charalambous was entitled to appeal the decision to the British Columbia Supreme Court and he did so on June 15, 1988, complaining that the sanctions had been "harsh and excessive." According to Richard Peck, the college had erred in finding that Charalambous' conduct had been infamous. The doctor's lawyer told Justice Reginald Gibbs that the college had failed to identify which inquiry committee findings established infamous conduct, with the result that neither the court nor Charalambous could know what conduct the college had considered improper.

The penalties, said Peck, were harsh and excessive in light of the fact—known to the college at the time it imposed punishment—that the doctor and Shelley had continued their relationship since the inquiry committee hearing, and that they had married and had a child.

The inquiry committee, Peck contended, had failed to identify what it described as "material contradictions" between the evidence of the Jongkinds on one hand and that of Dr. Charalambous and Shelley on the other.

Peck complained that the committee had rejected the doctor's evidence "partly or wholly because of an inference of untrustworthiness based solely on his position as the subject of the disciplinary proceeding." Furthermore, the lawyer claimed, the inquiry committee had rejected the evidence of Shelley Joel simply because she was allied with his client and opposed to the position taken by her mother.

The lawyer also argued that the inquiry committee had failed "to accord to the evidence of Dr. Charalambous that measure of belief to which a professional man is entitled in the absence of compelling evidence to the contrary."

Peck said Charalambous never disputed the facts but felt he had been unduly penalized. The doctor had no money, said Peck, only debts. "If he's suspended from practise for six months, he's finished. He'll have no practise to come back to. They may as well have erased him. That's the effect of it."

College lawyer David Martin argued that the doctor's financial problems were of his own making because he had deferred paying income tax for two years and "now faces his day of reckoning." Martin filed medical plan receipts showing the doctor's gross income from 1986 to 1988 was almost $200,000 per year—approximately $60,000 per annum above the average doctor's income.

Charalambous, added the college lawyer, had incorporated his practise to obtain whatever tax advantages were available, and had mortgaged his $250,000 house for $191,000 to pay other debts and to purchase securities prior to the college hearing.

Six days after the legal arguments, Justice Gibbs dismissed the appeal on all issues other than punishment. Though he had strong criticism for Charalambous, the judge agreed with Peck that the college penalties had been "extremely harsh."

Gibbs, a tall, retired rancher who spoke with a slow western drawl, was hesitant to overrule the college findings, because of "the deference due to a council of the appellant's peers, who are in a position to know and appreciate the standards required to be maintained in their profession; and to judge the appropriate severity of the sanction to be imposed for infringing those standards."

Nonetheless, the judge set aside the suspension and financial penalties, ordering them referred back to the college for reconsideration. "The fine is the maximum which may be levied under the Act," he said, in his reasons for judgment. "The cost award is double the amount of the fine. The obligation to find and pay $30,000 after tax while suspended from the means of earning a livelihood represents potential financial ruin for this relatively young family.

"It appears to me that insufficient regard was given to record and reputation and to the subsequent marriage and to the appellant's family responsibilities as mitigating factors.

"How is Dr. Charalambous to pay if he can't practise?" the judge asked. "The objective is to punish, not to destroy."

Gibbs did, however, uphold the remainder of the college findings, and disagreed with Peck's contention that the college had been remiss in failing to single out any particular instance of what had constituted infamous conduct.

"What they found to be infamous was the entire course of conduct," said the judge, "the bare bones of which were itemized in the charge, proceeding from the family-doctor relationship, to the singling out of the fifteen-year-old daughter of the family for concentrated personal attention, to cohabitation and sexual intercourse with her.

"I am not under any misapprehension and neither was the council—and neither, I am sure, is Dr. Charalambous—about what conduct of his fell within the category of infamous."

The judge referred to a doctor who'd been disciplined for seducing a married woman, and found that the Charalambous case involved "moral turpitude" that was even worse. "Here, the family doctor—over the strenuous objections of the mother and stepfather—took a fifteen-year-old child into his home and cohabited with her and had sexual relations with her.

"The fact that he subsequently married her and that they now have

87

a family does not, in my view, erase the abuse of trust and confidence implicit in the course of conduct which the doctor undertook at the material times. There was an honorable course which he could have followed if he had exercised patience; but he did not and, thereby in my opinion, he elected to accept the risk of the fate which has now befallen him."

Gibbs disagreed that Charalambous' testimony should have been afforded special consideration because of his professional standing. "There is no principle of law," the judge said, "that the mere fact of a professional qualification puts the evidence of an individual on a higher plane of credibility than that of an individual without professional qualifications."

In light of the split judgment, Gibbs declined to award costs of the appeal to either party, even though the matter was raised by Martin in his capacity as the college's lawyer. Each side would have to pay their own legal expenses.

Though the judge's decision represented a partial victory for Charalambous, any celebration in the doctor's camp was relatively short-lived. Within three months, the college reconsidered the penalties—as required by the court order—and delivered its rejoinder.

Although it cut the $10,000 fine in half, the college upheld the $20,000 in costs as well as the six-month suspension. The college did give Charalambous more time to pay, but all the other sanctions remained in place. Privately, a college official said Charalambous was being treated leniently, and that some council members had wanted his license permanently erased.

Peck and his client, however, contended the "marginal change" in penalties did not comply with the spirit of the court order, and complained that it merely reduced the financial portion of the sanctions from $30,000 to $25,000. The doctor considered a further appeal but eventually found little choice other than to prepare for the suspension and take his medicine.

According to Shelley, the doctor was bitter, angry and deeply humiliated as he began serving his six-month college suspension on January 1, 1989. He was forced to re-mortgage his house for a second time, but managed to keep his Surrey office by renting it for $1,500 a month to another doctor in the same building.

Charalambous recorded a new, outgoing message on his telephone answering machine giving the impression that he was merely on vacation, but college officials found out about it and insisted that the message be deleted. The doctor did, however, continue to employ his receptionist, Sharon Frank, as a subtle reminder to patients that he was still connected with the practise even if he was not physically present.

Shelley noticed a big change in her husband after the college decision. The doctor became withdrawn and no longer invited karate students over to the house as he had in the past. He gambled away a good part of the mortgage proceeds, once putting $6,000 on a horse that came in dead last.

"The college is out to get me," he told Shelley. "I don't know what gives them the right. I didn't do anything wrong."

Charalambous found the whole affair "traumatic" and continued to blame it all on Jacqueline Jongkind. Fearing for the family's safety, Rick Jongkind arranged a job transfer to Alberta.

Now totally cut off from her mother, Shelley grew closer to her husband's friend Gail Pikker—a dark-haired, heavyset woman who walked with a cane and lived close by with her cat Lily—but life with her new husband was a constant turmoil. "He was always stressed out," Shelley recalled. "If it wasn't one thing, it was another." But when it came to other people's problems, she learned, her husband generally showed no emotion at all. And Shelley didn't know whether to believe her husband's continual threats or not. "There were many times," she said later, "when he threatened to hit me or beat me—which he did—so I can't say he didn't mean them."

Begrudgingly, Charalambous arranged to attend the course he had been ordered to take in medical ethics, flying to Washington D.C. to sit in on classes at the Kennedy Institute of Ethics at Georgetown University. "It was a course in bioethics," he smiled on his return. "It had more to do with organ transplants. It wasn't really applicable to their intent."

Before he could get back his license, however, Charalambous was required to report for an interview with college officials and to supply them with details of the course as it had applied to him. The late college registrar Dr. Arnold had been succeeded by an affable Englishman, Dr. Tom Handley, who together with Dr. Jack Harrigan, of the college's ethics committee, questioned Charalambous about the course contents and the large folder of course materials he had brought with him.

Handley, a slightly balding man with gold rimmed glasses, dwelled on the serious nature of the offenses, informing Charalambous he had been fortunate not to have faced more severe punishment or criminal prosecution. The registrar also reminded Charalambous of the condition that his future practise would have to be beyond reproach in all respects.

Upon his return to practise, the doctor's receptionist Sharon Frank recalled that Charalambous had a much different outlook on life from anyone she'd ever known. "Laws didn't apply to him," said Sharon. "He seemed to have more guts than anybody I ever knew. Nothing ever fazed him."

Charalambous rarely paid his rent or his taxes on time. "They would always be chasing after him and he'd say, 'I'll send it, I'll send it.' It didn't seem to bother him that he owed money. Other people in the building would turn their noses up at him. He said himself, 'I am a very hated man.'"

Charalambous had kept his receptionist while he served out his suspension but, one month later, he replaced her with a young married patient who had been a friend of hers. "Don't bother coming back tomorrow," he told Sharon after work one day. "I have to make some changes in my life. We don't get along very well."

Sharon was hurt and surprised but realized she was no competition for the younger woman. "Karen was quite pretty and had a very nice body," the receptionist said. "She carried herself like she knew she was a looker." Unknown to his wife, the doctor expressed his appreciation for Karen by buying her a black leather miniskirt. But Sharon would later be proved to have been correct in one of her assumptions; as Karen's thirtieth birthday approached, Charalambous fired her too.

Shelley knew full well why Charalambous had married her, but felt she had little choice now other than to help him rebuild his practise, as he set out to add more patients and double his dollar volume. Hoping it might squelch rumors about his licentious practise, he tried a partnership for a while with a woman doctor, but she quit after a few months when she realized why she'd been hired.

But the practise was busy and he did have discussions with a male physician nearing retirement about coming in on a part-time basis. Since buying the practise, Charalambous had added a fourth examination room, but now entertained thoughts of further renovations so as to create six examination rooms by juggling things around with a new floor plan.

By calling Shelley his office manager, the doctor was able to split his earnings with his wife for income tax purposes. Shelley continued to come to the office on weekends, but she was pregnant with her second child, and soon presented Charalambous with the son he had always wanted. Office photos of Shelley and the children on the walls showed the patients glimpses of an ostensibly happy family. "You're so lucky to be married to such a kind, generous man," patients told her.

It had been some time since Charalambous had seen his friend Brian West. Shelley observed that the two of them would sometimes lose touch with each other for as long as three years at a time, but then get together for a beer at a sports bar in Vancouver or for a game of cards at the home of Charalambous' mother, in North Burnaby. Although it went back twenty years, it was that type of friendship.

West had been grateful, Shelley noted, when her husband gave him a character reference in 1990 pertaining to an assault on the biker's estranged wife. Charalambous kept blank reference letters for patients in his medical files, but for his best friend had the letter redone and especially typed by an office services company in Surrey. Charalambous wrote that he had known West since the early 1970s and that his friend had been very helpful in the karate schools that the doctor ran in his spare time.

Shelley knew that Charalambous hated authority but no matter where he went, he seemed to run straight into the forces of officialdom. Firstly, it had been the police, then the College of Physicians and Surgeons—and now the authorities at the racetrack had suggested he forget about renewing his owner's license. His legal problems, it was explained, might conflict with the strict provisions of the provincial Horseracing Act.

Shelley observed that her husband didn't fight the disqualification—some of the track officials, after all, were ex-policemen—but it didn't stop him continuing to bet heavily or eventually from getting around the ban by having his wife withdraw $16,000 from his bank account to register a horse in her own name.

In martial arts, Shelley went on to get her purple belt but then quit karate altogether. Now pregnant with her third child, she had become increasingly anxious to get out of the relationship, but didn't tell her husband this. She had always been extremely quiet and compliant, but her resentment was growing.

The simple fact was, though, that the suspension seemed to have had few adverse effects. The Charalambous practise was growing by leaps and bounds. Shelley listened as Charalambous bragged how much he cared for his patients, but some of them had come to distrust and despise him almost as much as she did. One of them, a bespectacled young woman with long, lank hair, felt the doctor should have been charged for roughly grabbing her infant son by the ear to make him sit down. "He should be a good boy and stay with his mom," she recalled Charalambous telling her. According to the same patient, the doctor and his staff were not dressed professionally either. Instead of wearing lab coats or nurses' uniforms, the doctor's assistants were inappropriately clad in high heels and miniskirts. Nor did she think it was proper that the doctor was invariably dressed in casual pants and unbuttoned shirts. Another patient said Charalambous once implied she could get better quality marijuana and cocaine by coming to him, rather than buying it on the street.

Charalambous also seemed to have developed some unusual, diagnostic techniques. Even if they went to see him with a sprained ankle, several of his female patients found, now, that he often inquired if they were happy with their sexual relationships.

11 Stolen Dreams

You will give no drug, perform no operation for a criminal purpose, even if solicited, far less suggest it....

Standing in the kitchen of the split level house in Willoughby Hill, Sian Simmonds put down the telephone. In her teens now, she was no longer an awkward child, but had blossomed into the blonde, blue-eyed beauty accurately described by her sister Katie as the envy of every girl in her school.

"That was my doctor," Sian frowned, redirecting her attention to a visiting friend. "Just checking up on me while Mom and Dad are in England." Sian seemed flattered but puzzled. If she hadn't had company, it had almost sounded as though Dr. Charalambous was suggesting he could make a housecall. And she wasn't even ill....

Sian thought little more of it, however. There was no reason to suspect anything untoward. She knew that the doctor had a young wife and family. She'd met Shelley as his weekend receptionist at the office, and had seen photos of their children smiling happily from the walls of his waiting room. Besides, he was the family doctor, and she certainly wasn't interested in wasting her holidays speaking to someone of his age. She was having far too much fun with her own friends.

As he took a break from stocking shelves in the Coquitlam Center Safeway store, Dave Sella observed that the new cashier with the "big blonde hair" was attempting to explain why she was late for her very first day at work. The tall, young grocery clerk did a double take. He could see the girl was flustered, but went out of his way to read her name tag. "Hi Si-Ann," he interjected. "Twenty minutes late, eh. I guess you've been driving around trying to find the store?"

Sian glared at him. She may have been concerned about getting fired before she even started, but she was nothing if not self-confident. Everyone said she got that from her mother. "It's not Si-Ann," she corrected haughtily. "It's Sian (S-h-a-w-n)."

Two months later, when she arrived for work plastered with ointment for a bad sunburn, Sella got up the nerve to try again. "Gee Sian!" he said, seeing the skin peeling off her nose. "You're looking a bit pale. You should get a tan!" Hearing this, Sian fired back about the facial blemish that Sella had as the result of a birthmark. "At least I don't have a big scar on my face!" she fumed. But when she apologized and confided that a rival male employee was "nothing but a loser," Sella could barely conceal his delight. "I could have told you that," he beamed. "If you'd just stop flirting around, we could have a nice time."

After work, the two of them went to see a Stephen King horror movie at Coquitlam Center, Sian giggling when Sella jumped at the scary parts. "She was very outgoing," Sella recalled. "Everyone always had more fun when Sian was around." Male colleagues at the store congratulated Sella on his find. "She looked great walking down the aisle at work," he agreed later, "but when she got dressed up, she looked like a million bucks."

When his girlfriend invited him to her parents' home, David wasn't sure who intimidated him more: Sian's stern father, Chris Simmonds, or Bear, the family's big German Shepherd who bounded up to greet David, barking loudly. "Sian had a lot of respect for her parents," Sella recalled. "She and Katie jogged a little bit and kept pretty fit; but she also smoked and she kept that a secret from her Mom and Dad."

Eventually, however, David and Sian split up. Sian transferred to the Safeway store in Langley and agreed with her parents to stop moping about him. Soon afterwards, she enrolled in courses at Kwantlen college for a career in environmental health, and took a waitressing job at Boondocks Seafood Broiler in Langley. But Sian was fiercely loyal. Occasionally running into her ex-boyfriend at local nightclubs, she still brooded about him. Finally, Katie took Sella aside one day for a big sister talking-to at a Coquitlam restaurant. "You hurt Sian," Katie admonished, "I don't know if you're good for her, but she's still willing to see you."

"We still love each other," Sella conceded, looking more serious than usual. "I'd like to talk with her and give it another whirl."

After that, Sella felt he had to walk on eggshells around Katie. She was so protective of her younger sister that he'd never want to risk offending her. Katie told Sian what she'd done, but the sisters got onto other topics. And it was then that both opened their eyes widely in shared recognition, as they discussed the similar experiences they'd both had through the years during their visits to Dr. Charalambous. "Just after New Year's," Katie said to Sian, illustrating her point, "I told him I had quit smoking and he put his arms around me and gave me a big wet kiss. It was gross."

"Really," Sian concurred. "He did that to me, too. I never realized it when we were younger, but now I can see he's always been *way* too friendly."

Sella was stunned when Sian told him that her family doctor had made passes at her. He wanted to pay the doctor a surprise visit, but Sian convinced her boyfriend that that was "not a good idea." Instead, Sian and Katie discussed the matter with their father. After Chris Simmonds listened to their story, he did what any other thoughtful and responsible parent might do. In September 1991, he picked up the phone—and initiated a formal complaint about Dr. Charalambous to the British Columbia College of Physicians and Surgeons.

When he received the complaint, college registrar Dr. Tom Handley immediately realized it had been only two years since Charalambous had finished serving his previous suspension. The registrar was shocked. He made sure that the complaint was put on the agenda for the very next meeting of the college council. He also immediately notified the college lawyer and staff.

Daryl Beere, the college investigator, was now back on the trail of Dr. Charalambous. The council had ordered an investigation into the doctor's conduct under Section 50 (4) of the Medical Practitioners Act and Beere had driven to the Simmonds' residence in the country to meet with Sian and Katie in person. As he interviewed them in the living room, Beere felt that Sian was nervous, but he was impressed that both she and Katie appeared to be thoroughly decent young women. Before leaving, the college investigator talked with Chris Simmonds about a mutual acquaintance in the RCMP, then—in the driveway—he took the girls' father into his confidence. "He got away from me before," said Beere with contempt. "He's not going to get away from me this time."

Charalambous was not unduly concerned, however, when he first learned of the complaint. He confided to Shelley that he had phoned Sian at home while her parents were in England, but denied having fondled either of the sisters in his office. Even if he had kissed them, he told Shelley, it would be no big deal. "The complaints are baseless and frivolous," he said.

From his wife's perspective, it appeared Charalambous felt the complaints would end up being dropped long before they ever went to a college hearing. The college was notoriously slow in scheduling such hearings in any event. The doctor had often told his wife that his time was worth $150 an hour—apparently too much to bother fretting about the new allegations, or to dwell on all that had happened since the previous verdict.

Jacqueline Jongkind had felt mixed reactions at that time. On one hand, she hadn't wanted to see Shelley and her grandchild hurt by the college sanctions—but the doctor's conduct, she'd felt on the other, would fully have warranted the irrevocable loss of his license.

Shawna had moved back with her mother, and Shelley had begun hanging up on her too. "She was my idol," Shawna said later. "Every time she did that, I just bawled and bawled." Around her mother, Shawna felt that she had to take her sister's place and actually be Shelley. Moving with her mother and stepfather to Alberta, Shawna wondered if she would see or talk to her sister again. When new friends asked about her family, she bit her tongue and lied, a sad, vacant look in her eyes. "I did have an older sister once," Shawna conceded, "but she died."

Jacqueline Jongkind had always kept a framed photograph of Shelley in her bedroom. Alongside her daughter's picture, she placed Shelley's Barbie Doll, a smaller doll and her teddy bear. Each night, Jacqueline knelt beside her daughter's shrine and prayed for her safe return. Jacqueline continued to turn a deaf ear to any criticism of her eldest child, but soon was sorely tested when her father underwent heart surgery.

"Please," she implored Shelley by phone. "If your grandfather means anything to you, don't hang up!"

"What is it?" Shelley asked impatiently.

"He's had a quadruple bypass," said Jacqueline, "He's in critical condition."

Shelley listened to the news, but her voice was desolate and emotionless. "It doesn't matter," she said just before she hung up. "None of you even exist for me any more, anyway."

Jacqueline felt as though a knife had gone through her, her whole body shaking as she sobbed, torn between generations. She couldn't help but remember the futility of how her father, retired gospel minister Bert Lowe, had tried so gamely to reason with Charalambous early on. But the tall man with the regal bearing was no longer bolt upright. Tubes everywhere came out of his body, as he lay on his hospital bed, mercifully oblivious to his granddaughter's cold response.

Later, Shelley offered an explanation for her reaction by saying she was trapped, acutely depressed and that she had to bottle up her emotions to survive. The doctor had been careless not only with her, she felt, but had also demonstrated less than honorable concern for the health of their unborn third child. Just a few days before the baby had been due, Shelley had learned that her husband had been out with a hooker, and later he had experienced pain when he'd gone to the ensuite. "It could be serious for the baby," he told Shelley.

"How could you?" Shelley asked angrily. "Now what?" Despite any other shortcomings she may have had, she was a devoted mother.

"I'll check with a specialist," Charalambous offered. "I'll say it's for one of my pregnant patients."

"I don't believe this," said Shelley. Thinking more about it that day, she wanted to leave him now, more than ever before. She was tired of his demands. Never once had he tried to please her, but he always expected, before her latest pregnancy, that she would do anything to please him. "I know you'd go down on another girl to please me," Shelley recalled him saying.

Her husband returned after work with two vials of penicillin. The specialist had confirmed that the "pregnant patient and her husband" should each receive a single dose. Raising her long T-shirt, Shelley leaned over the kitchen counter. It was a large volume of antibiotic, made even larger by the necessity of mixing it with anesthetic, and Shelley grimaced at the length of time it seemed to be taking.

It was now her turn to play doctor. Shelley looked at the long needle, and glared at the target presented by her husband as he lowered his trousers and bent apprehensively over the same counter. Despite being the office manager of a medical practise, Shelley had never given anyone an injection before. Under the present circumstances, however, she didn't much care whether she hurt him or not.

Without telling her husband, Shelley had the new baby girl carefully checked for any symptoms of his infidelity. She had already asked a second doctor for her opinion, and that doctor had been appalled that Shelley had received the injection outside a medical setting, in case she'd had an unexpected reaction. Though relieved to find that her baby was well, Shelley would never forgive her husband this particular trespass. It would be bad enough coming from any husband, doubly so from a doctor who, she felt, surely must have known better.

Almost six months after the Simmonds sisters had made their complaints, Daryl Beere called at Charalambous' office on March 30, 1992, to ask for Sian's and Katie's medical records. Accompanied by a junior lawyer, Charalambous still seemed unconcerned. "It's all lies," he told Beere. "These complaints are baseless and frivolous." Ten days later, Beere submitted his findings to college lawyer David Martin.

Charalambous was advised by his senior lawyer, Christopher Hinkson, that there were "inconsistencies" in the girls' statements and it would be his word against theirs. The doctor now admitted to Shelley and others that he was addicted to sex, as well as to gambling, but he didn't tell them that he'd begun an affair with yet another teenage girl—this one allegedly procured for him by her own father in exchange for prescription drugs.

The sixteen-year-old patient alleged that her father told her to "go in there and do everything the doctor asks" after getting his prescription on March 26, 1992 (just four days prior to Beere's visit). "I knew what he meant," she said later, "but I didn't want to make my father angry and face another beating. Dr. Charalambous asked me if I would join him for dinner that evening.... Dad told me it would be okay, to go ahead, that Dr. Charalambous was a good doctor."

According to the teenager, Charalambous drove her as darkness fell to a secluded spot on the University Endowment Lands, where he pressured her into giving him oral sex. "Come on," she recalled the doctor persisted. "Nobody'll know. I won't tell anybody." Afterwards, she alleged, he took her for a pizza and then drove her back to the same place for a repeat performance. "It was gross," she recalled.

The girl said she declined an offer to be a nanny to the doctor's three children and began working as a hooker on the street. "I no longer had any respect for myself," she said. "I felt hurt, used and dirty. He was supposed to be my doctor. I had thought he was somebody I could trust."

The doctor, she alleged, also visited the Surrey motel where she was staying with another street girl, offering her pills and cocaine in exchange for more sex. She had a final tryst with Charalambous, she recalled, after business hours at his medical office. "He pressed the security code to get in. We went into one of the examining rooms and the doctor asked if I would have sex with him.... He wouldn't wear a condom so I gave him oral sex instead. He was sitting on his examination table."

Eventually, the teenager returned to the small interior town where her mother was living, and went to the police to file a complaint. One day soon afterwards, she alleged, she received a telephone call from her father. "You should drop it," she recalled her father telling her. "Go to the police station where you made the statement and say that you lied. Tell them you were high." The girl told authorities she feigned agreement but secretly had no intention of withdrawing any of her statements, even though she said her father warned her of the consequences.

"If you don't drop the charges," she recalled her father telling her, "the doctor will have somebody come after you. He'll put a hit on you."

12 David Schlender

Constable Tom Robertson didn't know it yet—but he had just found another piece in the jigsaw puzzle that he'd begun almost seven years ago when he had charged Dr. Josephakis Charalambous with sexual assault. The Coquitlam RCMP officer had never quite forgotten Shelley and the doctor. He had even saved his notes on the case—but there was no reason for him to think of them now as he looked at the body of the Native Indian man lying in a pool of blood on the bathroom floor.

It was the morning of April 24, 1992, and no one would make the connection for another year. Eventually, though, Robertson would be able to fit the piece snugly into the bigger picture. Through the doctor, he'd learn, Shelley Charalambous knew as much or more about the murder as he did.

Looking at the lifeless body of Charles Kirton, the policeman realized he'd met him before. After the doctor's acquittal in 1986, Robertson had transferred to a six man burglary unit. He'd felt fortunate that his new wife had adapted to his frequent night shifts, one of which had taken him to a house occupied by Kirton in search of drugs and stolen property.

Kirton had since moved to the basement entry home on Shaughnessy Street, where evidently he'd been in the middle of shaving when somebody had come in and shot him. Blood was now beginning to dry on the hard bathroom surfaces as Robertson surveyed the obese corpse sprawled across the linoleum floor.

Robertson told himself that dealing in drugs and steroids could definitely get a person mixed up with some dangerous sorts of people. Kirton should have known he was at risk. He had been released on bail after a cocaine deal had gone sour, which had left his associates with the impression that he must have ratted on them. He would have recognized them—if he'd seen them coming—but things weren't that simple. For the past several days, they'd been having him cased by a total stranger.

David Walter Schlender had been furtively watching the house from a distance. He could see a truck and a boat in the yard and had learned that Kirton drove "like a maniac." Schlender had also learned that Kirton's wife left each morning, before her husband, to drive the children to school.

Schlender was thirty-nine years old with a drooping left eyelid, a Fu Manchu mustache, and long hair tied into a ponytail. He had grown up across the river in North Delta with a stepbrother also named Dave. To differentiate between them, friends called him "Big Dave" and his stepbrother "Little Dave."

Although clumsy in social situations, often using the wrong words to express himself, "Big Dave" Schlender excelled at sports and claimed to have pitched at a California ball game attended by the President of the United States. But he'd begun using drugs on the first day of Grade 8. "And that," he conceded later, "was the beginning of the end right there."

After Grade 12, Schlender had worked as a welder for mining and construction companies. His wife Colleen, whom he married as a teenager, had suffered permanent short-term memory loss, as a result of too many painkillers following hip replacement surgery. "You can talk to her in the morning," Schlender explained, "and at nighttime she can't remember what you've talked about."

Schlender graduated to cocaine in the late seventies. His wife, he said, would do just one hoot but not him. "I went through pounds and pounds of the stuff. If I had an eight ball or a quarter ounce or whatever, I would just stay there until it was all gone. One time I ran through a double plate-glass window and dove off the third floor of an apartment block, got right back up and went upstairs, did some more. Once you're completely wired on it, you're in bad shape. It's the worst fucking drug in the world. If you're a heavy user, you get to meet the people that score large quantities so that you can support your habit because, when you are on that stuff, you go through vast amounts of money that no job could pay for.... You have to move the product and be in that lifestyle in order to keep your habit going."

It had been through a mutual involvement in drugs that Schlender had met the man who had asked him to watch Kirton. "After we got to know each other, he realized that I had some connections and he seen that I could move the product. It furthered into doing things for him and delivering stuff and so on...cocaine, delivering pot... picking up money, and stuff. He would come over or phone, and he had a pager that I could get a hold of him through."

Schlender wasn't especially flattered that the man who'd hired him for the surveillance job had described him as a "clean-cut, smooth talker with big feet." But Schlender *was* a con artist. Despite convictions for theft, possession of narcotics, failing to appear in court, and uttering forged documents, he'd never spent more than thirty days in jail. His last welding job had paid well, but he'd arranged for his family to collect welfare at the same time so he could buy more cocaine. "Fraud is good," he admitted. "There's a lot of money to be made out there by fraud."

But it was never enough. Schlender had accepted the surveillance job hoping to collect sufficient money to get Colleen and his daughters, aged eleven and fifteen, out of the apartment they had rented in Surrey. "A guy threatened to knife my wife in the hallway," he recalled. "I went out and had an altercation with him."

Schlender had now completed his stakeout. The way Schlender remembered the incident later was that a stranger called on Kirton to report a "minor altercation" with his wife's car. "Your wife told me to come see you to settle the insurance," said the stranger, according to Schlender. It seemed Kirton had asked the stranger to wait while he finished shaving, but had been gunned down in the bathroom before he could pick up his razor.

As far as Schlender was concerned, the ruse had worked well. Police arrested a big-time coke dealer named Art but had to release him for lack of evidence. Relieved that neither he nor his contact man were caught, Schlender figured he could use the same subterfuge again in the future.

The RCMP, however, were not above a little clever deception themselves. Hoping to flush out information that only the killer or his associates could have known, Robertson and his colleagues purported in a "Crimestoppers" TV reenactment that Kirton had been shot while reading a newspaper at his kitchen table. And later, they discovered that Shelley Charalambous knew otherwise. Not only was the doctor's wife aware that Kirton had been shot in his bathroom, she also knew about the bogus insurance claim. Her husband, she said, had told her all about it.

Schlender, when he talked about the incident later, didn't say how much he was paid for his role, but claimed the man who had hired him got $15,000 and bought himself a Harley. Afterwards, said Schlender, the two of them and their wives had bought cocaine and gone out and partied.

The doctor's wife, it subsequently transpired, also had considerable knowledge about Schlender's next "altercation"—two months later—with one of his drug suppliers. If there was one thing that angered David Walter Schlender, it was dealers buffing his coke. His supplier had ripped him off one time too many. Schlender checked the .380 automatic he'd borrowed and looked at the ugly cylindrical attachment that had come with it. Someone had welded in a bunch of washers—spaced apart to act as baffles. It didn't fit exactly like a glove, but as far as homemade silencers went, it would have to do the job. There was one more thing to do before meeting with Manjjyet Nareg on Surrey's 108 Avenue as arranged. Schlender cut up several pages of the June 15 *Province* newspaper, and smiled as he stuffed the bogus "cash" into a large white envelope.

Schlender waited north of Guildford Town Center, sweating in the hot noon sun. The late spring had been one of the warmest in memory, as the currents of El Nino swirled around in the Pacific Ocean altering the normal weather patterns. Schlender took off his denim jacket and placed it beside him on the sidewalk. It was a scorcher, but he'd had to bring the jacket to conceal the loaded Browning.

But Manjjyet Nareg, driving his two door Chevrolet Cavalier, with his wife Varsha beside him, was dressed appropriately in a vest and white shorts. As they stopped to pick him up, Varsha thought it strange that Schlender had brought his jacket with him on such a hot day. She also thought she caught a glimpse of the gun as the big man with the ponytail stooped carefully to pick up his jacket with both hands before climbing into the back seat.

The twenty-one-year-old Nareg was a slight man with a mustache and black, collar-length hair. Driving eastbound, he flashed his pearly white teeth as he twisted round in the driver's seat to hand Schlender an ounce and a half of white powder in a plastic Ziploc bag. Suddenly, Varsha screamed. The passenger in the back seat was holding a gun to her husband's head. "Turn here!" Schlender ordered.

Heart pounding, Nareg drove into the underground parking garage of an apartment building on 154 Street. As he stopped the car, he felt the end had come. Nareg switched off the engine, leaving the key in the ignition. He hoped Schlender just wanted to steal the car. If that's all he wanted, the drug dealer figured, he could have it. But, as Nareg turned, Schlender was already squeezing the trigger. "Dave, don't shoot!" Nareg pleaded. He held up his right hand in self-defense. He'd never been shot before, and didn't know what it might feel like, but something had sliced through his thumb, and there was now a perfectly circular hole in the windshield.

Schlender was still trapped in the back seat of the small, two-door car. Forgetting his jacket and the white envelope, he slammed Varsha against the dashboard as he forced his way out. Nareg frantically tried to wind up his window and lock the door as Schlender circled the vehicle. But it was too late. Another bullet tore through Nareg's cheek, taking out two of his molars, then ripping through the base of his tongue before lodging half way down his throat. It felt as if somebody had punched him in the mouth.

Nareg tried to start the car but his thumb was so swollen he couldn't turn the key. The gunman squeezed the trigger again but this time the Browning jammed. "I've had it with you buddy," Schlender bellowed. Using the gun as a club with his powerful left arm, he hit Nareg over the head, but the silencer fell off the gun as he did so, and dropped into the passenger compartment of the car.

Somehow, Nareg got the car started and jammed the Cavalier into reverse. As the car lurched backwards, its open driver's door slammed against the gunman, sending him flying. Two of its wheels ran over him, leaving tire tracks on his legs and torso.

Nareg screeched from the concrete tomb into daylight, his wife whimpering beside him as he drove to Surrey Memorial Hospital, less than five minutes away. Ditching the car on the main street outside, Nareg ran into the hospital's front entrance, patients recoiling in horror as he stumbled forward, face and white shorts covered in blood.

"What happened?" asked a nurse.

Spitting out blood and chunks of flesh, Nareg could barely talk. His gums had turned white. He was feeling weak. "I think I've been shot," he murmured. Conscious again on a gurney downstairs, Nareg observed the concrete floor. "Am I dead?" he wondered. "Am I in hell already." Out of nowhere, a policeman wanted to speak to him.

"I dunno what happened," Manjjyet lied. "We were just driving down the street when this guy comes outta nowhere with a gun...."

But Nareg could no longer breathe, frantically putting his hand in his mouth to choke up more blood as the emergency room physician opened his airway by tracheotomy. Praying, Nareg could hear fragments of bullets pinging, one by one, as the doctor removed them from his mouth, dropping them into a metal tray beside him. The young Asian, Dr. Lai surmised, had arrived at the hospital just in time. Apart from two scalp lacerations, the wound at the base of Nareg's tongue was sutured only with great difficulty. Three weeks later, when the swelling failed to subside, Nareg was x-rayed, and a doctor removed another bullet fragment from his neck. Afterwards, the patient had second thoughts about selling drugs and went into the restaurant business. He had learned in the meantime that his wife was pregnant. Born on their anniversary, the baby was a girl, and Manjjyet and his wife named her Raina, an Indian word meaning "To Stay."

Upon arriving back at his apartment, Schlender had called the Surrey RCMP to report his version of the events. Apart from the hospital report, the police had also received word that Schlender had been seen fleeing the parkade and hurling some object into the bushes. In Nareg's car, police then found the white envelope containing the pieces of newspaper, as well as the silencer and Schlender's denim jacket with the bag of cocaine still in its breast pocket. Apparently, there had been enough excitement without it. After a police dog sniffed it out, an RCMP firearms expert tested the weapon, as well as the silencer. The silencer worked well, the firearms expert noted, but the gun functioned only sporadically until it was cleaned, a stroke of good fortune to which Nareg apparently owed his life.

Charged with attempted murder, Schlender appeared in court the next day to hear his lawyer, ex-policeman George Wool, request that he should be released on bail. Wool hastened to correct media reports that an innocent couple of motorists had been waylaid for no apparent reason by a gun-toting madman. His client had no record of violence, said Wool, while the victim was a drug pusher motivated solely by money and greed. It might be a year before the trial could proceed, but his client would agree not to own, possess or carry any weapons in the meantime if he could be granted bail on his own recognizance. Having tried to kill someone only the day before, even Schlender must have expected to spend longer than his usual thirty days in jail. His lawyer, however, seemed to have done the impossible.

The request for bail was granted.

13   Matching Jeeps

A fter her father confounded the experts by making a full recovery, Jacqueline Jongkind traveled from Alberta each summer to visit her parents at their mobile home in Surrey. Still concerned that Shelley was being beaten, Jacqueline was desperate to see her daughter and, at least once every week, set out in hopes of catching a glimpse of her. Waiting until after dark on these occasions, Jacqueline would drive north across the Pattullo Bridge into Coquitlam, park her car two or three blocks away and position herself behind a hedge across from the house on Foster Avenue.

The doctor had once done all he could to invite Jacqueline and her daughter to this house, but now Shelley's mother trembled outside as she concealed herself ever deeper in the hedge, an unwelcome interloper stalking his palace. Trembling, she felt her nerves on edge lest anyone discover her suspicious roost. But then, fleetingly, all was worth the risk. In an upstairs window above the front door, there she was, looking out, illuminated by a hallway light—Shelley!

Jacqueline held her breath, yearning somehow to reach out and touch her. She craned her neck as she attempted to see if her daughter looked well. It was too far away, but at least Jacqueline had seen her; at least she was alive; at least her mother could finally return to Alberta with the smallest of satisfactions.

Before departing, however, Jacqueline also yearned to see her grandchildren. Other than briefly holding Allison more than four years earlier, she hadn't even seen photographs of them. Learning that there were portraits of the children at the medical practise, she waited until Wednesday—the doctor's regular day off—before going there to see them. Jacqueline looked at photographs of the children taped to the glass of the reception area, and was about to take a framed portrait from the wall when she was interrupted.

"Can I help you with something?" asked a new receptionist, looking up at Jacqueline after being on the phone.

"No, it's okay," said Jacquie. "I'm just straightening it. I guess if the doctor's not in, I'll come back some other time."

Unknown to Jacqueline, the doctor was on a losing streak. He was gambling now more than ever, finally stiffing his bookie out of $30,000 for refusing to accept one of his football bets. For the next several nights, her husband told Shelley to bring the children to the master bedroom, so that all could sleep in a circle within his reach of a loaded shotgun.

Shortly afterwards, Charalambous sold his beloved house on Foster Avenue for $325,000, telling Shelley the decision involved a temporary restructuring while he straightened his finances. In the meantime, they would rent a small, dismal bungalow almost hidden by dark, mature evergreens on nearby Robinson Street.

Uncharacteristically, Charalambous took his son for a day's bird-hunting in Ladner, then went on a hunting trip in the fall of 1992 with his Greek friends to Osoyoos in the southern interior. While there, he told Shelley excitedly, he and his friends had avoided trespass charges, eluding the police by hiding at length in a ditch. He'd always been fascinated, Shelley knew, by the concept of the perfect crime.

All levity came to an end in November, however, when Charalambous was notified that the college was indeed proceeding with the complaints of Katie and Sian Simmonds. By letter from his old nemesis David Martin, he was notified that the college would hold two separate hearings, one for each of the sisters on March 4 and 5, 1993, respectively.

The hearings were still four months away but, to the Simmonds sisters after waiting almost a year since filing their complaints, the news was a big relief. Only recently, Sian had suggested dropping the matter. "I don't want to go through with this any more," she told Katie. "It's taking too long for our cases to go through."

108

"Just stick it out," Katie replied. "There's something wrong here and we have to speak up in case it happens to somebody else."

With the uncertainty out of the way, the sisters could get on with other things. Sian was still living at home with her parents, but Katie had been living for the past two years in the basement suite at her Aunt Gillian's house on 160 Street in Surrey. Chris Simmonds had gone on title with Gillian to help his sister buy the house after she went through a marriage breakup. The small, modest property was closer to Katie's new full-time job as a teller at Richmond Savings Credit Union, affording her independence as Gill usually kept to herself upstairs with her seven-year-old son.

Sian loved and admired her parents, but often stayed overnight with Katie and was ready for her independence too. Her decision to move out began while their father was on one of his hunting trips, and the girls got to talking about trading in their vehicles. Katie owned a 1973, orange VW bug, which her sister had dented, and Sian was the registered owner of an older Mustang.

"I know what I'd like to trade my car for," Sian said. "I'd like to get one of those Tracker type jeeps."

"Me too!" agreed Katie. "How about if we get matching ones?"

"Yeah!" said Sian. "Two matching black ones."

"Mmmm. That's outrageous," said Katie. "We're not making that much money—but let's talk to Dad about it when he gets back."

Chris Simmonds returned to the Willoughby house from his hunting trip. He still hadn't shaved or had dinner. The girls knew better than to approach their father on an empty stomach, and waited for him to finish his first home cooked meal in two weeks before ganging up on him.

Chris Simmonds listened patiently as his daughters explained how they didn't want to get ripped off, besides which they might need him as a cosigner. "Tell you what," he smiled. "Because Katie's got a full-time job, we'll go and have a look for her first."

Sian looked disappointed but accepted the decision as her parents went out with Katie looking for a jeep. The first one they saw had a good stereo but wasn't new. On the way back, Katie spotted two brand new Asuna Sunrunners on sale at one of the Langley dealerships—one black, the other red.

Katie looked at her parents plaintively. "We can't just get me one," she pleaded.

"How can either of you afford the payments?" her father asked.

"Well Sian could move in with me," said Katie. "That would help me with the rent and it'd be closer to college for Sian."

Chris Simmonds knew when he'd been had. He nodded in agreement. Katie and her parents headed home to get Sian, wanting to know how much the dealer would allow for her Mustang in trade. Katie couldn't wait to break the news. As soon as they stopped in the driveway, she ran into the house where Sian was pouting in the front room.

"Did you get it?" Sian asked expectantly.

"Yes," said Katie, "and you're getting one too! Act surprised!"

As they drove home in their new jeeps, the Simmonds sisters could barely contain their glee. Chris Simmonds cosigned the loans. He was a good father but, then again, he and Sue were blessed with two good daughters. Katie showed how much she and Sian appreciated him by ordering a personalized license plate: "DAD IOU." Sian had her picture taken with her red jeep, smiling proudly behind the open passenger door. Sian gleamed, like her new vehicle. She radiated happiness. Her future seemed full of promise.

Moving out was a big step for Sian. Katie had always been an independent sort of girl, but Sian was a real homebody. Even contemplating a sleepover at a friend's house would make her homesick. Her parents had encouraged Katie and Sian to live at home as long as possible by giving them their own suite in the basement, but now it was time for Sian to move out with her sister.

Sian and Katie descended to their basement foyer via a concrete stairwell. Their suite consisted of an adjoining living room, two bedrooms, and their own bathroom and kitchen. It was modest and inexpensively furnished, but the sisters were delighted with it. Family photos on the walls made it seem like home. Over tea, the sisters sat at their kitchen table, talking of future plans.

There was no driveway access at the front because of the busy main road. Instead, the house was approached by a rear lane, where the girls could park their jeeps. The lane also served three or four neighboring properties. Sian and Katie noticed that the landscaping was sparse. Unlike their father, Aunt Gillian wasn't much of a gardener. Out back she had a set of lawn chairs and a table, its umbrella down for the winter. It seemed a safe enough neighborhood, but there had been quite a few break-ins. The neighbors, a little more than usual, were alert for anything suspicious. The noise of the passing traffic, however, might muffle the sounds if anyone needed help.

But Sian and Katie had no such concerns. Both had their new jeeps, Sian was doing well at college, and she and her boyfriend Dave Sella were planning to get engaged in the summer. "Her mother and I were very happy for her and ourselves," recalled Sian's father. "We were looking forward to grandchildren, all part of our family growing about us and fulfilling our lives."

The only cloud on the horizon was the upcoming hearing. Sian looked at the letter from the college and put it in her bedroom. The matter had been dragging on for more than a year, and the thought of having to testify at an official tribunal was a daunting prospect. She and Katie would be glad when it was all over, but they knew they weren't the only ones. Recently, there had been shocking allegations against two other doctors—one, an elderly Vancouver psychiatrist accused of whipping female patients at his home on the Gulf Islands; the other, a doctor accused of raping a patient after drugging her during a housecall.

Although Sian and Katie had a new doctor and hadn't seen Charalambous for more than a year, they were about to hear from him now. After receiving his notification of the college hearings, Charalambous went to Radio Shack and bought a telephone tape recorder. He looked up Katie Simmonds' phone number in his medical records and phoned at 2:00 P.M. on November 11, 1992. Picking up the phone in the suite on 160 Street, Katie was unaware that her former doctor was recording their conversation.

Charalambous opened with a friendly enough sounding inquiry as to whether Katie and Sian liked their new doctor. Then he got down to the point. "Listen, um, you know I got this letter from the College of Physicians and Surgeons.... I guess you know about that, eh?"

"Uh-huh," Katie responded cautiously.

"Yah," Charalambous continued. "no, the reason, you know, the reason I called you is because, you know, I was your doctor for a long time, right?"

"Uh-huh," said Katie.

"And, um, I never hugged and kissed you on the mouth, right?"

Katie now understood the reason for the call. "I really don't think I'm supposed to be talking to you," she said.

"I know," Charalambous pressed, "but...the point is that, you know, this thing is going to get out of control now. It's going to go to like a college hearing, and we're going to subpoena your parents, and it's gonna, you know—it's gonna really—it's gonna become a lot bigger than just making a complaint.... I don't know why you guys did it because I thought you were, you know, you were a nice person and I didn't do anything like that, right Katie?"

Again, Katie told her former doctor that she couldn't talk to him about the matter.

"Yah," Charalambous acknowledged, "but I didn't do anything, Katie, and it's not fair, is it? A lot of times when you came into the office and you were upset about things that were going on with your boyfriend or your life or your parents or whatever, I was there for you and I tried to be as good as I could for you. I thought of you—you know—as a good person and you are, I believe, and I don't know what happened to set you off, you know, against me like this but, if you don't like me for whatever reason, and you want to leave, you know, that's, that's okay.... It's a free country, but when you go and you say I did something that I didn't do, you know, it's just not right.... You wouldn't like it if I said something, or somebody said something about you that you didn't do.... It's just not the right thing to do and, I want you to think about it, and your sister too.... I never did anything to your sister or to you that had anything to do with sexual overtones. I never touched her breasts. I never kissed her, okay."

The doctor wasn't finished. "I liked you as patients," he added. "I looked after your parents and I looked after both of you well, and especially you. You needed me and I was there for you. Okay? Isn't that true?"

As he continued to protest, Katie again told him: "I'm sorry, Dr. Charalambous, I can't talk to you about this. I really don't think that I should talk to you.... It will be dealt with in another way and if there is any question on your part then it will be dealt with...."

"I know but Katie, you know," Charalambous persisted, "I didn't do anything and you're saying I did."

"Well," said Katie, "I don't really think that you've said anything."

"I never kissed you," Charalambous protested. "I never hugged you. I never...."

"You did," insisted Katie. "You did kiss us both Dr. Charalambous ...and that is something that is going to be brought up later, but I really don't think that you should be phoning me and having this conversation with me and that is totally unfair on your part."

"Well, I'm not," said Charalambous. "I'm not with you, okay. I'm not—I just want to understand why you said those things, because I didn't do that."

Katie wanted her former doctor to know she bore him no malice. "The last thing that we want to do, and something that we took into consideration was, what this was going to do to you."

"Yes," said the doctor.

"We felt that there was a wrongdoing," Katie continued, "and we proceeded with a complaint...they took it as a justifiable complaint and, you know, they've basically taken all the steps. All we've done is said what has happened."

"Katie," the doctor insisted, "I never kissed you on the mouth."

"You did, Dr. Charalambous," Katie retorted. "It was just after New Year's."

"Okay," said the doctor, "well anyway Katie, listen, I'm not angry with you, okay, but I think you're not remembering things correctly, all right. I never kissed you on the mouth, I never examined you or your sister in the wrong way and I was there for you all the time, when you needed me, and I treated you with respect. I looked after your parents well."

Katie was losing her patience. "That's okay, that's fine but I really—I don't want to have this conversation any longer," she said.

"Okay," said Charalambous, "all right, bye."

"Bye," said Katie.

Both parties hung up. During the call, Katie had put her hand over the receiver and whispered to Sian: "Psst! It's him. It's Dr. Charalambous." As they talked about it later, Katie and her father considered the call had been a blatant attempt to interfere with Sian and Katie as witnesses, and they reported the conversation to the college.

Charalambous had told Katie that he wasn't angry with her, and that was true. He wasn't angry, he was *livid*. At his home, the doctor rewound the cassette tape. He walked purposefully out of the bedroom, looking for Shelley. "I can't believe those girls," he told her, shaking his head. "They really believe what they're saying. There's no way to prevent them from testifying except to kill them."

Charalambous handed the tape to his wife. "Just put the date and time on it," he told her, "and put it in the desk with my other stuff." He told Shelley again that he had never touched either of the sisters in a sexually inappropriate way. "I never kissed them or touched either of them on the breast," he protested. "They're lying." Even if a doctor did kiss a patient, he repeated, it was no big deal. He never would have expected the college to hold a hearing over such a minor and insignificant complaint. Obviously, he reiterated, it was just more proof the college was prejudiced against him.

Charalambous told Shelley that the college probably would either suspend him for up to two years or erase his name altogether from the medical register. The complaints, he said, would ruin him financially. If the college took away his license and never gave it back, it would be the end of his livelihood. It was unfair. The hearings simply could not proceed. "They would never hold a hearing and find me not guilty," he told Shelley. "Maybe I should just go to the hearing with a gun and shoot the whole panel."

Shelley listened dispassionately. She was accustomed to her husband's wild threats. She remembered how he'd ranted and raved seven years ago about alternative ways of taking revenge against her mother, including threats of killing her. He hadn't done so, and Shelley wasn't sure that she really believed him now, either.

But there was always that nagging doubt.

It wasn't only the physical abuse that upset Shelley. Joe was selfish and inconsiderate in other ways, too. He was a hard worker, but that meant he had little time to spend with the family. Shelley resented the fact that, when he did take two or three weeks off work during the summer, he spent most of that time playing cards or gambling at the racetrack. Only once had he taken the family on a vacation, packing them all up for a brief look at the Oregon coast.

"The children and I did not suffer financially," she recalled, "but his gambling had a lot of disadvantages—like mood swings. If he came home and lost while he was gambling, it was just impossible. It would be one little thing that triggered him." The family suffered emotionally, she added, and it was a typical sort of addiction that affected everybody in the family, not just her husband.

Yearning ever more to leave her dictatorial husband since the birth of their third child, Shelley realized now that, other than the children, she had very little to show for the marriage. Joe had promised their son that he could have his $12,000 Rolex when he reached eighteen, and there were some family rings and necklaces from Joe's mother. Despite his big earnings, however, that was about all.

Charalambous did want back into the real estate market, though, and had been making inquiries about getting preapproved for a $500,000 mortgage. He considered buying property closer to his office. "There's some nice houses in Surrey next to Bear Creek Park," he told Shelley.

Despite her unhappiness, Shelley and the children accompanied Charalambous on Sunday drives as he looked at houses in Surrey, and at acreages north of the freeway in Langley. Shelley dutifully jotted down the numbers of various real estate agents, whom she would phone later for the prices and details as Joe requested.

Although Katie had rebuffed his telephone call several hours earlier, Charalambous was still fretting at dinner time. He seldom drank, but tonight he asked Shelley to share a bottle of wine with him. Following that, he drained a glass of Grand Marnier, then had two or three more. After the children went to bed, he spent the evening rehashing ways of preventing the college hearing from going ahead.

"Joe's like that," Shelley said later. "He's very obsessive whether it's about restaurants or whether it's about somebody who has done something wrong to him. He dwells on it for days at a time. He has a very obsessive personality. When he does get a thought or a plan, he just obsesses over it constantly for days and days or weeks."

Charalambous was unable to sleep that night. There would be a full complement of patients to see in the morning. A couple of times he might have nodded off, but the enormity of the situation would awaken him in a cold sweat. The Grand Marnier was wearing off. *If he couldn't practise medicine, where would he get the money to gamble?* Finally, he gave up trying to figure it all out and took some sleeping pills.

After the College of Physicians and Surgeons received word that the doctor had phoned Katie Simmonds, it acted with surprising dispatch, almost immediately sending Charalambous a letter warning him not to tamper with college witnesses. "That," recalled Shelley, "just started him off all over again. He was very upset and very angry that they had complained to the college."

"All I did was phone them," her husband protested, "and they complained about that too. They have to be taken care of. If I could just

115

lay a beating on them, I would. But rats are rats, and if you don't get rid of them, they just complain about that, too. There's no choice. I'll kill them both."

Charalambous consulted with Chris Hinkson, the lawyer he'd retained to represent him at the college hearing. The large, portly lawyer firmly told the doctor not to have any further contact with the complainants. Hinkson was unable to assure him that he could get him off, but felt it was advantageous that the complaints would be heard separately. That way, the sisters could not corroborate each other's evidence.

"I've reviewed the files on these patients and the statements taken by Mr. Beere," the lawyer told his client. "There are a number of inconsistencies. It's going to be your word against theirs."

Charalambous was a gambling man. "What do you think are my chances?" he asked.

"Fifty-fifty," the lawyer replied.

Hinkson was aware of his client's prior history with the college, but he held out a ray of hope. He didn't think Charalambous would be erased altogether, even if he were found guilty. No doctor to Hinkson's knowledge had ever been permanently erased and a psychiatrist recently convicted of sexual intercourse with a patient for the second time—obviously a more serious offense—had received a suspension of only three years. "If it goes against you, it's likely that you would be suspended for a period of time," Hinkson told Charalambous. "Probably between six months and one year."

Hinkson agreed that Shelley Charalambous could deliver the tape of her husband's phone call so that one of his legal secretaries could have it transcribed. While delivering the tape on November 20, Shelley found the lawyer reticent about speculating on the outcome of the proposed hearing, either way.

Shelley also recalled that her husband considered making a last ditch appeal to Sian's and Katie's father. Charalambous liked Chris Simmonds and respected him as a fellow martial artist. "He said that when he was suspended from practise, the Simmonds family had stuck by him. And that Chris said that he supported him, and he felt that he and Chris were very close. He thought they (Sian and Katie) had complained to the college without their parents' knowledge."

"Sian's the instigator of the complaints," the doctor told Shelley, adding she was angry with him for releasing medical information to her parents that she didn't want them to know. "She's trying to get back at

116

me," he reasoned. "And Katie's just going along with it on a 'Me, too' basis."

But Hinkson had advised Charalambous against any further contact with members of the family. Despite the lawyer's otherwise cautious optimism, Charalambous wanted another opinion—not from a lawyer, but from his friend Brian West.

Shelley remembered that Charalambous had also consulted West seven years ago. "He was trying to get revenge on my mom and talked about a lot of different things then," Shelley recalled. "He talked about just having her beat up...he talked about getting revenge on her some-how—and then also he was in contact with Brian West, or Brian was in contact with him."

According to Shelley, however, her husband had lost track as to West's whereabouts. "He phoned his (West's) mother and left messages with her for Brian to call him," Shelley recalled. "He kept phoning another telephone number he believed Brian was at, but the people there wouldn't admit whether Brian lived at that house or not. And he dropped by Brian's last known address. He would instruct me to stay home to be able to answer the call when Brian did call."

Over the next week, Shelley remembers being interrupted in her housework more often than usual by her husband phoning her from work, three or four times each day, with the same question. "Has Brian called yet?" she recalled him asking. "If he does call tell him I'll be home at six o'clock...." A few days later, recalled Shelley, her husband was in the living room when he got the call for which he'd been so anxiously waiting.

"Oh hi, Brian," she heard him say into the phone. "I've been trying to get a hold of you. What've you been up to?"

Shelley couldn't hear the reply, but overheard as her husband continued. "I need to get together with you," she heard him say. "Can I get together with you....? Oh, okay, yah, whatever, it's just up the street from where I am, Hailey Street. It's right by our house."

Up until that time, Shelley observed, her husband had talked frequently about having the Simmonds sisters killed. "He talked of it, talked about it often," but after contacting his old friend he seldom if ever voiced his threats again.

Charalambous, according to his wife, had found a new obsession. Instead of healing patients, his priority now became stalking Sian and Katie Simmonds. He wanted to find out where they were living and what vehicles they were driving. The doctor expanded his weekend househunting activities to include driving past and gazing curiously at the Willoughby Hill home of Sian's parents in Langley, memorizing the license numbers of vehicles parked in the driveway.

He also dug Katie's address out of his medical files and drove with Shelley and his children past the house on 160 Street in Surrey. In the lane behind the house were a black jeep and a white, older model car. He wasn't sure which vehicle Katie drove. "He knew that Sian Simmonds owned the red jeep," said Shelley, "and he never did pinpoint which vehicle Katie drove."

Shelley recalled her husband's chilling activities as a midnight stalker. "He told me that sometimes in the middle of the night...that he would drive past Katie's house and that he would park a block away. Behind her house, there was a dead-end street. He couldn't drive back there, so he would walk back at three or four o'clock in the morning to see what vehicles were parked behind the house. Those weren't the only times that he would drive past their house. He told me that he would leave early to go to work in the morning to drive past their house. He told me that he had driven by on his lunch breaks and after work...."

Before work on the morning of November 24, the doctor apparently took another detour past the Langley house, trying to find out whether Sian still lived at home with her parents or whether she had moved in with Katie. While driving in the 7200-block of 200 Street in Langley, he was stopped shortly before 8:00 A.M. by the police. Constable Al Dengis of the Langley RCMP detachment clocked him by radar going 30 percent over the speed limit. The officer did a U-turn, made a note of the black, 1989 Pontiac Trans-Am, bearing B.C. license plate PVS 698—and gave Charalambous a ticket.

While Charalambous was stalking them, members of the Simmonds family were busy dealing with another tragedy. This time it involved Chris's youngest brother John, who had also gone on title with Chris to help Gill buy the house on 160 Street.

John Simmonds was a successful Edmonton painting contractor. He was always generous and would buy everyone a round of drinks. Never married, he had a reputation as a bit of a playboy. In November 1992, while Charalambous plotted against his nieces, John Simmonds was thirty-three, almost the same age his father had been when he was killed. Chris Simmonds recalled that he and his other brothers also experienced emotional difficulties at that age.

"It seems to have been a crisis point," Chris suggested, although the official reasons for the tragedy at the time were that John perceived he had business problems and he had just had a trivial argument with his girlfriend. She was with him at home in Edmonton when he shot himself. Later, Chris would feel angry at his brother for committing suicide, but at the time he didn't know what to think. When he and his younger brother Brian drove to Edmonton to sort things out, they found that John had been in great financial shape and should have had nothing to worry about.

If John had foreseen the tragedy that would strike his brother two months later, he might never so frivolously have ended his life.

14   Conspiracy

Despite being on bail, David Walter Schlender continued to sniff out cocaine at every available opportunity. Since his release, he had found better accommodation for his family in a new basement suite—just a mile from the Simmonds sisters whom he didn't yet know—but his drug bill was getting out of reach. With winter just around the corner, he and his family had just settled down in their suite to watch television, when they were startled by an unexpected knock at the door.

It was late in the evening, Schlender recalled, and he had opened the door with apprehension. The visitor, Schlender claimed later, was a biker whom he and his wife had got to know because the biker's girlfriend had lived in the same apartment block. "Oh, how are you doing?" Schlender asked, not entirely relieved to see the bearded, tattooed man standing on his step. "Do you want a drink?"

"No, no," the biker growled. "I have to talk to you." Schlender put on his shoes. He owed the man between $3,500 and $7,000. He'd been fronted more than that in the past but it wasn't a good idea to owe that much money, especially not for drugs.

He accompanied his visitor outside, getting into the bearded man's red Honda Civic with trepidation. "Maybe I'm gonna get the fucking shit beat out of me," Schlender thought.

"What the fuck's...what, what's this?" he asked, looking around at a crowded back seat as the bearded man pulled away. Schlender wasn't inquiring about the black leather jacket that the biker always wore, nor about two balaclava ski masks. As he recalled, he was looking at an oblong wooden box, two garbage containers, and two red plastic, five-gallon cans of gasoline.

According to Schlender, his companion explained the box contained a fuse that wouldn't go out in the rain or the wind. Otherwise, he recalled, the bearded man only grunted. With his mane of unkempt hair, he looked like a wild man. When he did talk, it was a guttural sort of growl. He was driving, it seemed to Schlender, to a specific location, somewhere southeast of Guildford Town Center in Surrey, and Schlender's questions would have to wait.

Within a few minutes, according to Schlender's recollections, the bearded man pulled over. He parked a few houses down the street from the residence at 9340 - 160 Street. "The people in that house are gonna testify against a friend of mine," Schlender recalled him saying.

Schlender turned to look at the house. It was a small home with two scraggly fir trees in front, surrounded by the new houses of a recent subdivision. "Why?" he recalled asking. "What's it about?"

The bearded man, he recalled, only partially answered the question. His friend was a karate instructor whom he'd known for many years. Two girls in the house were going to testify against him. They had to be stopped. The bearded man, Schlender recalled, handed him a piece of paper with the address, telephone number, and names of the girls. Schlender squinted to read in the darkness: Sian and Katie Simmonds.

"What are they testifying about?" he asked. "Did he rape them or something?" Schlender recalled asking the same question over and over but his companion, silhouetted against the streetlight, gave only the same reply. The girls were testifying against a longtime friend, a karate instructor.

Schlender recalled that the biker and the karate instructor had planned to burn down the house earlier that night, but thought someone had seen them by floodlight in the rear lane. Because of that, they couldn't do the job themselves, so the biker had come to Schlender.

Schlender recalled how the gasoline was supposed to have been used. "This is absolutely insane," he said. "They were going to dump it through the mail slot and put one end of the fuse through. Then the other garbage can on the porch was going to be full of gas.... Somehow they were going to light it and God knows how it was going to end up."

As he sat in the Honda, Schlender declined to participate. "Well there's no way I'm fuckin' burning down their house," he recalled

121

telling the biker. "That's arson. That's a fuckin' heavy, heavy charge, man."

The biker, Schlender recalled, had replied in a tone of voice leaving no doubt that the job was essential. According to Schlender, it seemed that the bearded man himself was being forced. "He was choked," Schlender claimed. "Visibly pissed off. It was like he thought I would just jump right on it and do it. We drove around for a while, and he drove me home and dropped me off."

Unaware anyone was stalking them, Sian and Katie Simmonds had taken advantage of new powder snow to get in a day's skiing at West Vancouver's Cypress Bowl. An Arctic front had swept over the Lower Mainland. The roads were icy and dangerous; but the Simmonds sisters had no difficulty driving through the snow in their new jeeps. It was going to be a white 1992 Christmas.

Sian and Katie joined their parents for Christmas dinner, exchanging gifts at the Willoughby family home. But Sian still hadn't told her parents that she had begun seeing Dave Sella again. On Boxing Day, the young couple secretly boarded a ferry, and spent the night watching logs burning in the big stone fireplace at the wooded retreat of David's grandparents on Saltspring Island. After breakfast the next morning, David and Sian stepped outside into the snow, breathing air that was fresh with the scent of the surrounding forest and ocean as they set out for a walk. Sian, bundled up in a ski jacket, scarf and mittens, laughed and squealed as David chased her with a snowball. When he caught up to her, David stared intently into her sparkling blue eyes. "You know what I did today?" he said, after their laughter had subsided. "I woke up and I was happy."

"You were happy?"

"Yeah. I woke up thinking of you, Hon, and I was happy. I want to be happy forever."

"Honey, it's about time you figured that out," Sian smiled, suddenly turning to hug her boyfriend. "I knew from the moment we met that you were the one for me."

It seemed to David that his pretty, fun-loving girlfriend always knew what he was thinking. Often, he would start a sentence and Sian would finish it. On their way back to the house, the young couple detoured to look at some land that Sian's parents owned on Saltspring Island, and it was not until late that night that they got back to the mainland. Sian told her mother and father she'd been on a skiing trip with some friends, but soon everyone—including her parents—knew she and David were dating again. Struggling to keep up with his girlfriend while skiing down Mount Baker in Washington state, David bruised his heel and had to take several days off work, but he had finally realized that Sian was the one for him. "You'd better like her," he told his parents. "She's going to be around for a long time."

"Don't worry son," said David's mother. "We love her too."

Soon after that, David gave Sian a promise ring with a gold heart and a tiny diamond. For hours, they talked together, planning to get married. They'd announce their engagement, they decided, on August 19, which would be the second anniversary of their movie date. "We talked about buying a house and having kids," Sella recalled. "I said a boy would be fine but Sian said she'd like about three children, including at least one girl. Those few weeks after Christmas were the best time we ever had together."

David Schlender, meanwhile, checked his answering machine. There were several messages, he recalled, from the bearded man, but Schlender didn't return them. Although he had the biker's pager number, he deliberately avoided calling him back. Within a week, he recalled however, the biker dropped by to see him again.

The two men went outside. They always did that, said Schlender, whenever the biker called. Schlender didn't want anyone in his family to overhear their conversations. "I don't know if it was the first time or the second time," Schlender tried to remember, "but then it was beyond burning of the house...at that point both those girls were to be killed."

Schlender still asked for reasons. "Why?" he wanted to know. "What did the karate instructor do? Why do they have to be killed?" The biker, he said, again refused to explain but pestered and threatened him over the ensuing weeks, reminding him he owed money. The way to eliminate his debt was to kill Sian Simmonds. "Look, you've got to do it!" he recalled the biker telling him. "You owe.... You must do it and you've got to do it, now!"

Schlender claimed he procrastinated until the New Year, when the biker told him to look at some pictures in the glove box of his car. "They were Polaroid pictures of slaughtered people," said Schlender. "I was in the Honda sitting in the passenger seat. I picked them out of the glove box and looked at them, and I threw them back in there. You could tell these people were dead. I don't know if they were shot or what the hell happened to them but they were definitely dead. Pretty messy-looking photographs."

"That could be your family," he recalled the biker telling him.

"Okay, okay," said Schlender. "I'll do it."

Schlender said later his family was all he had. "I know it's not an excuse," he added, "but after seeing those pictures...of slaughtered people I said I would do it. And at that time it was just the one girl, the girl that drove the red jeep. She was to be gone.

"And that's after four or five weeks of being pestered and phoned and threatened. At that point I was so far gone and so screwed on cocaine and so terrified.

"I don't know how to explain it...there was just no other way. No matter if I died, if my whole family died, those girls were going to be gone. There was no doubt in my mind."

Schlender recalled that the bearded man then gave him $700 to rent a car. "If I needed a car, I'd borrow one," Schlender said later. "I blew the $700 on cocaine." When he returned home, he recalled, Colleen was anxious to tell him that the biker had visited and dropped something off for him. "I put it under the hamper in the bedroom," Schlender's wife told him.

"What is it?" Schlender asked.

"I dunno," said Colleen. "I never opened it."

Schlender recalled finding a plastic garbage bag under the hamper, with something inside wrapped in cloth. "And there it was," he said, "the gun, the silencer, the bullets." Schlender said later that he hid the gun outside. "I didn't keep it in the fuckin' house," he stated. "I didn't want my fuckin' kids or old lady to ever see the fuckin' thing."

Shortly afterwards, according to Schlender, he got a phone call from the bearded man. "Have the tools arrived?" he recalled the biker wanting to know.

"Yes," Schlender confirmed.

After that, said Schlender, he phoned Sian's and Katie's number. He got an answering machine, he recalled, and hung up. Several times in January, he added, he borrowed cars and drove by the house on 160 Street, unaware that his activities had briefly aroused the suspicions of the neighborhood mailman. Because of a spate of break-ins, he learned later, the mailman had recorded the license number of the car that

Schlender was using, but had discarded his note after hearing of no further problems.

In the lane behind the house, just as Schlender had been told, there were the two jeeps. The red one belonged to Sian Simmonds. The biker's words echoed in Schlender's mind. "The girl with blonde hair that drives a red jeep and lives at that address. You are to go there and you are to kill her."

Schlender added that neither he nor the biker realized that Sian lived in the basement. Both of them, Schlender recalled, thought she lived in the upstairs of the house. "I went there many times," Schlender recounted. "I drove around and tried to get up enough nerve to do it and I couldn't. Every time, I just went home and got completely drunk out of my mind and did hard drugs and almost went off the deep end. It was not easy, I'll tell you that."

The biker, he recalled, was becoming more insistent, phoning more frequently. "Have you done the job yet?" Schlender recalled him asking. "I need the tools back."

"No, not yet," said Schlender.

"Look," he recalled the biker telling him. "You're gonna get out there and do it or things are gonna happen to your family. I'm under pressure. There's no more time on this. It has to be done. You are going to do it or else."

"There's something insane going on here," said Schlender. "You won't even tell me why she has to die."

"Are you gonna do it?" he recalled the biker repeating. "Just get out there and do it. Do it the fuck today."

"Okay," said Schlender. "I'll do it."

Later, he recalled the pressure. "It was five or six weeks of torment," said Schlender. "You're sitting in a box and something comes over you...you just can't deal with it, man. You've got to get it out. It just went on for weeks...the threats and all the bullshit that led up to it.... I just couldn't handle it any more."

On January 26—two days before Sian's twentieth birthday— Schlender invited a friend named Brian McCann* to drop by his house to do some freebasing, but the real reason for the invitation was that Schlender wanted to borrow his friend's car. He'd known McCann since they were both teenagers growing up in North Delta. They'd lost touch with each other, but had recently become reacquainted. In the meantime, Schlender noticed, McCann had lost much of his hair and now combed what he had left across his pate from one side to the other. Schlender leaned across the kitchen table. "I hate to do this to you," he said, sounding nonchalant, "but I was wondering if I could borrow your car again, just for an hour."

Brian McCann hesitated. His 1984 silver blue Dodge Omni was parked outside Schlender's suite, but he needed the car himself to drive into Vancouver to see his girlfriend.

"Well, what d'you want it for?" McCann stalled.

"I just gotta visit some friends and get a couple of things done," Schlender said. "I just need it for an hour. You can stay here for a while and visit with Colleen."

"No, that's okay," said McCann. "You can borrow it if you can drop me off at my girlfriend's place."

Schlender agreed, dropping McCann off in Vancouver. "Here," McCann said, "In case you need it, here's my girlfriend's phone number."

"Thanks, Brian," said Schlender. "I'll be back in an hour—two at the most."

Schlender failed to keep his promise, however. And, when he still hadn't returned the car by the following morning, McCann began to realize he hadn't known his old friend as well as he'd thought. All McCann could get at the Schlender residence was an answering machine. He shouldn't have loaned Schlender the car at all, McCann fumed. Obviously, the man wasn't too reliable. Briefly, though, McCann's anger turned to concern as he considered that his car might have been involved in an accident.

Because of his own drug record, McCann hesitated to call the police but finally did so in frustration, asking the Surrey RCMP to tell him if his car had been involved in an accident. He didn't mention Schlender's name, but gave them the car's registration and license number. When the answer came back negative, McCann phoned the Vancouver Police Department, asking them to check whether they had anyone in jail by the name of David Walter Schlender.

But Schlender wasn't there either. He was on bail for attempted murder, but the person assisting McCann with his inquiries at the Vancouver police station had never heard of him.

15   A Blunt Instrument

Into whatsoever house you shall enter, it shall be for the good of
the sick to the utmost of your power....

One of the reasons Dr. Charalambous had been so successful re-
building his practise, Shelley knew, was the fact that he took
Wednesdays rather than Saturdays off. It was easier for patients to see
him on the weekend, and his $450,000 income for the past year had
proved his point, placing him among the top-earning general practitioners in the province.

It would be Shelley's twenty-third birthday in two days' time, and
her husband wanted her to go shopping with him on the morning of
Wednesday, January 27, 1993 so that they could select her presents. At
lunchtime, he suggested, they could pick up their eldest child from
kindergarten, then go for a drive past the home of the Simmonds sisters
in Surrey. Shelley, as usual, went along with his plans.

The morning had dawned overcast, but the temperature was mild,
in the mid-forties, after one of the coldest winters in memory. It was still
too early to say spring was in the air but the worst of the winter
definitely was over. In Surrey, light rain fell but Katie Simmonds felt
warm and snug as she woke up, still elated that Sian had been able to
move in with her.

Getting ready for work, Katie reminded herself that it was Dave Sella's birthday, and that she and her sister would have a party for him tonight to overlap with Sian's twentieth birthday tomorrow. Katie would also have to remember to pick up a birthday present for her sister before returning home.

Katie crept on tiptoe into Sian's darkened bedroom. Her sister didn't have any classes until the afternoon and Katie didn't want to disturb her, but Sian awoke to the sound of her sister scuffling in the bottom of her closet. Sian sat up in bed and smiled. "Katie," she yawned, good naturedly, "what are you doing?"

"Morning," Katie said, breezily, looking over her shoulder. "I'm borrowing a pair of your shoes."

Sian propped up her head. "You know they're three sizes too big," she giggled. "They won't fit you."

"They do, if I put cotton in the toes," Katie replied. But stopping for a moment to think about it, Katie decided to make do with a pair of her own. She stood up and smiled, thinking her sister showed surprising logic for someone who had just woken up. "You're right," said Katie. She reminded her sister about tonight's party. "I guess you'll remember to pick up a cake at Safeway?" she asked.

"I haven't forgotten," said Sian. She got out of bed, intending to do her laundry and squeeze in some studying before going to her classes. She smiled again at her sister. "Have a good day at work, Katie. See you tonight."

"You too," said Katie. "See you then."

Katie closed the basement door behind her. She walked into the lane and climbed into her black jeep, turning on the windshield wipers as she pulled out onto 160 Street, heading south then west on her way to work.

Although it was a dreary, wet day, Katie still felt warmed by the conversation with Sian. She loved Sian more than words could say. Nothing could be further from her mind than the thought that she would never see her sister alive again.

Just over a mile away, David Schlender woke up listless and lethargic after being on the needle the night before. Not bothering to shave, he got dressed quickly and freebased some crack. Leaving his wife still in bed, he went into the kitchen and opened a can of beer.

Schlender took the cloth-wrapped Ruger out of the garbage bag and loaded it with trembling hands, hoping it would work better than the

Browning. At least the experts seemed to think it would. In a *Gun Digest* article, an instructor for the National Rifle Association had written that the silenced Ruger was the favored tool for "up-close-and-personal-diplomacy" of Israeli intelligence agents as well as the U.S. Navy SEALs. Defending silencers as a legitimate way for sportsmen to reduce noise pollution, the writer added that U.S. government records indicated not one registered silencer had been used for an illegal act since 1934.

Schlender knew this silencer wasn't registered. It was obviously homemade and it was too shiny. It might attract unwanted attention so he wrapped it with black electrician's tape from his toolbox. He stuffed the gun into his jeans and walked out to the Omni. The car looked a more vivid blue than it had the day before, and the mountains in the distance looked closer. Coke had a way of doing that.

Schlender got in the car, started the engine, and turned on the wipers. Despite the cool weather, Schlender began to sweat, feeling beads of perspiration on his forehead. The coke was doing that too. His face was serious, his expression taut, as he pulled out of the cul-de-sac. It would take only a few minutes to get to his destination.

Schlender lit a cigarette, smoke mingling with the faint scent of gun oil. It was important to keep a weapon well cleaned if one expected it to function reliably. He couldn't afford another fiasco like the last time. He pulled up outside the house on 160 Street. He saw the red jeep in the lane. As he watched, trying to get up the nerve to carry out his plan, someone pulled away in a white midsized car. Probably an Oldsmobile or Buick. But the cocaine was wearing off and Schlender felt a pounding in his temples. He didn't know it was Gill's boyfriend Colin leaving for work. Whoever it was, it had unnerved him. He watched and waited for a while longer, but began to shake. He needed more cocaine.

Schlender drove home. Everybody was still sleeping as he walked into his corner of the house. He opened another beer and did some more crack, his wife joining him sleepily for a couple of tokes. When he felt hyped enough, Schlender turned to his wife. "I'm just going out for a bite," he told Colleen. "Could you phone Brian McCann and tell him I've just gone out for breakfast. I'll bring his car back right after."

"I'll go into town with you," said Colleen. "I'll be ready when you get back." A meticulous housekeeper, Colleen was a short pleasant woman but amazingly naive when it came to some of her husband's activities. Schlender hopped in the car and drove back toward to the house on 160 Street. This time there'd be no turning back.

After finishing her laundry, Sian Simmonds picked up the phone to call her boyfriend. Dave Sella was wakened by the telephone ringing in his bedroom. By now, at midmorning, he wouldn't normally have been sleeping, but he was still on sick leave with his bruised foot from the skiing injury. Twenty-two today, he fumbled with the receiver, then smiled as he recognized Sian on the other end of the line.

"Happy birthday to you...." sang the voice on the phone. "Happy birthday...."

Sella, sat up in bed and interrupted with a grin. "Who is this?" he joked. "Tracy?...Susan?"

Sian Simmonds laughed, but finished her musical greeting. She was happy. After a rocky start, her relationship with the handsome young grocery clerk was back on track. Two kids in love. David was looking forward to being with Sian tonight for the joint celebrations, although he had delivered her birthday present two days earlier. It was a practical gift—a night table for Sian's new suite.

Sian hadn't yet wrapped David's present, but she could do that tonight. She had bought him a green rugby jersey while shopping with her girlfriend Kim Jones. At midnight, she figured, she and David could also exchange cards.

"I've got to clean up the kitchen and have a bath," Sian told her boyfriend. "But I'll call you back before I go to college at one o'clock."

At 10:45 that morning, Sian's mother phoned from work. "I'm just going to have a bath and get ready to go to class," Sian told her. Since moving, Sian had faithfully phoned or visited her parents every day, just to find out how they were doing.

Sian never did phone David back as promised. Sella waited until around 12:30 P.M., then called three more times. Each time, he got the answering machine. "She must be in the shower or upstairs still doing laundry," he thought. By the third call, Sella was getting a bit annoyed but left a message on the machine. "Well, I guess you're talking to your aunt and you can't hear me," he said, trying to sound calm. "No, gee, look at the time. I guess you've already gone to school. Oh well, I'll see you tonight."

David Schlender parked the Omni on the street about 100 yards south of the house and walked into the lane, furtively looking around to ensure no one was watching as he approached Sian's red jeep. Now at last he was ready to execute the plan that he had put off for so long.

The rain had stopped. The air smelled fresh and clean. Schlender took a deep breath. With his keys, he made a long, deep, deliberate scratch in the glistening paintwork of Sian's previously unblemished jeep. Then he stood back to admire his work. The scratch was parallel to the ground on the driver's side door. It didn't look particularly accidental but he was satisfied that it would do the job. No one had seen him. He walked round the house, climbed the front steps, and knocked boldly on the front door.

Gill Phelps, who had been busy paying bills while she cleaned her oven, opened the door, blinking inquisitively as she got a good look at the stranger on her porch. The man needed a shave, Gill thought, but he looked pleasant enough. He was about thirty-eight, approximately six-feet tall, one hundred and eighty pounds, wearing a checked shirt, jeans and a brown jacket.

"Do you own that red jeep at the back of the house?" the stranger asked.

The question caught Gill by surprise. "What red jeep?" she asked, absentmindedly. "...Oh, sorry, no I don't. Why?"

"Well I scratched it...." the stranger began.

"You what?" Gill squinted.

Schlender suppressed his impatience. "I accidentally scratched it," he said. "But I've got my insurance papers and everything."

"Ohhh!" said Gill, comprehending. "It doesn't belong to me. It belongs to the people downstairs. If you go to the side entrance, they'll look after you."

The stranger seemed satisfied with that, thanking her as he descended the front steps. Gill closed the door quickly, hurrying back to the kitchen where she could peer out of the side window. Overlooking the basement stairwell, she could see and hear the stranger repeating his story to Sian.

Gill looked out at the jeep, an unsettling thought flashing through her mind as she did so. "If he'd been passing by and scratched the jeep, as he'd said, wasn't it a bit odd that there was no sign of his car in the lane too?"

"But everything must be all right," Gill decided. Deep in thought, she carried on with her chores, cleaning the bathroom and washing the floor.

After her bath, Sian had looked at her schoolbooks as she lay on her bed, unaware of the terrible danger this dreary day would bring. Still in her white bathrobe, she had already laid out what she would be wearing for college including her favorite large, gold earrings.

She was talking on the telephone for the third time that morning with her friend Kimberley Jones, whom she'd known since kindergarten, making plans for the weekend. Sian's telephone was in the entrance foyer to the suite. Abruptly, the conversation was interrupted by an unexpected knock at the door.

Kim, a slender, pretty girl with long, dark hair, knew the suite well. Suddenly, over the phone, she heard what she took to be the sound of the Venetian blinds on the door rippling as Sian opened it. "Oh! You freaked me out," Kimberley heard Sian saying, apparently startled by an unknown male visitor. Over the telephone, Kimberley heard a male voice reply to Sian: "I accidentally scratched your jeep." Whoever it was, thought Kim, he sounded sincere and apologetic.

The sudden intrusion had startled Sian. "Kim, I'll call you later," she said. As Kim put down the phone, she felt an inexplicable chill. She called back after half an hour but all she heard—just as Dave Sella had—was Katie's voice on the answering machine.

Sian regarded her jeep much the same way a mother might feel about a new baby. Forgetting she was still in her bathrobe, she pushed past the stranger and hurried out to the lane to inspect the damage. She shouted at the man with the ponytail as she looked at the scratch. "For crying out loud!" she yelled. "How could you do this?"

"Sorry," said Schlender, meekly. "I was just driving by and...."

Sian was swearing at him and Schlender was feeling uneasy. He hadn't figured on this. The last thing he wanted was to attract all this attention. He hadn't reckoned on Sian being so assertive. Nor did he realize the commotion was already being witnessed by two of the neighbors.

Cheryl Batista* looked out of her kitchen window as she heard the disturbance. She knew that the bathrobe-clad woman in the lane lived across from her, and watched her strike her own forehead with the palm of her hand as she yelled at the man with a ponytail standing beside her jeep. He was quite a stocky man, wearing blue jeans, and he was carrying a piece of paper. The man followed the woman back into her basement suite across the lane.

Immediately next door to Sian's house, Darlene Kennedy* was changing sheets in a bedroom overlooking the lane when she also heard

132

the commotion. At first, she thought Katie was yelling at someone. Brushing aside her long red hair, she looked out of the window but didn't see either Katie or Sian. The man with a ponytail, however, looked up at her as he walked around the jeep towards the entrance to the girls' suite. She got a good look at him, but had darted back from her window not wishing to appear nosy.

"Mind if I use the bathroom?" asked Schlender. The basement foyer was furnished only with a chair and a wicker desk but it was cramped. Schlender had the Ruger stuffed in his jeans and he needed more room to get ready. Two doorways led from the vestibule, one to the right going into Sian's bedroom, the other leading to the living room and the remainder of the suite. Absently, Sian directed the stranger through the second doorway, telling him where he'd find the bathroom. "It's through there," she said, pointing over her right shoulder. "Just behind that wall unit."

The big stranger handed Sian the insurance documents. "Here," he said. "While I use the bathroom, you can write down the details so you can put in a claim." The ruse worked perfectly, even better than Schlender could have hoped. Sian would never normally have let a stranger into her suite, let alone allow him to use her bathroom, but she was preoccupied with the damage to her jeep.

Schlender disappeared into the bathroom. He took off his jacket and pulled the long gun from the waistband of his jeans, scarcely believing it was him—himself the father of two girls—in the bathroom mirror. In the foyer, Sian Simmonds sat down to copy the name and address from the insurance documents, unaware that her visitor was creeping up behind her.

Suddenly, Sian turned to see the stranger holding the big gun to her head. Dropping the pen, she let out a piercing, unintelligible scream. She turned and leapt to her feet as Schlender coldly fired the first shot, a contact wound that shattered the left side of her jaw. The hot shell casing flew from the automatic, falling to the floor beside the chair. In a futile attempt to escape, Sian backed up toward the living room door, raising her hands defensively as Schlender fired the second shot. Screaming hysterically, she lunged at her assailant, kicking him in the groin.

The second bullet seared through the back of Sian's right arm, lodging deep in the muscle near her shoulder blade. As the shell casing

133

flew through the doorway into the living room, Sian still struggled for her life. The gunshots had not killed her. Cleaning the bathroom upstairs, Gill Phelps thought she heard the muffled shots. But the silencer did its job. Thinking the sound was coming from outside, Sian's aunt carried on with her housework.

The veins stood out in Schlender's neck and forehead as he gripped the silencer of the gun in his left hand. With all his might, Schlender swung the big weapon against Sian's head. Although the blow was cushioned somewhat by the girl's long, blonde hair, it was still delivered with such force that it split her right ear. Tough as she was, Sian was no match for the six-foot, ex-baseball pitcher. She reeled backwards against the doorframe, splinters of wood tangling in her hair as blood splashed against the wall behind her.

Sian fell to the ground, the big man losing his balance and falling with her in a macabre dance of death. Again and again, Schlender swung the weapon, gouging the linoleum floor as he missed his target. But still, another six times, the big man clubbed Sian's face and head until the screaming stopped.

The left tip of Sian's index finger was severed from her hand as she tried to protect her head. It was no use. She was quiet now. One of the blows had lacerated the main artery exiting her brain. Permanent imprints from the gun were embedded in Sian's face and scalp. As she gave up the fight, bleeding to death, brain substance was coming out between the fractures in Sian's skull.

Schlender turned to run, forgetting his insurance papers and within minutes, as Gill Phelps continued to clean upstairs, Sian Simmonds was dead.

16   Code 3

Letter carrier Todd Martin*, a slim young man with a red beard and mustache, pulled up outside Darlene Kennedy's house next door. He always parked there to make his deliveries because it was the first place where the shoulder was wide enough to pull safely off the busy two lanes of 160 Street. And just as he walked to the back of his red, white and blue van to fetch the mail, Martin was intrigued to see a man with a ponytail running towards him from between the houses.

Knowing one of the residents had recently been burglarized, Martin was already on the lookout for anything unusual, and the tall stranger, carrying his jacket and wearing black gloves, certainly looked suspicious. As the man with the ponytail clambered over an embankment at the edge of the Kennedy property, he offered a seemingly unconvincing explanation for his haste. "Oh shit!" he muttered towards Martin. "Late for work."

Half way across the road, the man with the ponytail looked over his shoulder to ensure no vehicles were coming, then leapt into a silver blue Dodge Omni parked on the opposite side. There was a lot of junk in the back seat of the car, Martin noticed, and he now realized it was the same vehicle he'd noted when one of the neighbors had been robbed about a month ago.

Martin had discarded his note at that time because no further break-ins had been reported. The man with the ponytail looked very suspicious, however, and the postman peered through his glasses trying to see the license plate as the Omni sped away. On the back of an advertising flyer, Martin wrote down what he thought was the number, and put the flyer in his pocket. This time he kept it, in case he might hear of any more burglaries in the next day or two.

Gill Phelps, meanwhile, switched off her vacuum cleaner and wondered if the two loud bangs she'd heard might have been gunshots. But figuring the sounds had come from outside, she prepared a sandwich for her seven-year-old son. Matthew would be home any minute for lunch and afterwards she would go out for groceries. Gill kept to herself. She didn't like to interfere with her niece's business.

If Gill had not gone shopping, she might have observed Dr. Charalambous as he happened by with his wife and children in the family van. Although the doctor craned his neck to get a good look at the house, he could see no signs of life. Upon her return, Gill noticed a light was still on in the basement. Putting her grocery bags on the kitchen floor, she phoned downstairs, but got only the answering machine. She descended the stairs to check the light and found Sian propped up against the wall in the foyer. Gill screamed. She ran back upstairs and called 911.

Constable Harry Pokorny thought it was an unusual call right from the start. As a cop for fifteen years, the six-foot, 190 pound, uniformed patrolman couldn't figure out why Metro (police dispatch parlance for the ambulance service) wanted him to attend the scene of what had come over his car radio as a routine cardiac arrest.

The forty-year-old Pokorny, married with two teenage children, was a clean shaven, pleasant but no-nonsense type of guy who had just spent an uneventful day in court. As he had pulled his cruiser out of the parking lot, the most important thing on his mind had been where to go for lunch.

It was already 2:00 P.M. but for now his growling stomach would have to wait. Pokorny scribbled down the address. His first thought was that some distraught ethnic family might be impeding the efforts of ambulance attendants to revive a loved one. Whether by instinct or design, he decided to go Code 3. Turning on the cruiser's siren and flashing lights, Pokorny headed northeast towards Guildford, encountering only light traffic as he sped through the cold afternoon drizzle.

Pokorny turned onto a road lined by telephone poles and dirt shoulders. It was easy to find the small, gray house on 160 Street. Two ambulances and a fire truck were already parked just around the corner.

With dawning concern, Pokorny observed that the paramedics and firemen were still waiting for him outside. "Didn't you get the second call?" one of them asked. "There's blood involved. We were told to wait for you."

It was a fine time for a breakdown in communication, Pokorny thought. He didn't have any cover. He looked at the house. The upstairs front door was wide open. He warily crossed the front lawn, noticing a Caucasian woman in the living room as he did so. Visibly shaken, the woman came onto the porch to meet him.

"RCMP," Pokorny called out. "What's going on?"

"I'm Gill Phelps," said the woman, who appeared to be in her mid-thirties. Shaking almost uncontrollably, she confirmed that she had called 911. "My two nieces live downstairs," she explained. "I think one of them has been murdered. I found her on the floor in the basement suite. Her skin felt cold."

"Where's your other niece?" Pokorny asked, concerned for her safety.

"I think she's at work," Mrs. Phelps replied. She told Pokorny about the stranger who had scratched the jeep two hours previously. Noticing the basement door was slightly ajar, Pokorny descended the concrete steps. The policeman had arrived less than ten minutes after receiving the call, but was about to discover that he was already far too late.

Whenever he was involved with fatalities, Pokorny was acutely aware of his surroundings, his emotions controlled but on edge, his hearing super sensitive, his eyesight clear and fixed, olfactory senses ready for that faint but unmistakable smell of death. Feeling the hair rising on his scalp, he pushed the door open. In the small foyer, he saw a well-proportioned young woman lying on her back, naked beneath a white terry cloth bathrobe that was up around the top of her thighs. She had long, blonde hair matted with blood. To the right of the motionless body, Pokorny noticed a pair of black dress boots.

"More than likely a prostitute," the police officer thought. "Possibly brought a john back to her suite and got murdered as a result." Everything added up. Black boots. Male caller unknown to the aunt. Girl still in her housecoat at lunchtime.

What little light there was in the foyer—this dark, cloudy winter afternoon—shone obliquely and eerily through the opaque amber window panels in the double doors to the suite. The foyer also was eerily quiet. Pokorny switched on his flashlight.

The girl's skin, he could see, was an ashen color. There was a large amount of coagulated blood beneath her head. Her eyes were milky and lifeless. "Just wait there," he told the paramedics and firemen at the door. "I'd rather you didn't come in."

Veteran ambulanceman Roland Russell and his partner Bill Weston had arrived at the scene as an advanced life support unit, but all their skill in the present circumstances would be useless. The victim may have been alive when she had fallen backwards against the wall, Russell figured, but the forward position of her head would immediately have cut off her breathing from that time. After thirty years as a paramedic, Russell still felt dejected by not being able to help.

Pokorny was careful not to step in any blood as he skirted the body to check the remainder of the suite. After talking to Mrs. Phelps, it was obvious the murderer was long gone. There was no need to draw his gun. Although it was bad enough already, the policeman dreaded possibly finding a second victim in another part of the suite.

Still shining his flashlight, he checked an unfinished area of the basement but found nothing of concern. There was one light on in a back hallway, but otherwise the suite, like the foyer, was bathed in semidarkness. Room by room, Pokorny toured the remainder of the suite, its adequate but inexpensive furnishings typifying it as somebody's first home. In the living room were a couch and chair, an octagonal coffee table and a wall unit, housing silent stereo components. Pokorny also checked the bathroom, the kitchen, and two bedrooms. In one of them there was an apparently new night table beside the bed. In the corner was a TV, which was switched off.

No one else was present. There were no other bodies. Although the bed was unmade, Pokorny did notice that the suite was clean and tidy. Absolutely immaculate. On the walls, almost everywhere he looked, there were framed photographs: photos of happy, smiling people—portraits of a loving family. Pokorny knew then that his first guess had been wrong. Now, he felt ashamed for having even thought it.

To the police officer's trained eye, it looked as though the victim had put up a struggle. It seemed probable she'd been fighting off a molester. Pokorny crouched for a few minutes looking at the body. He had been in similar situations many times before. Never, though, for a murder victim had he felt so much compassion as he did here and now.

This girl, lying on the ground with the life drained out of her, seemed to be communicating with him about her own mortality. *Help me*, she seemed to be saying to him. *Look what's happened to me. Let's get to the bottom of what's going on.*

Pokorny reached for his portable radio, which up until then had been working just fine. Unbelievably, true to Murphy's law when things were most needed to go right, the radio was dead. Pokorny pressed the squelch button several times but it was no use. He desperately had to communicate with headquarters but he couldn't leave the scene unsecured. Pokorny noticed a phone in the far right corner of the foyer but decided against using it. The phone might yield fingerprints of a suspect. The policeman paused for a moment, then realized his cruiser was parked in such a way that he could use the car radio while still keeping watch on the door to the suite. Pokorny's call was answered by dispatcher Carol Wooldridge. He was glad for that. Carol, married to a sergeant at headquarters, was an experienced dispatcher. "I have a confirmed 58," Pokorny radioed. (The code number meant sudden death).

Pokorny felt no sooner had he finished calling for reinforcements when the first TV camera crew arrived at the scene. Someone had monitored the calls but it still seemed unbelievably fast. Pokorny scratched his head. "Must be telepathy," he mused. Gill Phelps was shivering, not hysterically, but in a state of obvious and extreme discomfort. Although one of the ambulances had left, the other was still on the scene. Paramedics remained in the kitchen in case they might be needed. Though her voice was breaking, the distraught woman was able to explain to Pokorny the events leading up to her call.

"I was cleaning the bathroom," Mrs. Phelps recounted. "Around 11:00 A.M., there was a familiar, friendly type of knock at the back door." The woman demonstrated against the kitchen table: rap, rappety raprap, rap, rap. "I opened it and there's this fellow holding his car insurance papers in his hand. He looked like a fairly nice-looking, clean-cut sort of guy."

She had looked the stranger right in the eye and was confident she could identify him if she saw him again. "He asked me if I owned the red jeep in the lane. He said he was driving by and accidentally scratched it. I said, 'Oh, you mean the little red jeep? It belongs to the girl downstairs.'"

The woman paused in her narrative while Constable Pokorny

139

looked out the window to see the red jeep parked in the lane behind the house. The scratch, he observed, was about twelve inches long, running parallel and below the driver's side door handle.

Gill continued. She had looked at her niece's jeep from the kitchen window, she explained, but hadn't been able to see any car. If, as he'd said, the stranger had been driving by, where was his car? It had seemed strange, but she hadn't wanted to be accused of prying. She had peered through the Venetian blind at a side window to observe the man standing in the basement doorway. "I heard him say, 'I'm really sorry. I scratched your jeep.' Then I heard my niece exclaim, 'Oh my God. Oh Lord.'"

As well as police reinforcements, curious members of the public and the media had now also arrived on the scene. Using trees and fenceposts, Pokorny and another uniformed member cordoned off the house with yellow tape. After briefing the GI (General Investigation) people on what he'd found, Pokorny returned to headquarters to fill out his report. He got home for a very late supper, realizing the young woman's death was still very much a mystery. "Her profile didn't fit," he recalled. "She wasn't into drugs. She wasn't mixed up with any seedy characters. She hadn't been fighting with her boyfriend. None of it made any sense."

17   Corporal Straughan
Starts a File

Corporal Gary Straughan's pager went off while he and a dozen of his colleagues from the RCMP's serious crime unit were attending a seminar on child sexual abuse in nearby Langley. A pleasant sandy-haired man in his mid-forties, Straughan excused himself from the meeting and went to the nearest phone to learn that headquarters in Surrey was appointing him file coordinator on the latest murder case.

Recently, the plainclothes General Investigation Section of which he was a member had been solving better than 80 percent of the murders in Surrey, but the latest case sounded like a real whodunit. Straughan was relatively new to the section, but Staff Sergeant Bob Briske in charge of GIS obviously had a lot of confidence in him.

Muttering apologies, Straughan gathered up his colleagues from the lecture room, briefing them outside before heading for his car with Constable Deanna Kohlsmith. Without realizing it, he had always walked everywhere at full speed and sometimes found himself apologizing if people had trouble keeping pace.

Constable Kohlsmith, a large, pretty woman who had been a plainclothes investigator for the past four years, caught up with him as he started his car on the far side of the parking lot. Straughan was a friendly and sincere man, but Deanna knew he had little patience for anything other than the logical. "Well, what would you suggest we do?" he would say, in his deep voice, and soon everyone would be back on track.

Straughan had almost been thwarted in his attempts to become a

Mountie because of a teenage marriage. New recruits in the days before Charter rights had to be single, but he got accepted seven years later in 1975 after his first marriage ended in divorce. A crack shot with small arms, Straughan was one of a four-man team of Mounties who won a police combat-shooting competition in Bismarck, North Dakota, sixty rounds from his .38 Special hitting the target for 299 points out of a maximum 300.

Posted on Vancouver Island, where he married his present wife Paddy, he spent several years investigating bar fights and other minor incidents before his knack for more complex cases got him back into plainclothes in Victoria. There, Straughan was one of the Mounties who proved "the butler did it" in 1986 when a wealthy American socialite was murdered aboard her cruiseship as it sailed through Canadian waters.

Straughan had transferred to the mainland in 1992, and was one of thirty-nine members in Surrey GIS, where he had worked alongside Deanna Kohlsmith for the past year. After driving from Langley, the two of them now observed the yellow tape cordoning off the house on 160 Street.

As they descended the basement stairwell and looked inside, both were shocked and saddened by what they saw. The victim, so young and beautiful, appeared to have been attacked with such savagery. There was no need for Straughan, as file coordinator, to go inside but Deanna borrowed his car keys so that she could get a "bunny" suit to work alongside members of the identification section. Dressed in their head-to-toe, white cotton suits, Corporals Dave Flamank and Gene Krecsy had already found two spent .22-caliber cartridges and were now searching for even the minutest of fibers.

Straughan saw no reason to enter the foyer and possibly disturb anything. Instead, his steel gray eyes focussed on a wicker desk just inside the door on which someone had left a set of car registration and insurance documents. Enclosed in a plastic holder, the documents described a blue 1984 Dodge Omni, license number WDS-577, registered to a person named Brian McCann. Straughan looked at the package, but didn't touch it. Neither, for the time being, did anyone else. It would be dusted, in due course, for fingerprints.

"Seems too obvious, doesn't it?" one of the officers suggested. "Almost like it's some kind of ruse."

"Mebbe not," responded Straughan. "Perhaps he's just a bumbling, fucking idiot."

Learning that his colleagues had found two eye witnesses in addition to Gill Phelps, Straughan assisted for a while with further neighborhood inquiries before heading back for his car. The investigation was now well in hand and it was time for him to return to police headquarters to begin coordinating the file.

Using the back porch as a command post, police officers shivered outside as they waited in the gathering darkness for the coroner and the pathologist. They were also waiting, however, for Katie Simmonds. The victim's sister was on her way home from work and would have to be intercepted before she could go inside.

But Katie didn't drive directly home. After work, she bought Sian some apple bubble bath and a white camisole for her birthday. Katie then visited friends on her way home, leaving the unwrapped presents in her jeep. Alerted by news bulletins, she now arrived, heart pounding, to see the *U.TV* Winnebago with its big satellite dish outside her home. Katie jumped out of her friend's car almost before it had stopped. Just in time, two policeman caught her as she leaped the yellow tape cordon,

"You're Katie?" Constable Nels Justason confirmed breathlessly. "I'm sorry. You can't go inside."

"Is it Sian?" asked Katie, the knot tightening in her stomach. "I have to know what's happening."

"Your sister has met an unfortunate demise," Justason confirmed.

"What do you mean?" Katie demanded, suddenly sinking back in the Justason's police car. "Tell me what you mean? Is Sian dead?"

"Yes," Justason replied, almost choking on his words. "I'm sorry. Sian is dead."

From experience, Justason knew the young woman would want to know everything in thirty seconds or less. But he also knew she wouldn't hear him, even if did have the answers, and it would be useless for him to attempt giving details now. "We don't know," he said. "We're still investigating."

As he drove Katie to police headquarters, Justason asked her if either of the sisters had had any problems with boyfriends, past or present. Katie knew of none. As far as she was concerned, none of the questions seemed real. Shortly, her boyfriend Dean arrived at the police station and drove Katie to her parents' home. "I must be in a movie," she thought. "This isn't really happening."

143

The terrible task of notifying the victim's parents had already been given to Constable John Gould, a compassionate and gentle 200-pound weightlifter, who had gone to the Willoughby Hill house with two victims' services volunteers behind him in a second car.

Gould walked past the manicured grounds to the front door and rang the bell. Himself the father of three young children, he dreaded this job. He identified himself clearly enough when a petite woman with long hair opened the door, but he still hoped somehow to avoid the confrontation. "Is your husband home?" Gould inquired. "No," Mrs. Simmonds replied. "What's wrong?"

"Do you have a daughter named Sian?" Gould continued.

"What's the matter with my Sian?" Mrs. Simmonds screamed. "What's the matter with my Sian!"

"I am sorry to tell you Mrs. Simmonds," Gould began, speaking slowly, trying to overcome the lump in his throat, "that Sian was involved in an accident earlier today. She was seriously hurt and, as a result of her injuries, she has died."

Gould had learned in police training how he was supposed to break such news, but there was no such thing as being able to do it properly. Sian's mother accused him of lying. The dark, curly-haired policeman stood back now as she assailed him, screaming, sobbing, punching him in the chest. Nothing could have been worse. He had just taken away one of her reasons for living. Following Sian's mother inside, Gould had to wrestle the phone from her hand to stop her calling her husband. If her husband was at work, he suggested, they would drive there together. Then, he held her for three, four, perhaps five minutes.

Other than discussing directions, Gould and his passenger were silent as they drove to meet Chris Simmonds at work. As darkness fell, the drive seemed to take an eternity. Arriving at the Safeway truck maintenance yard, Gould took Susan Simmonds to the car of the victims' services volunteers, who had followed. The policeman was told at first that Chris Simmonds was busy and could not be disturbed. "Someone in his family has been hurt," Gould insisted. "Don't tell him that. Just bring him here!"

Gould waited until a well-built man with gray hair pulled up in a golf cart. Chris Simmonds was about average height. He got out, looking at Gould curiously. The officer established that he was talking to Sian's father and gave him the news. Sian had been involved in an incident today, he repeated. She was seriously hurt and he was sorry to say that she had died....

Before Gould could add "as the result of her injuries," Sian's father fell to the ground like a sack of potatoes. When Chris Simmonds rose to his feet, he punched at everything within reach. "Not again!" he cried. "We just went through this. My youngest brother just committed suicide, two months ago."

Gould listened with compassion. After a moment, he spoke: "I've got Sue in the car," he said. "You've got to be strong for her." After they embraced, Gould left the sobbing parents with the victims' services volunteers. "They'll take you home," he explained. "I'm going back to the office but I'll come over and see you this evening as soon as we know more."

Meanwhile, David Sella had returned from a Vancouver car show to the home of his friend, Jason Van Strepen. Sella still planned to visit his girlfriend in an hour or two and he phoned his own answering machine at home to check for messages. *Strange*, Sella thought, there were about twenty calls but most of them had hung up without saying anything. There were a couple of the messages to call Katie at her parents' home, but the Simmonds' line was busy. Others he phoned in the meantime acted strangely, telling him he should call the Simmonds family immediately. Finally, after what seemed an eternity, he got through to Katie.

"David," Katie said. "Where are you?"

"I'm at Jason's."

"Can you come over?"

"Tell me what's the matter."

"I just think you should come over."

"Katie," Sella persisted, "what's the matter? What's happened to Sian? Tell me."

"Is Jason there?"

Sella handed the receiver to his friend. "Jason," Katie said. "I want you drive David over. I want you to bring him right now, but don't let him drive."

Under normal conditions, the drive from Coquitlam to the Langley residence of Chris and Susan Simmonds—most of it on the heavily travelled Trans-Canada Highway heading east from Vancouver—takes about twenty-five minutes. Dave Sella did it in ten. Accompanied by

145

Jason, he had ignored Katie's exhortations and jumped behind the wheel of his blue Nissan pickup, his mind racing as he sped in excess of 100 miles an hour. "Will I still love Sian if she's been disfigured?" he was thinking. "What if she's been disabled?" With its emergency lights flashing and occasionally veering onto the shoulder, the small Nissan passed every vehicle in sight.

Eventually, Sella and his friend approached the Simmonds' residence on 83 Avenue. The long driveway was filled with cars, and still more vehicles clogged both sides of the street outside. As he entered the house, David noticed dozens of pairs of shoes that visitors had taken off just inside the door. There were all kinds of shoes, he observed, summer and winter shoes, all colors and sizes, lined up in row after row by the door. It seemed oddly inappropriate, but someone had started it and everyone else had followed suit. David yanked off his shoes and left them there with the others.

In the house, he spotted Sian's friends, her cousins, aunts, uncles, her mother sobbing at the kitchen table, and a lot of people he didn't know: all of them with the same dreadful look on their faces, an unforgettable look that would haunt him for ever more. "You don't know what's happening, do you?" said a familiar voice. David searched Chris Simmonds' face for an answer.

"What's happened to Sian?" David asked. "Where is she?" Sian's father guided David away from the kitchen, where most of the visitors were assembled. "Somebody broke into Sian and Katie's today and shot Sian," Chris Simmonds said.

Blankly, David stared at Sian's father. "Is Sian dead?" he asked.

"Yes," Chris Simmonds replied. "Sian is dead."

At the dining room table, Constable Gould was interviewing Kim Jones about her last telephone conversation with Sian. Dave Sella introduced himself. Gould seemed satisfied with David's explanations as to where he had been that day. "Why was she shot?" Sella asked. "Was she raped?"

"We don't think so," said Gould, "but there'll be an autopsy and a bunch of tests." Although Gould didn't regard Sella as a suspect, he advised him that he might be asked for a blood sample if the autopsy indicated it necessary. In the basement, meanwhile, Sian's cousins and her younger friends were trying to come up with some reason why Sian might have been murdered. Some thought it may have been a would-be suitor from the restaurant where she worked.

146

It was close to ten o'clock as Gould got up to leave. Chris Simmonds escorted him to the front door. Even at this early stage in the investigation, Sian's father already had his suspicions. He didn't know if was relevant, he explained, but Sian and Katie had accused their doctor of molesting them and the girls had been scheduled to testify against him in March.

Gould listened skeptically. "Heck, no," he suggested. "I wouldn't think that's got anything to do with it." As he stood in the open doorway, however, Gould turned back. "It sounds pretty bizarre," he said. "I'm sure it's got nothing to do with it, but what's the doctor's name?"

"Dr. Charalambous," Chris Simmonds replied.

Constable Gould asked how the name was spelled. Simultaneously, he wrote it down in his notebook. "I'll check it out," he promised.

As she worked at the murder scene, Deanna Kohlsmith also was interested in knowing more about the family doctor. After applying adhesive tape to the body in hopes of lifting hairs or fibers from a suspect, the detective had done a perimeter search of the murder scene. Looking for clues in Sian's bedroom, Deanna had found a letter addressed to the victim from the College of Physicians and Surgeons. The policewoman had absorbed it contents. Could it have been relevant? She reexamined the letter and took another look at the doctor's name. Dr. Josephakis Charalambous. It was not an easy name to absorb. Subsequently, it would be a name she would never forget.

Deanna had been a police officer for almost twelve years. She could tell this was two young girls' first home away from home. The girls' photos were all over the walls, some of them blow-ups from the time they were two to the time they were sixteen. They looked so alike. They looked like a pair of twins. Deanna could tell they were close.

The suite wasn't expensively furnished, but it was meticulously neat. Sian's schoolbooks were open beside her bed. Deanna couldn't help feeling personally involved. Sian was a true victim, murdered in her own home. On an emotional level, it was the hardest case she'd ever worked on. Along with the others present, she felt a personal sense of dedication to see it through to the end. Sian was a beautiful young college student murdered in her own home. It was a shock, a real whodunit. Deanna and her colleagues had quickly sobered up as the dreadful reality sank in.

Meanwhile, the task of locating Brian McCann and his 1984 silver blue Dodge Omni had been assigned to the likable Constable Brian Fleming, a short, slightly pudgy officer from the robbery detail. Working with Corporal Jim Larke, Fleming had fed McCann's license plate number into CPIC, the police computer information system, which would reveal if there had been any police inquiries concerning the Omni within the previous seventy-two hours.

CPIC would produce answers from anywhere in the country (as well as some parts of the United States) and Fleming couldn't believe his luck. The computer did indeed have the information he wanted. The Omni, he learned, had not been stolen, but only that morning its owner had reported it overdue after loaning it to an unnamed friend. The computer had yielded a major break. Finding McCann and discovering the identity of the person to whom he had loaned his car was now Fleming's top priority.

Fleming and Larke arranged for the vehicle's license number to be broadcast to all police departments in the metropolitan area. They also discovered that McCann had a past record for two minor drug offenses and—by yet another stroke of luck—there was a photograph of him in the police files.

After mounting McCann's mugshot along with seven others, Fleming and Larke returned to the house to show the photo lineup to Mrs. Phelps. Sian's aunt pondered the eight color photographs but the picture of Brian McCann meant nothing to her. "Whoever it was looked a bit more like number three," she said, handing the photos back to Fleming. "But it wasn't any of these guys." It had seemed like a good lead, but Fleming and Larke already had a good idea that McCann wasn't their man.

The insurance documents listed McCann's address as an apartment in North Delta. Leaving the Phelps' residence, the two policemen drove to what turned out to be a ground floor condominium owned by McCann's mother. "A witness saw Brian's car earlier today at the scene of a serious incident," Fleming began. McCann's mother was a well-groomed, pleasant woman, and she seemed cooperative. "He usually calls about eleven o'clock," she said. "He calls me almost every night. I'll get him to contact you but you might want to try his girlfriend's place."

As she gave Fleming and Larke an address in east Vancouver,

Fleming handed the woman his card. "If he does show up or call," the policeman stressed, "tell him it's urgent."

The two policemen drove into Vancouver. McCann's girlfriend was able to corroborate something Fleming and Larke already suspected. "Someone—I don't know who it was—dropped him off here last night and borrowed his car," she said. "Brian was ticked off this morning that whoever had his car still hadn't returned it."

Unknown to any of them at the time, McCann had finally got back his car—and it was now parked for the night in Surrey. "Sorry I'm late," Schlender had told him. "I was drinking paralyzers last night. I got pissed and I passed right out." After placating McCann with a beer at the Biltmore Hotel, Schlender and his wife had invited him back to their suite in Surrey. "We can watch some videos and have a bite to eat," Schlender had offered.

McCann had stopped his car on the way back so that Schlender could buy some cocaine. They had also stopped at a liquor store where McCann bought beer, while Schlender picked up a forty ounce bottle of rum. Then they had visited an old man's house to borrow some videos. Schlender and the local bikers liked the old man and often hung around his house to protect him.

While Fleming and Larke were looking for him, McCann sat talking with the Schlenders in their basement suite. Colleen fixed something to eat but none of them did get around to watching videos as planned. At about nine o'clock, a heavyset man named Brian dropped by to visit with Schlender. McCann had seen the man at the house once before. He had curly hair, a beard and several tattoos on his hands. Schlender and his bearded visitor went into another room and closed the door. After the bearded man left, McCann noticed that Schlender had a roll of banknotes in his shirt pocket.

Folding bedroom laundry in Coquitlam, meanwhile, Shelley Charalambous overheard her husband as he answered the telephone in the living room at about 9:00 P.M. After a brief telephone conversation, Charalambous hurried to join her in the bedroom to listen to the radio. The station was announcing details of the murder earlier that day of a nineteen-year-old woman in her basement suite in Surrey. Her husband turned off the radio. "I'm going out," he told Shelley. "Don't answer the phone till I get back."

Shelley continued folding her laundry. When her husband returned

149

thirty minutes later, he seemed to be very agitated, stressed out and jittery. He spent the rest of the evening flipping back and forth between radio and television stations. Eventually, the late night TV news showed the scene of the crime.

"That's Sian and Katie Simmonds' house," said Shelley.

"Yah," her husband agreed. After the news ended, he switched off the TV and went to bed.

Constable Deanna Kohlsmith, meanwhile, was still at the scene of the crime. As she worked late into the night, she was joined by Staff Sergeant Bill Silvester, from the RCMP's regional forensic laboratory in Vancouver. As a blood spatter analyst, Silvester had attended numerous university courses in mathematics and physics, learning the laws of fluids in motion and studying the specific characteristics of blood with respect to viscosity, clotting and drying factors. Silvester had spent a further fifty ghoulish hours doing experiments with bovine blood, as well as his own blood, at the Canadian Police College in Ottawa. Often, he could ascertain the number of blows and/or shots sustained by the victim; where a victim had been located while being struck; and the approximate location of the assailant. Sometimes, the staff sergeant could also glean the movements of the victim and of the assailant after blood had been let.

Silvester quickly ascertained that the victim, in addition to being shot, had been attacked with a blunt instrument, primarily in the same spot where the body was now lying on the floor. Taking careful measurements of blood drops cast off by the murder weapon, the staff sergeant was able to determine that the assailant had been swinging the weapon at about twenty-five feet per second at the time of the attack, somewhat on the high side of medium velocity. But while such details might be of interest, Silvester had also attended for another reason: the Mounties wanted to try out a new process that, until then, had never been deployed anywhere else in the world.

The staff sergeant explained the process to Deanna as the two of them followed the body removal people to the morgue in New Westminster. Using a new technique developed in Ottawa, Silvester intended to see if he could lift fingerprints of the attacker off the body itself.

Some of the RCMP chemistry whizzes at national headquarters had found that Crazy Glue was a good medium for picking up fingerprints from many types of porous surfaces, including cadavers.

At the morgue, Deanna watched with wide eyes as the staff sergeant constructed a plastic tent over the lower half of Sian's body. The success of the experiment, he explained, would depend on whether the victim had rapidly cooled off after being touched. On living skin, fingerprints would quickly evaporate and be impossible to detect.

Silvester placed several drops of Crazy Glue in a metal tray. Using a hygrometer to monitor the humidity, the staff sergeant carefully slipped the tray and a small electric heater under the plastic tent.

He and Deanna waited. Once the glue vaporized, he explained, it might stick to any fingerprints that anyone else had left on the body. The prints could then be seen under ultraviolet light after being treated with fluorescent dye.

It took Silvester about an hour to complete the cyanoacrylete fuming of the corpse and, indeed, the process appeared to work. There were marks around Sian's ankles. But then the elation of Deanna and the staff sergeant quickly subsided as both of them realized the marks had obviously been made by the body removal people as they had picked the victim up. No other prints were apparent. Sian's attacker, it seemed, had been wearing gloves or had not touched her at all, at least not her lower body.

The staff sergeant helped Deanna lock the body in the crypt. By the time Silvester and Kohlsmith left for home it was two in the morning. Having been up since 7:00 A.M. the previous day, Deanna was physically and emotionally exhausted but there was time for only an abbreviated night's sleep.

In just a few hours, Deanna would have to attend the autopsy. And perhaps it, she hoped, might shed some light on the mystery.

18   Stakeout

Early next morning, Dr. Charalambous showered and shaved in his ensuite as usual, getting ready for work in under twenty minutes. On work days, he didn't stop for coffee or a doughnut until he got to the office. Today was no different, but he did have something out of the ordinary to tell his wife as he towelled his hair. "You have to leave the house when I leave," he told Shelley while he got dressed. "Don't come back until you phone and find me home first."

Shelley pulled on her long T-shirt. With her right hand, she brushed her long hair away from her face. She would do as she was told, but wasn't immediately quite sure what her husband had in mind. "Well I guess I won't take Allison to school then," she proposed.

"No," her husband stressed, his gray hair still damp. "Don't do anything different from your normal routine. Take her to school. Just don't return to the house until you phone and find me at home before you."

Constable Deanna Kohlsmith also got up early, to meet Dr. Sheila Carlyle in the morgue at the Royal Columbian Hospital in New Westminster, for the unpleasant task of taking notes at the autopsy.

The pathologist, Deanna observed, projected an air of competence, not surprising in light of her background and experience. Dr. Carlyle had graduated from the University of Ottawa, in 1972, with the Governor General's Award for the highest standard in her class. She was now

152

a heavyset, middle-aged woman with glasses who had attended courses in forensic pathology, both in Canada and in England at the University of Leeds.

The pathologist had inspected the body the previous day at the murder scene, where she had observed that the victim had been lying on her back with arms and legs extended, her head wedged up against the door frame behind her.

Sian's body temperature, Dr. Carlyle noted, had been cool—31.7 degrees centigrade—and the pool of blood beneath her had attested to considerable head injuries, partially obscured by blood tangled hair around the victim's face.

At the murder scene, Dr. Carlyle had observed shell casings on the floor, but it hadn't been immediately apparent that there were indeed gunshot wounds to the body. On cleaning blood from the victim's face, however, the pathologist was able to show Deanna that Sian had been shot in the jaw from very close range.

Working deftly, Dr. Carlyle recovered first one bullet from the soft tissue between Sian's jawbone, and the inner lining of her mouth, then a second bullet from the victim's back. Using forceps, she passed both projectiles to Deanna, who placed them in a plastic bag. The pathologist pointed out extensive skull fractures and brain injuries, showing the policewoman a distinctive pattern of bruises that appeared to have been made by the same blunt instrument.

"There are at least seven blows to the head," she noted authoritatively. "Possibly more."

The blunt force lacerations on both Sian's hands, she confirmed, were consistent with injuries the victim would have sustained attempting to defend herself. Sian, her autopsy indicated, had been facing her assailant as the shots were fired from close range, and evidently had raised her arms in a futile attempt to protect herself.

Much would have depended on the relative positions of the victim and her assailant at the time of the attack, but it seemed likely from the location of the wounds, primarily on the right side of Sian's head, that the murderer had been a left-handed individual, and a strong one at that.

The doctor explained to Constable Kohlsmith that death had resulted from tearing of the venous sinus, draining blood from the brain into the deep jugular vein of the neck. "Laceration of this vessel was the source for the most part of the external blood loss at the scene," the pathologist said. "In effect, it is major hemorrhage from this laceration which would be the most immediate cause of death."

But the post mortem did little to shed much light on motive. Despite initial indications at the scene, Dr. Carlyle could find absolutely no evidence that the victim had been sexually molested.

Constable Kohlsmith digested the autopsy findings and returned to the police station, anxious to give her report to Corporal Straughan. Both she and the file coordinator agreed that, rather than explaining things, the autopsy had compounded the mystery still further. Until now, a sexual attack had seemed the most likely motive. "There's got to be more to this than meets the eye," said Straughan.

The file coordinator was praying that Fleming and Larke would find the 1984 Dodge Omni and its elusive owner, Brian McCann. As the two policemen resumed their inquiries that morning, McCann's mother told them that her son had indeed phoned the previous night as expected and that she had passed on the urgent message to call them. For reasons, however, that the officers could not imagine, McCann had still not contacted them. It was a puzzle.

The policemen decided to pay McCann's mother another visit, Fleming getting her to sign a consent in his notebook allowing the installation of a trap on her telephone line. It wouldn't record conversations, Fleming assured her, but it would reveal the origin of any incoming calls. The officers were driving into Vancouver to make the same request of McCann's girlfriend when, at 9:57 A.M., Fleming's pager went off. "That's him!" the constable said to his partner. "About time!"

To find out what was going on, McCann was calling from the Turf Hotel, a strip bar where one of the patrons had recently been shot in the back of the head while drinking his beer. Fleming dialled the hotel number. "I understand you want to talk to me," said McCann.

"That's right," said Fleming. "Just make sure you wait for us. We'll be there in half an hour."

At 10:29 A.M., Fleming and Larke walked into the hotel lounge. Sitting at one of the tables was a slightly built man with a mustache, bulging eyes, and long, thinning hair. Introducing themselves, the officers told McCann why they had been looking for him since yesterday afternoon. "Why didn't you call back till now?" Larke asked.

McCann was nervous, but it was quickly apparent that he was not a party to the murder and that he was only too anxious to cooperate.

"Who had your car yesterday afternoon?" Larke continued.

"I loaned it to a guy named Dave Schlender," McCann replied. "He's a guy I knew about eighteen years ago, but we lost touch and only met again just recently. I'm sure it was about that long ago I used to know him because he didn't have kids back then but now he's got a nine and a fifteen-year-old."

The officers told McCann that his car would have to be impounded for twenty-four hours so it could be checked for evidence. It might yield clues tying it to the murder scene. As the three men continued chatting in the lounge, Constable Jim McNamara arrived at the Turf to have the vehicle towed to the police compound. Meanwhile, McCann agreed to accompany Fleming and Larke back to the police station to give a detailed statement. "Can you tell us where Schlender lives?" asked Fleming.

"Yeah, okay," said McCann. "I can show you on the way."

In Fleming's notebook, McCann drew a sketch of a cul-de-sac. It was a section of 99A Avenue in Surrey, showing the position of Schlender's house, and the location of his basement suite in the left-hand corner of the building. McCann also gave police Schlender's unlisted telephone number.

With McCann directing them from the back seat of their car, Fleming and Larke stopped to look from a distance at a modern, two-storey house, only about a mile from the scene of yesterday's grisly murder. Police work didn't get much better than this. It had been a productive morning.

Constable Wayne Rideout had returned to the scene of the murder to continue with neighborhood inquiries, hoping to find and talk to people who had been in the area the same time yesterday.

Rideout's hunch paid off.

At 11:20 A.M., Todd Martin pulled up in his postal van, outside Darlene Kennedy's house next door. The officer reached into his hip pocket, showing the postman the black and gold police badge pinned to the inside of his wallet.

"We're investigating a murder," he began. "If you were here yesterday, I was wondering if you saw anything suspicious."

"Yeah, as a matter of fact, I did," Martin replied. "I have some information for you."

Rideout could scarcely believe his luck. Martin handed Rideout a flyer on which the postman had written down what he thought had been the license number of the suspicious car he'd seen the day before. He also gave the policeman his description of the suspect.

Back at police headquarters, Brian McCann began his statement at 11:38 A.M.

McCann explained how Schlender had borrowed his car and failed to return it until the following day; he had stayed overnight at Schlender's house; he had been there when Schlender had received a visitor named Brian; afterwards he had stayed up for a while, chatting with Colleen.

McCann told Fleming and Larke that he'd stayed overnight at the Schlenders because he had been drinking beer and had been "feeling no pain." He had called home to let his mother know; his mother had told him to call Constable Fleming about a serious incident involving his car. Not wanting to alert Schlender, he had felt it best to wait until morning.

"Did he have any scratches, marks or blood on him?" asked Fleming.

"No, not that I noticed," said McCann.

"Is there anything you can think of that was unusual?" Fleming added.

"Well," McCann replied, "there is one thing. I noticed he had quite a bit of money. He had several bills in his shirt pocket and I seen that the outside one was a $100."

McCann got his car back the next morning. It had failed to yield any useful forensic evidence. Afterwards, though, McCann would find it hard to sleep for months to come.

Dr. Charalambous continued to see his patients. There were about 4,000 of them, all relying for their health on the enigmatic Greek Cypriot karate expert. They included newborn babies waiting to take their first breath, elderly patients about to take their last breath, and patients with just about every other type of condition in between.

The practise had already been a thriving concern when Charalambous had bought it, and he had built it up still further since then. He was seeing perhaps too many patients now, but he could be charming and soft-spoken and most of them didn't realize even if he was rushing them.

The office was a bit shoddy and showing signs of age, but recently the diminutive Charalambous had again been talking about renovating, making it even larger by bringing in another doctor, and turning the four examination rooms into six smaller ones. He had called for estimates from building contractors and inquired about arranging a bank loan to cover the cost.

Other than that, it was business as usual. As Charalambous returned to his office after lunch, someone may have made reference to the apparently increasing crime rate and the fact that one of his patients had been murdered, but he didn't seem overly worried.

The doctor might well have been concerned, however, if he'd known what had been going on at that precise moment just over two miles away, where a team of police officers had begun their stakeout of the Schlender residence at the end of the cul-de-sac on 99A Avenue. The tense, three-hour siege had begun almost as soon as Brian McCann had finished making his statement at police headquarters. Although police could have moved in on Schlender immediately, they had decided to wait for a search warrant to get more evidence.

Policemen tensed as a Yellow Cab pulled into the driveway and came to a stop at 1:30 P.M. A man and a woman matching the descriptions of Schlender and his wife got out of the cab. The man had a ponytail and was wearing a sleeveless Mac jacket. The woman, with short dark hair and blue jeans, was carrying plastic bags of groceries. After paying the driver, the couple walked to the rear of the house and went inside.

Constable Justason was watching from another street behind the house with Corporal Kautzman, the officer who had arrested Schlender the previous year for the attempted murder of drug dealer Nareg. The two officers were slouched behind the headrests of a rusty, old car that police sometimes used when they wanted to blend inconspicuously into certain neighborhoods. Had it not been for the serious nature of their mission, they felt they would have looked comical but, suddenly, there was another tense moment. As they watched, a young girl appeared at the back of the house followed by the man with a ponytail. He appeared to be admonishing her for being outside with bare feet. The man looked over towards Kautzman and Justason. He seemed to be staring directly at them. The officers felt themselves holding their breath.

Just moments earlier, Constable Gould had brought his colleagues heaping portions of takeout Chinese food. Being a weightlifter, Gould tended to overestimate other people's appetites, but Kautzman and Justason decided now would be a good time to tuck in like two ordinary guys who'd just stopped for lunch. The man with the ponytail glanced at them again, seeming unconcerned as he and the girl went back inside the house.

It wasn't until just after four o'clock that Constable Fleming arrived with the search warrant. Wanting to be sure that the man with the ponytail was indeed David Walter Schlender, Constable Gould called from a cellular phone to the unlisted number that had been provided by McCann.

Colleen Schlender answered. "I'm not sure if I've got the right number," Gould began. "I'm looking for a Dave Schlender I used to go to school with....."

"It's an unlisted number," said Schlender's wife, hanging up before Gould could finish.

Conferring briefly, the officers decided nothing was to be gained by waiting. They drew their guns and crept around to the back of the house, each of them in turn ducking beneath a kitchen window. "Here comes the cavalry," said Justason, watching from the other direction. "Let's join 'em."

Gould knocked on the basement door.

The white, metal door was opened by the man with the ponytail. "Police!" Gould yelled. The officer leapt at Schlender's throat with a surge of power, grabbing the man's ponytail and hurling him across the entrance to the suite. Other members of the arrest team piled on Schlender to handcuff him.

Thinking the intruders might be drug dealers, Schlender's panic-stricken wife tried to intervene. Rideout screamed at her at the top of his lungs. "Get on the ground!" he shouted. With a snub nosed .38 pointed directly at her face, Colleen Schlender did as she was told.

The sudden intrusion interrupted the amorous activities of a six-teen-year-old girl and her boyfriend in one of the bedrooms. The girl screamed obscenities at the police officers as she ran to the foyer to see her parents on the ground, just in time to hear Constable Fleming reading her father his rights.

"We're arresting you for the first degree murder of Sian Simmonds." Fleming told Schlender above the screams. "You have the right to retain...."

"What are you guys talking about?" Schlender protested. "I don't know what you're talking about."

The policeman finished reading Schlender his rights, the latter continuing to protest his innocence as he was hustled to the back of Fleming's and Larke's unmarked car. "This is Five Delta Fourteen," Larke radioed from the maroon, four-door Plymouth Acclaim. "Suspect under arrest."

Little more than twenty-four hours had elapsed since Constable Pokorny had been called to the basement suite on 160 Street. The RCMP now had the main suspect under arrest. When it came to murder investigations, it didn't get much better than that. As Fleming and Larke drove back to police headquarters, Schlender sat silently in the back seat.

When they arrived at the police station, the suspect was taken to the basement booking area, where the concrete floors, ceilings and walls were all painted the same depressing gray. It was like a mausoleum, modern but suffocating in its silence.

Schlender surveyed his cell. Except for a meager bedroll and a one-piece aluminum sink and toilet, everything else was concrete, including a raised ledge on the back wall that was meant to be a bed.

The suspect had been booked and stripped of his personal belongings. In place of his own clothing, he was given jail issue, white paper coveralls. Police were still hoping to match his clothing with any fibers that might have been retrieved from the murder scene. They already had a good hair sample. In the scuffle during the arrest, Constable Gould had grabbed a clump of Schlender's hair.

Schlender was also asked to provide a sample of pubic hairs. He was asked to pluck them out himself. He didn't raise much objection. If the police suspected him of a sexual attack, they had it all wrong. Maybe his lawyer could get him out of here yet.

At 5:17 P.M., Constable Fleming escorted the prisoner to the telephone room. He asked Schlender which lawyer he wanted and dialed George Wool's number for him. Wool arrived at 6:14 P.M., hotly objecting to being placed in a closed interview room, where he was separated from his client by a glass partition. After his outburst, he was allowed to meet with his client face-to-face.

As a former cop himself, Wool knew the ropes. He'd worked in the Arctic and had been frostbitten a few times. Once, he'd been blithely hooking up his police dog sled when his partner had warned of an approaching polar bear. He knew he couldn't stop the police from interrogating his client, but he also knew how to make things a bit more difficult. At 6:55 P.M., as he was getting up to leave, Wool dropped his caveat. "I don't want my client to be interviewed by the police," he told Fleming.

"What's that?" Fleming asked incredulously.

"I'd like a written acknowledgement that you've been requested not to ask my client any questions," Wool said.

"Okay," said Fleming, "whatever you say." Never before during his career had the policeman encountered such a demand but he made a signed notation of Wool's request in his police notebook. It wouldn't make any difference anyway, he figured. The police, he knew, had a duty and a right to interview a criminal suspect and Fleming fully intended to ask all the questions he wanted.

As Wool departed, Schlender eyed a package of cigarettes in Fleming's shirt pocket.

"How's your smokes?"

"Not bad," replied Fleming, "would you like one?"

"I'd love one," said Schlender.

"Here you go," said Fleming, holding out the package. "I'm going out for dinner. I'll be back later if you want to talk to me."

Fleming, accompanied by Larke and Gary Straughan, went to the nearby Greek Taverna restaurant, where they discussed the case with the file coordinator, over a meal of lamb souvlaki and rice. "There's something real strange about this murder," said Fleming. "He's not just some crazy guy off the street."

"I agree," said Straughan. "There's more to this than meets the eye."

The file coordinator sat back for a moment to think of a strategy. "Tell him we don't need an admissible statement," Straughan suggested. "The evidence is overwhelming. I just want to know what the motive was."

Fleming and Larke returned to the police station at 9:00 P.M. It had been a long day. Schlender had finished picking at a TV microwave dinner and was being photographed and fingerprinted by Constable Rideout. "He wants to talk to you when I'm finished," Rideout told Fleming.

Fleming and Larke placed three chairs and a tape recorder in a small interview room, with a window that was a two-way mirror. In accordance with regular procedure, the tape recorder was placed in full view. Then the prisoner with the ponytail was escorted from his cell. "Dave, I understand you want to talk to me?" Fleming said.

A relaxed Sian Simmonds.

The sisters with Sue Simmonds in the driveway of the Willoughby home.

Katie and Sian as little girls.

Sian and Dave
Sella dressed
up for
Halloween.

Sian Simmonds

Dr. J. Charalambous, his bride, and his winning horse.

Joseph Charalambous in his karate class: front row, second from left.

164

Charalambous with his baby daughter during her first swim.

Jacqueline Jongkind and her younger daughter Shawna.

Below: The hammer that Charalambous kept in his bedroom with a threat to hit his wife's head "until there is nothing left." The hammer was found left carelessly beside the clothes hamper when a search warrant allowed police to investigate his home.

The house in Coquitlam that Charalambous later gambled away.

Playing the odds—Charalambous secretly photographed by police surveillance at the local casino.

Angela Street outside Charalambous' office at 9808 King George Highway.

Joseph Charalambous under surveillance.

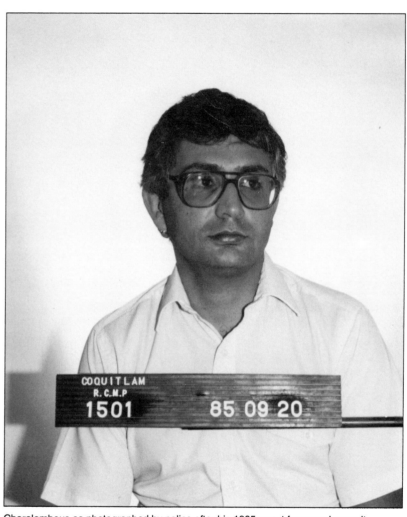

Charalambous as photographed by police after his 1985 arrest for sexual assault.

David Schlender

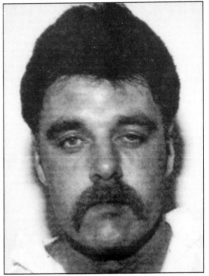

Brian West

Dr. Joseph Charalambous

Corporal Gary Straughan takes time to smile after the grueling investigation.

The prosecutors Terry Schultes and Sean Madigan.

Sian's aunt's house where the murder took place.

Entrance to basement suite on 160 Street, Sian's bedroom is on the right.

Chris Simmonds and daughter Katie give media interview during 1994 murder trial.

Angela Street will always wonder if her
1986 complaint to the College of
Physicians and Surgeons could have
saved Sian's life.
*Photo courtesy Sharp Shooters,
New Westminster, B.C.*

Sian's Asuna Sunrunner Jeep. The scratch made by Schlender is on the driver's side door.

The Ruger pistol and homemade silencer.

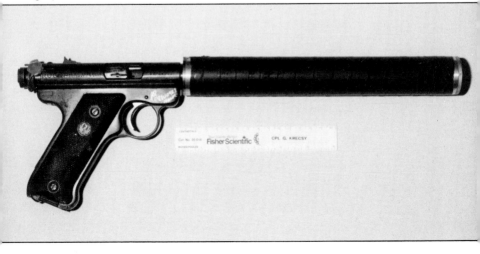

Constable Harry Pokorny with cruiser similar to the one he was driving on January 27, 1993.

After attending the murder scene, Constable Deanna Kohlsmith felt a "personal sense of commitment" to see the case through to the end.

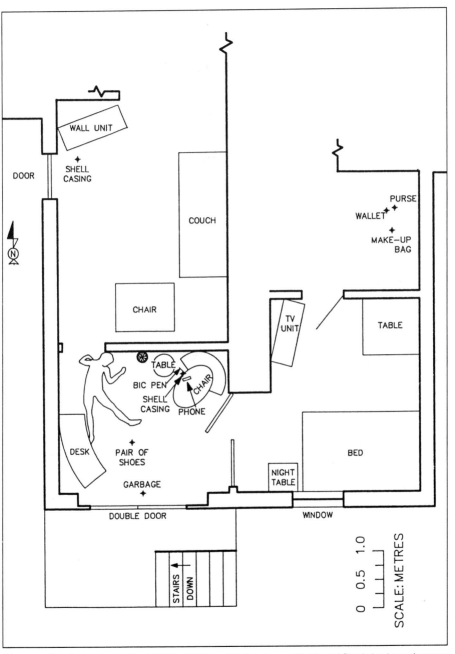

Diagram of the basement suite at 9340 - 160 Street. This is how police found Sian's body on January 27, 1993.

Sketch by one of Gary Straughan's colleagues, "Campbell," Corporal Straughan at right with, left to right, Schlender, Charalambous, and West.

"Yeah, I want to know if anyone has told my wife what's happening?"

"Let's go down and see about it," said the officer.

Fleming, forty-two years old, had been trying to quit smoking with the help of a nicotine patch. His efforts had left him edgy, but Schlender seemed to understand. Smokers these days had to stick together. Fleming carried three styrofoam cups of coffee into the room, one of which—when empty—would have to do for an ashtray.

Soon, though, it became apparent that the interview was going nowhere. Schlender said he'd never been convicted of any violent crime and insisted that definitely he was not a sex offender, but otherwise he wasn't saying anything. The officers did note that he was left-handed but for two hours and four minutes Schlender maintained he knew absolutely nothing about Sian Simmonds. He steadfastly denied he'd committed the murder. At one point, Fleming stepped out of the six by ten room to confer with Corporal Straughan. When he came back, he suggested to Schlender that the prisoner owed it to himself to be truthful.

"But I'm looking you right in the eye and telling you that I didn't do it...." said Schlender.

"You didn't kill that girl?" repeated Fleming.

"You can put me on a goddamn lie detector," Schlender insisted. "I don't care, put me on it."

But when Fleming offered to arrange the polygraph test, Schlender backed off. Again and again, Fleming and Larke informed Schlender that the evidence against him was overwhelming—but it was to no avail. The room was filled with a smoky haze but one thing was abundantly clear. Schlender had heeded his lawyer's advice. He wasn't talking. As they gave up for the night, the interrogators resolved to try again. There was at least a glimmer of hope. While Fleming was showing him back to his cell, Schlender asked the policeman to revisit him in the morning.

177

19   Confession

David Walter Schlender jabbed his finger in the direction of the tape recorder and glanced up at Constable Fleming with a look of resignation before speaking.

"Can you shut that thing off?" he asked.

Fleming had been a police officer for fifteen years. He could sense when a prisoner was about to talk. He hit the stop button as requested.

It was January 29, 1993—Shelley's birthday—and the police officer's questions had resumed in Interview Room 11 at 8:27 A.M. after Schlender had consumed a microwaved egg and muffin concoction for breakfast. There were no kitchen facilities in the police basement.

Evidence that Schlender was responsible for Sian Simmonds' murder was piling up, and Fleming brought the prisoner up to date. A police dog, said Fleming, had sniffed out a plastic bag full of bullets from a tree stump in a vacant lot next door to Schlender's residence. The bullets were .22-caliber, the same type and caliber as those that had been removed, two days ago, from the body of Sian Simmonds.

Schlender was fighting a losing battle and he knew it. He slumped forward, shaking his head from side to side.

Schlender looked at Fleming. The police officer seemed like a good guy. Perhaps it was time to help him out with some of the answers. Fleming could find the murder weapon, said Schlender, in a vacant lot beside a Chinese restaurant, near Guildford. He had hidden it in some bushes there while on his way home after carrying out the murder.

Dressed in plainclothes, Fleming had a way of talking to people like Schlender on their own level. He could gain their trust before wearing them down, but he still didn't know Schlender's motive. "Did you sexually assault that girl?" the policeman asked.

"No, I didn't sir," said Schlender.

"Call me Brian."

"Okay, Brian, I didn't. I didn't touch her."

"Yeah, I believe you because I was right up front about that last night as well, wasn't I?" said Fleming. "And I told you our preliminary indications were that it in fact she wasn't assaulted."

"Yeah," said Schlender. He lit another cigarette. "I'm not asking for anything for myself but you have to do something for my family."

The police officer listened intently. The big man with the ponytail was offering to tell him everything if the RCMP would guarantee protection for his wife and daughters. But when it came to Canada's national police force, Fleming didn't want the prisoner thinking deals could be made that easily.

"I have to talk to my boss about it," said Fleming. "We have to be able to show him beyond any reasonable doubt that a danger exists."

"I just want to know that my fuckin' family has got a chance," retorted Schlender. "That's all I want. I want you guys to say a few good words for me somewhere down the line, too."

In return for the information, the prisoner suggested, the RCMP might consider moving his wife and daughters to the United States and giving them a new identity. "And hopefully when I get charged," he added, "I don't know how you guys do it, I'd like to fuckin' go to another jail out of B.C., somewhere, if it's possible. I don't know if it is but...."

Gary Straughan was at the courthouse across the street, laying the information with Crown counsel Lothar Kiner, in preparation for Schlender's first appearance in court. The two men were in the midst of discussing what little they knew about the case, when Corporal Al Kautzman came running breathlessly across the street.

"Hold it," said Kautzman, as he broke the news of Schlender's confession. "He's going to be telling us all about it and a whole lot more."

The normally pragmatic file coordinator was taken by surprise. Both he and the prosecutor were ecstatic at the sudden turn of events, but Straughan wanted to make sure that police could continue to question Schlender over the weekend. He didn't want the accused being remanded in the provincial jail after his court appearance, just a few hours from now.

"It's no problem," said Kiner. "He won't be getting out on bail this time. We'll request that he be remanded back into police custody."

Fleming wasn't taking any chances. The policeman returned to the interview room with Schlender at 12:41 P.M., this time in the company of Sergeant Rinn. Fleming began the conversation. "Dave, I have read your rights to you a number of times," he said. "Is that correct?"

"Uh-huh," replied Schlender. "Yes sir."

"If you wish, I can go through them all again."

"I will waive my rights to talk to you at this moment."

"Okay, you and I had a discussion some time ago this morning....?"

"Uh-huh."

"...With regards to some information that you wished or you wanted to tell the police, myself?"

"Uh-huh."

Fleming was deliberately vague. The tape recorder was back on. "...And in lieu or not in lieu, but you asked for a favor from us....?"

"Uh-huh."

"And you have no objections to Sergeant Rinn sitting here with us?"

"I have none whatsoever."

The sergeant interjected. Compared with Fleming, Staff Sergeant Don Rinn was the bad guy. He wanted it made clear to Schlender—or anyone seeing a transcription of the tape—that the police were offering no favors. "Okay," said Rinn, "there's maybe one thing we should clarify here when you are asking for protection for your family...."

"Uh-huh."

"We certainly can't sit and babysit your family."

"They've got to be moved!" Schlender protested. "They've got to be relocated."

Fleming was more sympathetic as he picked up the conversation. "You were given assurance by Inspector Larry Gallagher, who is the operation support officer at this detachment, that in fact...."

"I would be helped," said Schlender. "And I am charged with second-degree murder."

180

"Okay," said Fleming. "So is there any question in your mind whatsoever with regards to your family's safety?"

"Not at this moment."

Schlender said he would tell his story from the outset. "I will start from the beginning," he said. "I have been wired on drugs for at least eighteen years, probably more. I've been a coke addict for at least ten. Probably done $2 million to $3 million of the shit."

The tape recorder continued to run. "I was on the needle for at least eight years," Schlender continued. "I also maintained, kept care of my family, but as the kids got older they figured things out. I've done a lot of little bad...you know...little shit, but never hurt anybody...."

Although Fleming and Rinn looked outwardly calm, both of them felt the inevitable rush of adrenaline as they listened expectantly to the information they so eagerly wanted. But despite Schlender's protestations to the contrary, the prisoner obviously wasn't ready to tell the entire truth, yet. The man might be confessing to murder but he was still a liar. A lot of the things he told them would have to be corroborated. Never hurt anybody? Only seven months before, Fleming and Rinn knew, he'd attempted to murder Manjjyet Nareg, but Schlender obviously didn't want the policemen thinking he was a cold-blooded killer. Denial, Schlender knew at the back of his mind.

"As the years went by," he continued, "I've met people and eventually I got so fucking far behind the eight ball that I am where I am today...."

"Uh-huh," said Fleming.

"And, through that, I have ended up meeting people that are very, very fucking heavy, and these people have things on me and I consequently was threatened, and I had to do things that were severely against the law, severely you know...and that's where I am now."

"Uh-huh."

Schlender admitted he had murdered Sian Simmonds on behalf of one of his drug suppliers to whom he owed between $3,500 and $7,000 for cocaine. He then went on to describe Brian West.

"I don't know him," said Fleming. "Is that the big heavyset guy?"

Schlender confirmed that it was. He described West as a "big fucking rat and fucking thief." The biker, he alleged, had offered to wipe out his cocaine bill if Schlender would burn down the house on 160 Street to deter Sian Simmonds and her sister from testifying against one of West's friends.

181

West, he alleged, had come to his house with the proposal three weeks before the murder. "He took me out, drove me right down to the fucking house and said, 'You do this and...I will square off your bill.'"

"Brian told me that...the broads are going to testify against his best friend...he has known for over twenty-five years. He didn't want her killed, just wanted her scared. He wanted me to first dump five to ten gallons of gas through from the front door and torch the place. I says, 'I ain't gonna do that to nobody.'

"Then he took me home, very pissed off. He came back and says, 'Look, I got in contact with him and this is the way we're gonna go now.' He went back to this guy. The guy said, 'Scare the shit out of them.' He said, 'You do that and your bill will be square.'"

Rinn wanted to make sure he had everything straight. "Just going back over this again...." said the sergeant, "your coke source is West?"

"One of them, yes," said Schlender.

"And it's through him that you'd built up this debt that you had to pay off, is that it?"

"Yes, yes sir."

"And so West coming to you to go and threaten this gal, that was helping to pay off that particular debt?"

"Uh-hmm, uh-hmm."

While Rinn was seeking clarification, Fleming was making notes of questions still to be asked. "Did he front you some money?" the policeman inquired.

"Before I did it?" asked Schlender. "Yeah."

"How much did he give you?"

"Seven hundred dollars. He gave me the money first, and then two or three days later he brought the gun over."

"And that's the one that we now have?"

"That's the one, that's the one."

"The one with the silencer on it?"

"Yeah, yeah, and he wiped it all off, wiped off the bullets and everything before...he gave it to me."

"Okay, so then what did you do with the gun after you got it? Did you keep it in your house or hide it outside or....?"

"I didn't keep it in the fucking house, man."

"No?"

"I left it outside."

"Yeah."

"I didn't want my fucking kids or old lady to ever see that thing."

"Had you tried to shoot it, or did you know how to load it or anything about it?" asked Fleming.

"Oh he...showed me that," said Schlender. "We went for a drive, he showed me and he blasted off the fucking thing. You know.... He says, 'Just fucking go in there, put it in her head, tell her to shut her mouth or she is going to get it the next time.' And I tried that. She started screaming and freaking out. She didn't give me a chance to talk and I just lost control. I didn't want to shoot. I was only supposed to terrify her."

Schlender assured the two police officers he was telling the truth. "That's the straight goods," he told Fleming, "right to the fuckin' wire, man." Schlender said he had specifically scratched the red jeep with a key to make sure he got the right woman. "That's why I knocked on the front door first," he added.

Fleming interjected: "And got the wrong lady, and then you went downstairs?"

"That's right."

The policeman asked what Sian had been doing when Schlender had first approached her.

"She was on the phone," said Schlender.

"Then you walked back in and that's when you were going to scare the shit out of her?"

"Uh-huh."

"So then you told her you scratched it and...the two of you went inside?"

"You got it. You got it."

"Okay, she walked in ahead of you?"

"Uh-huh."

"And she turned around and saw you pulling the gun out?"

"That's right. She was looking at the insurance papers and she seen me making an erratic move for the gun and she fuckin' freaked out and came at me."

"That's when she got the one scream out of her right?" Fleming asked.

"That's when she started screaming, yeah."

"What did she say?" asked Fleming. "Do you remember?"

"It wasn't words. It was just hysterical screaming."

"Yeah, so what did you say?"

"I freaked out. She started screaming and I panicked. I thought I could just knock her out, but I got carried away."

"And you shot twice?"

"Before I could get the jump on her to scare her, to get her on the ground with the gun, she seen it and started screaming and freaking out and the thing went off. I didn't want to shoot her again...I just wanted to knock her out and get out of that place. I was supposed to scare the shit out of her and threaten her and tell her that if she did testify, we'd be back. I thought I'd go in and just, you know, get in and just scare her, but she caught me before I could get the jump on her and she started screaming. I was just going to stick it in her and 'You say one word, bitch and you're outta here.' And things got out of control and that was that. That's exactly what happened. If she wouldn't have screamed everything would have been okay...."

"Okay," asked Fleming. "So then things got out of control?"

"Uh-huh."

Fleming turned towards Rinn, then summed up Schlender's statement. "That's obviously why you forgot to pick up the insurance," he suggested, "and that's exactly what I said probably did happen."

"Yeah, you are right," said Schlender. "You are pretty smart. I know there's fuck all I can do for her family...(but) by coming clean...and getting on with my life...it's the beginning."

Schlender alleged that West had returned to his house the night of the murder to give him an additional $1,200. "He said, 'What the fuck happened?' I told him. He says, 'Well, I'm going to get you more fucking money.' After he found out that I freaked out and killed the broad, he went back to the guy, and he was going to get me more money because he said 'No one does something like that for that amount of money.'"

Fleming asked about the shells that had been found at the scene. "Are they the same shells?" he asked.

"Yes sir, yes Brian."

"Yeah, so it was a case of a...."

"A case of she started screaming. Like, a lot of people you threaten them and they don't, they just fuckin' hit the ground and then fuckin' tremble, they don't say a fuckin' word."

"Yeah, overreaction," agreed Fleming. "Were you clean when you did it? Were you coked up?"

"I was on drugs, yeah. I'm always on drugs."

"Okay," continued Fleming. "When had you started?"

"Oh we...based about fuckin' ten, ten-thirty in the morning, free-basing."

"We've got to get you to court here pretty soon," Fleming said.

Schlender asked the question that concerned him the most. "So by what I'm telling you here, is it enough?" he inquired. "My wife needs protection."

"Well," mused Fleming, turning up the pressure, "I'm just trying to digest and run everything over in my mind. You've told us all this stuff but from the way I see it at this point anyway, Dave...."

"Uh-hmm...."

"...Is that there's really no...even if you were to tell that story in court, like on West...."

"Uh-hmm ..."

"...Blow the whistle on West, I don't, unless I've missed something Don, I can't see where at this point where we can tie West in, really, to any crime. It sounds like he's on the outside."

Schlender was getting more concerned. "Co-conspiracy?" he asked. "Are you saying this is no good?"

"Oh, no, no, no, no, no, no, no Dave, I'm not," said Fleming. "I'm not saying it's no good. I'm just trying to...to see, ah."

Rinn didn't want the interview coming to an end. He turned to Schlender and said, "What it would boil down to would be your word against his, type of thing, if we took action now."

"Yeah," Schlender agreed, "but now you guys can go and investigate him and you can come up with stuff."

Schlender offered to tell the two policemen about various other crimes. "I know where the guns are that have been used in homicides," he began. "The barrels haven't been—they do file the barrels after, though. I know the guy who pays the money out."

Schlender told the police officers about the murder of Charles Kirton on behalf of a big-time drug dealer named Art. "He does a lot of business on the island and he's done people. He's had people done in."

Fleming asked Schlender how he knew about the Kirton murder. "How do I know that?" asked Schlender. "My job was to keep an eye on him, trying to figure out his pattern."

Schlender wasn't finished with his free information. "And the Iranian," he said, "that Iranian that got wasted there about four or five

185

years ago, maybe a little more, the Iranian pimp. They emptied the whole fucking revolver on him."

"Don't get me wrong," said Fleming. "I'm not saying what you're telling us is of no value. It's of great value, but whether or not it's going to put somebody behind bars, I don't know at this point."

"You know," said Schlender, "I sure hope it's good enough to move my family, man, because fuck, they're going to toast me. You've got me worried here, again."

"No, no," countered Fleming. "What I'm saying to you is that if—would your wife and daughter be in a....?"

"Well, just by giving you guys the gun, that's it. I'm fucking toast right there. I'm fucked because I told him that the gun was out of the house. So he's going to know I fuckin' talked if he don't get that gun back...."

Fleming came up with a long answer, informing Schlender what the police would need in order to charge West in Sian's murder. "Where I see West has got his ass covered," Fleming began, "is that he never told you to go kill that girl, okay...what he told you to do was to go over and threaten the shit out of her, that's all he told you to do...the death of that girl was subsequent, okay, to the threat that you made to her. So far as the conspiracy aspect of it is, there really isn't one. You might get a conspiracy to commit threats.

"If West would have said to you, 'I'm telling you man, go over there and waste that girl,' or dust her, or put her six feet under, or whatever you guys might call it, ice her, then we've got a conspiracy to commit murder. But when all he's done is said, 'You go over there man and you threaten her'...it's of a very minor, minor nature that he's involved."

Schlender was worried. He was concerned West would know he had talked to the police, but Fleming continued to press him.

"What can we do?" Fleming asked. "How can we tie West into that gun?"

Schlender had been good at subterfuge in the past. He racked his brains. "Well, okay," he said after a moment. "This is what we do, this is what we do."

"Okay you tell me."

"We don't say a fuckin' word about it...."

"Yeah?"

"He'll come and visit me eventually...."

186

"Uh-hmm."

"I'll tell him where the gun is...."

"And leave it there and let him pick it up?"

"Yeah, yeah."

Schlender liked the sound of it but Fleming remained skeptical. "Still, what's he done?" the policeman asked.

"He hasn't done nothing then?" asked Schlender.

"No, you've told him where a gun is and he's gone to pick it up. It's no, no offense."

"Oh fuck, it's not an offense?"

"No, no."

"Holy fuck, I thought it was for sure."

Fleming again laid out as clearly as possible what the police would need if West were to be implicated. "If he had said to you, 'David, here, take my gun, you go over there and you kill that girl and you kill her now, because if you don't I'm going to kill you' or something to that effect, if he had instructed you to do it, you have a conspiracy. We've got him, okay, there'd be no problem."

Schlender pondered the bait but still wasn't biting. He wasn't about to admit that he had killed Sian Simmonds in cold blood. "Just because he told me to beat the shit out of her and scare her, that's not a conspiracy?" he asked.

"Well, it's a conspiracy maybe to commit threats, commit assault," said Fleming.

"Oh God," said Schlender. "Now I wish I hadn't have said a fuckin' word."

"Well no, no," Fleming began. He stopped pulling out the rug for a moment but the prisoner wasn't going to admit anything further.

"I had a feeling this would happen," cried Schlender. "Now my wife's in total fuckin' fear. You've got the conspiracy, you've got the guy that's paid the fuckin' money, you've got Brian bringing the gun and you've got me fuckin' carrying it out."

"Yeah."

"So he's tied in there, man."

"Yeah, but is he tied into the conspiracy as far as the murder is concerned?"

"Sure he is, because he's going back to the guy and saying, 'Hey, fuckin' yeah, he fuckin', he offed her and he freaked out' and he was going to get more money."

"Well, I don't think that's an offense, you know...."

"Oh God," cried Schlender. "See, there again, I don't know all the laws, now I'm fuckin' toast here. Oh shit. I can't live in here for the rest...waiting for trial, being in total fear of my family, you guys. That's my family out there, man, and I've opened up. I want to...deal with this."

"Yeah, I know," said Fleming.

"You know like, how can I have documentation, and fingerprints, and forensic evidence for you? All I've done is told you the fuckin' truth."

"Yeah."

"And the rest, you guys, you're the feelers and the finders, you're going to have to do the rest. This is very important to me Brian, very important. My wife is an emotionally weak woman and my children are defenseless compared to what's going on out there."

Fleming repeated his earlier concerns about arranging police protection. "We have to be able to show—Don and myself—after talking to you, we have to go and see Larry Gallagher...."

"Uh-hmm."

"...and be able to show him beyond any reasonable doubt that there is in fact a genuine danger for your family...."

"Uh-hmm."

"If we never act on anything—I burn these tapes for example, after we're out of here, if it's never used—is your family under a threat, are they going to be threatened?"

"I think there's a 75 percent possibility there. I can't go one hundred, but I can go a goddam good seventy-five and I hope you guys can convince your boss...I really do...."

Rinn: "But you see..."

"I should have just shut up, and dealt with it myself," Schlender continued. "I was just going to wait and go into the courtroom and fuckin' tell them the truth in there. Now I've hung myself out to dry and my family is in jeopardy, instantly, instead of months down the road. If I had just shut my fuckin' mouth and said not a word and went in there and dealt with it, they would have known nothing was said, no gun recovered.... Now I've hung myself by being honest with you."

But Rinn and Fleming convinced the prisoner they would see to it that his family would be safe for the time being. "You figure I'm covered until we go to court?" Schlender asked.

"I think you're covered, the way I see it, yeah. I think you are. I don't really see a...unless you, unless there's something more you haven't told me?"

"No," said Schlender. "I've told you everything."

"Well there is one other thing I'd like you tell me," said Fleming. "Where can we find Brian West?"

"I dunno," said Schlender. "The guy's a real nomad. You might have a helluva problem."

20 The Funeral

While Staff Sergeant Briske was in a celebratory mood, buying his investigators a round of drinks at the Legion, Dr. Charalambous returned home from work, looking tired, agitated and surprised.

"They got the guy that killed Sian Simmonds," he told Shelley.

"How did they get him so soon?" asked Shelley.

"I dunno," said her husband. "I don't understand it at all. He had all the right tools."

Shelley interrupted her housework. Her husband appeared animated by the sudden unexpected turn of events. "This whole thing has cost me about $20,000," he lamented.

Shelley said her husband told her that he had gone to Brian West's house and given his friend all the money he had on him, except for fifty dollars. The two of them, she'd been told, had allegedly washed the money in a sink to get rid of fingerprints.

Shelley recalled she had learned from her husband that Schlender was the same man who had shot his drug dealer in an underground parking lot in Surrey. And, according to her husband, Sian's alleged killer had also been involved in the murder of a Port Coquitlam man—who was shot while shaving—by an assailant reporting a bogus traffic accident with the victim's wife.

The smooth talking hitman, Shelley heard, had used virtually the same ruse to trick Sian Simmonds. "He scratched Sian's vehicle and went to her house kind of apologizing for damaging it," Shelley recalled her husband telling her. "Once he was inside, Sian was very mad."

The doctor had sounded vicariously thrilled as he had related Sian's struggle for her life. "He shot her but she was very tough and she kicked him in the groin and scratched him," Shelley's husband told her. "He was a mess because she fought back very hard. When the police arrested him, he had scratch marks on him. They tore up all the bushes around his house looking for a weapon."

Charalambous was still preoccupied with the case a day or two later. Shelley had just served him a cup of coffee when he commented on an obituary notice in the morning newspaper that said Sian Simmonds was to be cremated. "Just put this with the other newspapers by the TV," he said, handing the paper to his wife. "You never know when it might come in useful."

As always, Shelley did as she was told, but secretly she shivered with fear. Her husband had already told her far too much.

Scarcely a white rose could be found at a florist anywhere in the Fraser Valley on the day of Sian Simmonds' funeral. It was Sian's favorite flower and she had hoped it might adorn her wedding. In addition to family, more than a thousand people came to mourn her. There were friends from school, work and college, boys who'd admired her as a teenager and girls she'd known since kindergarten.

Those who could, jammed into the Valley View Funeral Home, on 72 Avenue in Surrey, while others spilled outside into the early darkness of a midwinter afternoon. To her family and friends, the fact that a funeral was taking place, when only a few days ago Sian had been so young, loving and full of life, made no sense at all. Sian had not died by accident; she had not been ill. In a chapel stacked with flowers and filled to overflowing, the predominant feeling among the mourners was: "We shouldn't be here."

Those attending the gut-wrenching, nondenominational service, as well as members of the public, had no idea why Sian had been murdered. At her home, Jacqueline Jongkind was saddened by the story, but was unaware as yet that the victim had been a patient of Dr. Charalambous. Sian's death was a mystery. Members of the Simmonds family had their suspicions, but the majority thought the murder had been the random act of some deranged killer.

Corporal Straughan mingled unobtrusively among the mourners, watching for anything suspicious. The investigation had barely begun but the fair-haired, unassuming policeman was already feeling a personal involvement in the unfolding tragedy, Straughan was not yet aware that the case would require his full attention at work and at home for months to come.

Among other mourners was Chuck Cadman, who had been campaigning for justice reform since his son Jesse had been stabbed to death by another teenager at a bus stop. Until that point, Chuck Cadman, a big, thoughtful man with long gray hair, had not known the Simmonds' family, but he joined them now, searching for answers to tragedy, bringing with him whatever support and compassion he could.

Susan Simmonds, sedated by her doctor, was valiantly supported by her husband, but her distress was painfully apparent when the television cameras showed footage of the funeral that evening. There was a deluge of public sympathy, but nothing could ever assuage the family's overwhelming grief.

The couple stood stoically at the front of the modern chapel, struggling to sing a hymn in tribute to their beloved daughter. In memory of her younger sister, Katie Simmonds performed one of Sian's favorite songs.

"I didn't want downer music," Katie said later, recalling the song. "Sian and I had practised it and we sang it together at our grandmother's eightieth birthday."

Unusual though it may have been, Katie had spent two days before the funeral lovingly redoing her sister's makeup, numb with shock. "For months afterwards, I felt like nothing was real," Katie recalled. "I still felt like I was in a movie."

Dave Sella told the congregation how he and Sian had planned to be engaged. "It looks like we'll be waiting a while to be with her again," he said.

Beside her coffin rested Sian's beautiful, framed graduation picture. The minister, the Reverend David Reuss, talked of random violence.

After the eulogies, the mourners stepped outside. The green, well kept cemetery grounds undulated downwards into the distance. It was not bitterly cold, but there was a chill in the air as the mourners gathered for the interment of the ashes, at the grave of Sian's aunt who had died nineteen years before.

Some murders take a long time to solve. Friends of the Simmonds family, as they left the funeral service, had but one consuming and fervent wish: whoever did this to such a warm, loving girl, bringing such devastation to an entirely innocent family, must surely be dealt with quickly and brought to justice.

They didn't know it yet but the answers, when they did come, would undermine the trust of the entire community—sending shock waves and demands for change all the way to the highest levels of the medical, legal and government establishments.

As they got ready to leave for home, members of the Simmonds family were approached by an elderly, gray-haired woman in baggy clothes. No one knew who she was. With a scarf around her head, she looked like a gypsy fortune-teller. Suddenly, the woman walked up to Katie and whispered earnestly in her ear. "They've got the wrong man," she hissed. "Don't you remember me warning you that you were in danger?"

Katie pondered the statement for a moment. A chill went through her. But before she could ask what it meant, the gypsy woman with the bandanna was gone.

At their home in Coquitlam, Dr. Charalambous and his wife watched coverage of the funeral on the late night television news. Chris Simmonds appeared on the screen to say that the justice system had let him down, followed by Katie singing a song for her sister. Then the camera focused on Sian's grief-stricken mother.

"She looks like shit," the doctor gloated to his wife. "She looks really depressed."

Shelley had already learned a long time ago that her husband didn't get emotional about other people's grief. Nonetheless, his self-satisfaction at the victims' grief made an impression she couldn't forget. It would be impossible to forgive him after that. "Yeah, she looks really sad," Shelley agreed.

"That's what they deserved," said her husband. "They were trying to kill me."

The funeral had taken place on Monday, February 1, five days after the murder. The following day, Constable Deanna Kohlsmith, following up on the college letter she'd found in Sian's bedroom, paid a visit to Daryl Beere of the College of Physicians and Surgeons. She wanted to know the ramifications of the complaint that Sian had made against her doctor.

The policewoman knew Beere had been a Mountie and she felt at ease as she sat down with the college investigator to take her notes. Deanna went straight to the point. "What were the possible outcomes if this hearing had gone ahead?" she asked.

Beere qualified himself before offering his opinion. "I'm not a lawyer," he began. "Speaking as an investigator for the college, I would say he might not have lost his practise, but he may have been suspended for some time."

"Couldn't he have set up practise somewhere else outside British Columbia?" asked Deanna.

"No," explained Beere. "It would be an automatic notification in all other provinces."

"What about the United States?"

"It'd be reciprocal in some states," said Beere, "but I can't comment on what would be the effect overseas."

Gradually, it was dawning on Gary Straughan that his chief suspect was a medical doctor. The policeman had investigated other unusual crimes in the past but was astounded that someone who was supposed to care about people's health had apparently been responsible for the killing of one of his patients. "This man is supposed to be a person of trust, a leader in the community," Straughan reflected.

Tapping into PIRS, the computerized Police Information Retrieval System, Straughan found that the Coquitlam RCMP had previous dealings with Dr. Charalambous. But the files went back eight years to 1985. The details were buried away in the archives and the officer who could tell him about it in the meantime was on a day off.

Nonetheless, someone managed to contact Constable Tom Robertson at home to advise him of the murder investigation. "When I was first contacted, I immediately recalled the investigation I had been involved in," Robertson said later. "I wasn't surprised that Charalambous would be involved in something like that, although it was amazing that he would go to that length."

Robertson advised Straughan, that, apart from the master file on PIRS, he'd retained all the working files he'd made during his earlier investigation. Normally, he would have shredded them, but he had kept all his notes because of the "bizarre nature" of the case. Straughan asked Robertson to drop by with his files as soon as possible.

The file coordinator also learned from Robertson and others that the doctor was heavily involved in the use of prostitutes. Early on in his

194

investigation, Straughan discovered that the doctor had made it onto the bad tricks' list, but there were other lists too—and they went on and on. The doctor, Straughan learned, had a prior conviction for common assault. His friends were individuals with known criminal backgrounds. And, only months before the murder of Sian Simmonds, another teenage patient had alleged that Charalambous and her father had exploited her for sexual purposes, coercing her to give the doctor oral sex on his examination room table.

Straughan wanted to find out as much as he could about this doctor, but he knew from experience that it was too early to risk speaking to the suspect's friends, employees or close associates. One or more of them could tip him off.

Gary Straughan phoned the president of the B.C. Karate Association. The police officer wanted to know more about the person he was up against but was careful to couch his questions in general terms.

From speaking with the karate official, Straughan learned that Charalambous and his brother both ran apparently successful and well established karate schools. The karate official was unaware of any complaints against either of them.

Straughan was about to have his life turned upside down. Every working day for the next seven months, the forty-five-year-old officer would work on little else.

Including policemen seconded from headquarters, as well as other police departments, an investigative core group of a dozen officers would put in many hours, plus a great deal of overtime, working exclusively on the case.

Each morning, Straughan and his team would meet for a file briefing. Sitting at the conference table with flip charts, the investigators would share the latest information and decide what had to be done next, selecting the most important and relevant items for immediate attention. It was an intense, intricate and long-term investigation and every angle would be pursued.

Straughan meanwhile had received a report back from the RCMP forensic laboratory in Vancouver. Tests conducted by Sergeant P. A. Ziegler, of the firearms' section, confirmed that the .22 shell casings found at the murder scene had indeed been fired by the Ruger pistol that police had found after being told of its whereabouts by David Schlender.

Police also had found a bloodstained shirt stuffed behind a night table in Schlender's bedroom, as well as a brown leather, blood-stained jacket.

Straughan had no need to request further scientific tests at this point. Not only had Schlender admitted the crime, his confession also had gibed with what the police knew from their own independent inquiries. Straughan asked Constable Kohlsmith to ensure that all the exhibits were identified, bagged and sealed. They could always be examined more closely if the need should arise.

Showing probable grounds for suspecting Charalambous of murder, one of Straughan's colleagues meanwhile obtained court approval for the installation of audio listening devices and telephone intercepts in Charalambous' home, car and office.

The court order would allow police to listen to all of the doctor's conversations except those with his patients. The installation of the bugs would involve three of the RCMP's most secretive divisions:

Special I (Special Installations) to put the bugs in place; Special O (Special Observations) to monitor the suspect's movements while the bugs were being installed; and Security Engineering Section to overcome security devices and to do whatever else might be required so that the Special I members could get in to perform their job.

Charalambous was clearly outgunned. The bugging of the doctor's office was set for February 9, less than two weeks after Sian's murder. Corporal Doug Comrie from the RCMP's serious crimes division in Vancouver kept lookout for the cloak and dagger mission after Special O had advised at 11:00 P.M. that Charalambous and his wife were both at their home, several miles away in Coquitlam. If he'd headed back for his office unexpectedly, Charalambous would have been arrested on some pretext, to prevent him from interrupting the work in progress.

But the police operatives were able to carry out their mission uninterrupted. Security engineering members had to break perimeter security at the medical building, so that the Special I people could get into the doctor's office to conceal an audio listening device connected to a monitoring room at RCMP headquarters. At 1:15 in the morning the mission was completed.

Members of Straughan's team also had permission to install bugs in the doctor's car, as well as his house in Coquitlam, but that would have to wait. For now, the main thrust of the police investigation, including the efforts of Special O, would be directed at discovering the whereabouts of Brian West.

Based on what Schlender had told the police so far, Straughan was troubled by some nagging concerns. The policeman weighed the pros and cons. Katie Simmonds had moved back with her parents. Straughan had asked the RCMP in Langley to keep an eye on the Simmonds' residence, but was that enough? Charalambous had already defied all logic. As far as Straughan was concerned, neither the police nor anyone else could assume that Katie and her family were out of danger.

And, in Coquitlam meanwhile, Shelley Charalambous thought her days were numbered too.

Part Two

Implacable Discord

Holding yourselves far aloof from wrong, from corruption, from the tempting of others to vice, you will exercise your art solely for the cure of your patients....

Hippocratic Oath continued

21 A Family Goes into Hiding

Katie Simmonds drove home, parked her black jeep in her parents' driveway, and went upstairs to change for dinner. It had been three weeks since her sister had been murdered and she had returned to her teller job at Richmond Savings Credit Union. In her own words, she had "just floated through work" and still felt numb to the nagging pain.

Katie was brushing her hair when there was a knock on the door. "I need to tell you something," said her father.

Chris Simmonds entered the room and sat at the end of his daughter's bed. "Dad, what is it?" Katie asked. Her father's countenance was filled with pain and sadness, but Katie could see too that his eyes simmered with anger.

"If I understand what the police are telling me, Dr. Charalambous was definitely involved in Sian's murder," her father said. "If I'm right, you'd be in danger too and we'd have to get out of here...."

"Till they can arrest him?"

"Yes," Katie's father continued, letting out a deep breath, struggling to contain his emotions. "They've suggested to me strongly that we should get you away. They've been making these hints, sort of helping me read between the lines."

Katie shuddered. She gave her dad a hug. He had always been a wonderful father. Now, in the family's hour of most desperate need, he continued to be a pillar of strength.

"Dad," she agreed, "whatever you think." The family had already been through so much. It would be good to get away anyway, thought Katie.

In the garage, there was the agonizing reminder of Sian's jeep, with a sheet over it. The dealership had repaired Schlender's scratchwork but no one could yet dispose of the vehicle. The jeep was registered in Sian's name and couldn't be transferred without her signature. Sian had been far too young to think about making a will.

"When do you want to go, Dad?" Katie asked.

"Tomorrow morning," said her father.

Chris, Sue, and Katie Simmonds got up early next morning—February 17—packing their truck and camper as they got ready to leave for their hidden destination. Katie's boyfriend Dean would stay behind. He and the police would keep an eye on the house.

Before leaving, Chris confided with his brother Brian, who lived less than two miles away. Brian Simmonds' house was on the same street. Lest his family might be endangered by a case of mistaken identity, the police would keep an eye on his house too.

A short, dark-haired man with a mustache, Brian had been a big comfort to his brother. After the murder, he had persuaded Chris to release a photo of Sian to the news media to show the world just how beautiful a person his niece had been. Brian and his wife had also gone to the house on 160 Street the following day to attend to the horrifying job of cleaning up the blood.

The ferry trip from the mainland to Saltspring Island was somber. Katie's parents owned a piece of land on the island but hadn't yet begun the summer home that they planned to build there. They had arranged instead to stay with their friends, Gerry and Barb Bourdin. Gerry was Chris' hunting buddy and he and his wife used to operate the pub at Fulford Harbour. Gerry had a loud, easy laugh. He was a short and stout man, who had always reminded Katie and Sian of Santa Claus. And he was about that friendly, too.

He and his wife had retired to a picturesque farmhouse beside a small pond, where lilies grew and frogs croaked, as sheep grazed peacefully on the surrounding acreage.

Barb Bourdin, a pleasant woman with short blonde curly hair, gave Katie a big hug, her eyes glistening as she attempted a brave smile. As far as Katie was concerned, Barb was "a good lady." She was also one of the best cooks anywhere on the island, even though these days she had to make sure her husband didn't get too much cholesterol.

"Don't you worry about anything," Gerry said reassuringly, as Katie unpacked her suitcase. "I'll be keeping a loaded shotgun under my bed to protect you."

Katie felt secure. There wouldn't be much to do here, however. She had brought several books with her, and tomorrow she and her Mom would take a trip into the town of Ganges to buy some oil paints and some canvas. That night, safe and warm as the wind howled outside, Katie picked up the phone to call her boyfriend Dean, as she did every night for the next two-and-a-half weeks. Although she would be unable to find much solace in its reflections and tranquil beauty, tomorrow Katie would paint the pond.

Back on the mainland, Constable Nels Justason continued to investigate the complaint of the young woman who'd alleged that her father had pimped her off to Charalambous in exchange for prescription drugs.

Justason was a studious looking man who looked more like a lawyer than a policeman. And when he called at the doctor's office on February 18, Charalambous obligingly produced the medical records that the constable requested. The doctor was cooperative, and agreed to follow Justason back to the police station to answer some further questions, driving his own car as he left his office.

It was exactly the scenario that Straughan and his team wanted. In one of the interview rooms, Charalambous blinked under the fluorescent lights as the bespectacled Justason informed him that he was being charged with sexual assault, breach of trust, and paying for sex with a person under eighteen.

Meanwhile, members of the RCMP's security engineering division had used a slimjim to unlock the doctor's car parked outside the police station. Working quickly, members of Special I installed the bug without a hitch—but then had great difficulty trying to get it to work.

In the interview room, Charalambous wondered what was taking so long. "Must be the paperwork," Justason suggested. The constable had to live up to his thoughtful appearance. Repeatedly, messages were being slipped to him urging him to find ways to keep the suspect just a bit longer. The battery-operated audio device, which Special I had installed in the doctor's car, was of a type that could be switched on and off much like a pager but it wasn't responding properly.

Five hours elapsed before the installers finally got the bug to operate. It was worth the effort though. Thereafter, the bug worked like a charm.

Afterwards, the newspapers reported news of the sex charges against the Surrey family doctor, adding he had been released on bail, on condition that he would make no attempt to contact the complainant while he awaited trial.

Shocked as he read of yet more complaints against Charalambous, Dr. Tom Handley, the college registrar, was far from satisfied with the bail conditions, and decided to take up the initiative on his own.

The registrar dictated a letter on April 4, 1993, demanding a written undertaking from Charalambous that he would not conduct any further examinations of female patients without the presence of a chaperon, pending the outcome of the charges.

If Charalambous did not agree to this condition, the letter added, the registrar would do everything possible to have yet another college inquiry committee appointed as soon as possible.

Under the college constitution, it was as much as the registrar could do for now, perhaps even more, but it elicited the response that the registrar wanted. Two days later, Handley was informed that Charalambous' written undertaking to comply with the request was on its way.

At her home in Coquitlam, Shelley thought her husband was especially late getting home from the racetrack. He didn't get in until 3:00 A.M., but woke her up to tell her of the charges. As his office manager, Shelley was extremely upset. She was embarrassed at the thought of having to face the patients. As she questioned him, the doctor went into a rampage.

Although the police still hadn't been able to find Brian West, the Simmonds family were now safely in hiding, and members of Special O could resume giving their full attention to watching the movements of Dr. Charalambous, the only exception being those times the doctor was at his office seeing patients.

Costs of the operation mounted astronomically as upwards of sixty Special O members took part in the operation, but no one ever suggested that any efforts should be spared. The Special O people were ordinary-looking men and women in all shapes and sizes who drove all types of nondescript cars.

The main objective in surveillance work was to watch a suspect without his or her knowledge. To accomplish this, Special O members operated in teams, keeping in touch with each other by radio. Instead of arousing suspicion by having to turn around, a member could thus allow a suspect to pass out of sight, radioing to another colleague to pick up the surveillance where the first member had left off.

It was all very much cloak and dagger stuff, the Special O members speaking in a jargon all their own. A member alighting from an unmarked vehicle to become a pedestrian was known as the "foot"; while the one actually observing the suspect was referred to as the "eye."

Throughout the investigation, Gary Straughan worked at the office from Monday to Friday, but often on weekends he would put in many overtime hours riding with Special O.

This gave the file coordinator the opportunity to see things firsthand and so it was that he was present on Saturday, February 27, when all of the costly surveillance effort paid off in a big way.

Until then, Special O had come up with little of interest except for the fact they had twice observed Charalambous picking up hookers after work in Vancouver's red-light district, but now the doctor was about to lead them to a major breakthrough.

It began after Charalambous had been followed to an apartment building in the 1300 block, West Tenth Avenue in Vancouver. There, at 3:40 in the afternoon, Constable Amy Bindon, a dark-haired member of Special O, observed the doctor getting into his black Trans-Am, with an unknown male companion.

The policewoman, accompanied by Constable Brian Marshall, watched from a distance as the two men went to Denny's Restaurant on West Broadway. She waited outside for forty-five minutes. Surveillance work was often boring. Finally, though, Charalambous emerged from the restaurant and drove away by himself. Bindon and Marshall followed the black Trans-Am through the streets of Vancouver, continuing in pursuit as the car turned eastbound onto the Trans-Canada Highway.

In another car, Straughan watched the taillights of the doctor's vehicle for more than sixty miles. "Where could he be going?" Straughan wondered. "He had never done this before." Charalambous continued to put distance between himself and Vancouver, still continuing eastbound, even after he had driven past Chilliwack. Finally, the black Trans-Am left the freeway between Chilliwack and Hope, taking the Laidlaw Road exit. It was a remote turnoff that didn't seem to lead anywhere except to a few farmhouses.

In their car, Bindon and Marshall waited as one of the Special O cars followed Charalambous off the freeway. Straughan waited with another member in another car, all of the police officers aware that the Trans-Am eventually would have to reemerge onto the freeway. There was no other way out.

Seeing the lights of the car following him, Charalambous made an evasive U-turn near the Jones Creek Bridge. But, just after 6:40 P.M., he returned to the freeway as expected, this time heading back towards Vancouver.

The Trans-Am and the cars tailing it crossed the Port Mann Bridge back into the heavily populated suburbs. Charalambous took the Brunette exit off the freeway into Coquitlam. He drove past his own house on Robinson Street before parking a few blocks away. Then, at about eight o'clock, Bindon and Marshall saw the suspect on foot, near a house at 715 Hailey Street.

Marshall got out of the car to do surveillance on foot as Constable Bindon watched the front door of the Hailey Street residence through high-powered binoculars. In the driveway, Bindon observed, was a red Honda Civic.

The policewoman watched for three hours, a large black dog running out of the house as visitors came and went. Then, at 11:11 that evening, Constable Bindon observed Charalambous. The doctor was leaving by the front door, carrying a cellular phone and walking in the direction of his parked car.

Constable Marshall also saw the black dog and heard it barking in the driveway as Charalambous left the house. From his vantage point on foot, however, the bearded policeman saw something of much greater interest. Just before eleven o'clock, Marshall had observed a heavyset man standing at the front door, stretching.

The man was wearing a white T-shirt. He had a beer belly and a full beard. From photographs with which he was very familiar, Marshall was able to identify the man, and to give Straughan and his colleagues the news for which they'd been hoping. "Guess who I just saw," he told his colleagues. "It was Brian West!"

At last, the police had found the elusive West. And all along, he'd been living less than a mile away from the doctor's house.

On March 4, Katie Simmonds returned home after two weeks on Saltspring Island. The College of Physicians and Surgeons was still scheduled to hear her eighteen-month-old complaint against Dr. Charalambous the following day. Neither Katie nor anyone at the college had phoned to cancel or postpone the hearing. Her parents had tried to dissuade her but Katie wanted to keep the college and the doctor guessing as to whether or not she would appear.

Charalambous, however, told his wife he had no doubt that the hearing would be called off. He wanted Shelley to go to the college with him, but lamented that it was a waste of time. It was ridiculous even to have to hire a babysitter, he said, because the hearing would never go ahead anyway.

"My lawyer told me to go buy a new suit for the hearing," Charalambous told his wife. "We're doing all this for no reason. They won't show up. Her father would never risk his second daughter for this."

As they went into the college building, Charalambous and his wife were watched by members of Special O. Inside, grim-faced college officials looked tensely at their watches as they awaited the arrival of Katie Simmonds. Finally, someone phoned and established that Katie wasn't coming and the hearing was cancelled.

Charalambous, looking as though a burden had been lifted, took his young wife by the arm, escorting her back to his vehicle for the twenty-minute drive home. On the way, he picked up his cellular phone to share the good news with his friend Gail Pikker. Recently, the dark-haired woman had become closer to Shelley than to the doctor. Nonetheless, Charalambous wanted her to know that he had been right all along.

"See," he gloated. "I told you she would never show up."

22 Surveillance

Although police now had Charalambous and his associates, including Shelley, under surveillance, they remained concerned for the safety of the Simmonds family, especially Katie whom they shadowed in squad cars each day, as she commuted back and forth to work.

"Make sure you always take the same route so we can keep an eye on you," Sian's sister was told.

Each day after work, Katie was escorted by a male employee to her vehicle in the parking lot. She wore a personal, electronic alarm and carried a cellular phone in her jeep.

Sometimes, she felt almost as protected as Fort Knox—but was annoyed by the restrictions on her freedom. Unless someone could go with her, she wasn't even allowed to visit the corner store.

And Katie's parents were warned to be cautious too. Chris and Sue Simmonds were also supplied with personal beepers and an aerial was installed in their house to relay messages if anyone in the family should call for help.

"This system was developed in Israel," explained the Special I people. "If you press the button, the alarm will go off at the Langley RCMP detachment."

The alarm would be loud enough to wake up even the sleepiest dispatcher in the middle of the night, the family were assured. In the event of a call, police immediately would phone the Simmonds' residence and, if all were not well, someone would arrive within minutes.

It was small comfort for a family already shattered by murder, and other concerns lurked just around the corner. Ignoring warnings not to mix tranquillizers with alcohol, Sian's mother almost became a casualty herself and had to be hospitalized. As Sue Simmonds put it, she had just wanted to be with Sian.

Katie found herself having to be careful not to snap at people. Both she and her mother were terrified every time there was a knock on the door. And Sian's father who had always been an easygoing and fun-loving member of his darts league became tense and withdrawn.

Chris Simmonds lay awake at night thinking of different ways of taking the law into his own hands, finally deciding he would wait outside the doctor's office in his truck and run his tormentor over as soon as he arrived for work.

Within a few days, Sian's father drove to the doctor's office and parked outside. But as Chris Simmonds waited, he learned something about himself: He was not a violent man. Sian's father was tough, but he was not a killer. Rather than exact his own justice, he would let the police handle things after all. Feeling thwarted, he turned around and drove away.

Even the most case hardened of police officers were reduced to tears. "I don't think one of us walked away without crying," recalled Corporal Straughan. "I have sat in their kitchen with Chris and Susan Simmonds crying with them."

Dave Sella had been unable to sleep much since the murder. Eventually, he dreamed that another girl had been killed and wondered how he could comfort her boyfriend. Then he'd wake up in a cold sweat, realizing he'd been trying to cope with Sian's death. Sella felt guilty, angry and afraid. Would Sian still be alive, he wondered, if he'd stayed with her the previous night? Like Brian McCann, he bought a knife and wore it under his jeans.

"I couldn't go to a mall by myself," he recalled. "I didn't know why Sian had been killed. I didn't know if it was something to do with me. Could we have offended someone in the traffic? I didn't know."

Stunned employees hugged Sella at the Safeway store, asking him all kinds of questions that he couldn't answer. He got a prescription for sleeping pills and visited a grief counselor. "Why did it have to be my Sian?" he asked.

Later, Sian's friend Kim gave Sella the green rugby jersey that Sian had bought for his birthday. He wore it a couple of times, but it evoked too much pain. Sadly, he put it in a box. At times, it seemed there was no end to the sadness. Bear, the aging Simmonds' family dog, had to be put down and Winston, the new pup, had failed to come home at 5:00 one morning after wanting to be let out. The family found him dead on the road outside, skid marks nearby.

Gary Straughan, however, had received some more encouraging news. Special O members—at 8:20 on the evening of March 8—had again spotted a short male wearing glasses, white pants, and a dark jacket circuitously approaching the home of Brian West at 715 Hailey Street.

Constable Janet Copp, an unlikely looking policewoman with long, dark hair, took down a description of the man in her small, red notebook, as she sat in her unmarked car in a church parking lot, a block away from West's house. She didn't recognize the man, but her partner told her who it was—Dr. Charalambous—and he was approaching West's house for the second time since the police had followed him there ten days ago.

The policewoman resisted the urge to crouch down as Charalambous turned around to look over both shoulders. Although she lost sight of him as he scurried into a darkened lane behind West's house, one of her colleagues picked him up in the high beam of an unmarked police car.

As Constable Rita Husted drove by, Charalambous was forced to draw closer to a chain link fence at the side of the lane. The second policewoman thought she saw him squinting, either from being caught in the headlights or from trying to see into her vehicle.

Constable Marc Mercier, a balding member of the team with a beard and collar length hair, heard a dog barking as Charalambous entered West's residence. The policeman could see light coming from the living room but the curtains were drawn. Then, at 9:50 P.M., the dog peered out between the drapes, and Mercier watched as a large person silhouetted against the light moved the animal away from the window, tightly shutting the drapes behind him.

Half an hour later, Mercier heard two faint gunshots. Were they fired from a gun with a silencer? Mercier couldn't tell. The shots were very muffled, apparently originating from the house under surveillance, but possibly coming from the neighboring house to the north.

At 10:53 P.M., Mercier watched Charalambous leave the house via the carport door, strolling up the driveway toward the street with his hand in his jacket pocket, again looking over both shoulders as he walked away.

Except between the doctor and his friend, whatever was discussed would remain unknown. Charalambous said later he had previously urged West to seek legal advice and that he had gone back to his friend's house to inquire if West had yet retained a lawyer.

The police had already installed audio bugs in Charalambous's car and office, but needed him to be at work, and for his wife to go out, before they could install eavesdropping devices in his residence on Robinson Street.

Special I members slipped into the house at 1:00 P.M. on March 9 after Shelley was seen loading her three children into her Ford van to go grocery shopping.

Shelley finished her shopping and took her children to a McDonald's Restaurant next door. Special O were ready to alert their colleagues when Shelley emerged at 1:53 P.M., but sighed with relief, as she drove to pick up her mother-in-law for an afternoon with the grandchildren in Confederation Park.

By the time Shelley got home, the bug had been installed in the living room wall and hardwired into the telephone line. She had the feeling something had occurred in her absence, but couldn't quite decide exactly what it was. Everything she and her husband might say in that room could now be monitored back at the police station. During the police investigation, Charalambous often gestured to her with a finger over his lips, but he'd never been electronically inclined, and apparently did not think to check out where any bugs might be hidden.

Three days later, Special I were ready to place a bug in yet another location, but the premises involved were guarded by a large Rottweiler dog. "This son of a bitch could be a problem," Straughan said to his colleagues. "What do you suppose we should do?"

"How about if we distract the dog with some meat?" suggested Constable Kohlsmith, returning shortly afterwards with a grocery bag in which the file coordinator expected to find a cheap cut of stewing beef. But as Straughan looked at the label, he recoiled in mock horror. Deanna had bought a sirloin steak. The policewoman blushed as everyone laughed. The officers cut up the meat and took it with them as they headed to the second location.

Carrying bear spray and wearing a padded arm guard, a dogmaster gingerly offered up Deanna's steak as security engineering members finished picking the lock. If things got out of control, the Rottweiler would have to be shot—but instead of any fierce attack, the dog winced and nervously backed away. It was a simple matter now, but everyone wanted to get the job done as quickly as possible and to beat a hasty retreat.

The bug in the doctor's house turned out to be a major disappointment. Asthma didn't prevent the Charalambous children from making a lot of noise, and they drowned out many of the conversations that the police were trying to overhear between their parents. Furthermore, the bug had been installed too close to the TV set, which was on almost constantly, further garbling the family conversations.

Eventually, the bug would be moved to the kitchen but Straughan and his investigators decided they wouldn't just sit back and wait for something to happen in the meantime. Almost two months had passed since the murder of Sian Simmonds—and it was time, Straughan decided, to confront Charalambous directly.

The job of going to the doctor's office and interviewing Charalambous fell to Corporal Doug Comrie and Sergeant Mel Trekofski, who were on loan to Straughan and his team from the RCMP's serious crime section, E division in Vancouver. At six feet, two inches tall, with his hair combed straight back, neatly clipped moustache and military bearing, Corporal Comrie was the archetype of the policeman. Trekofski, bald with a dark mustache, was perhaps a more lighthearted type, but both he and Comrie were serious as they pondered the task ahead.

At 9:05 on the morning of March 18, the two officers called at Charalambous's office. There were no patients yet in the waiting room, as Comrie and Trekofski introduced themselves to the doctor's receptionist.

After speaking to Charalambous on his intercom, the receptionist showed the two officers into the doctor's private office, all three men standing up as Comrie opened the conversation.

"We're investigating the death of Sian Simmonds," Comrie began. "She was a patient of yours. We'd like to ask you a few questions."

"So what's this got to do with me?" Charalambous asked.

Comrie and Trekofski didn't bother to warn Charalambous of his Charter rights. They hadn't come to his office with the intention of obtaining any admissible statements. Their aim was to turn up the pressure.

"Well we've charged this fellow named Schlender," Comrie said, "but we can't figure out what the hell he had to do with her."

Comrie paused, but the doctor showed no telltale reaction. "On the other hand," the policeman continued, "we know Sian did have a complaint against you."

"Look," said Charalambous, seeming unconcerned, "I'd be glad to help but the last time I saw Sian was in 1991. I've had no contact with her since then." The doctor told the policemen they could get a copy of Sian's complaint against him from the college. "It's not a serious matter," he added, as he showed Comrie and Trekofski the door. "Sorry I couldn't help you."

As they left the office, the policemen were glad to get outside into the fresh air. They headed back to the Surrey RCMP detachment to let Straughan know the results of their meeting.

The interview seemed to have accomplished its objective. The following weekend, Charalambous decided to take another daring risk.

When Shelley Charalambous got up on the morning of Sunday, March 21, she told her husband of her plans for the day. "I've arranged with one of my girlfriends to take the kids to the children's fair in Coquitlam," she said.

"No!" said Joe emphatically, getting out of bed and quashing Shelley's plans. "We're going for a drive to Vancouver. We're going to drive down to Stanley Park."

As usual, Shelley complied with her husband's wishes, Special O members watching as she and her kids backed out of the driveway in the family van heading towards Vancouver. Not immediately evident to the surveillance team members was the fact that Charalambous was also in the vehicle, slumped down in the passenger seat below the level of the window.

Special O members watched as Shelley drove into the downtown peninsula, heading towards Stanley Park via Robson Street. "Drive down this back alley and let me out," Charalambous whispered. "Pretend that we've had a fight and I need time to cool off."

"Where should I meet you?" asked Shelley.

Both Charalambous and his wife had cellular phones. Her husband had a portable and she had one in the van. "I'll phone you in about an hour and tell you where to pick me up," he said. Unseen by Special O, Charalambous alighted from the van, disappearing in the concrete maze of West End apartment buildings.

Shelley did what she could to kill the time. She was at a Mac's convenience store at Broadway and Hemlock to purchase refreshments for the children when the phone rang in her van. "Hello," said Shelley. "Hi," said her husband. "Are you near Stepho's?" "Yes," Shelley replied on her cellular phone. "I am not mad at you any more," said Joe, sounding a bit strained. "You want to come pick me up behind Stepho's?" "Okay," said Shelley, going along with the ruse. "Okay," said the doctor, hanging up. "Bye." Shelley headed for the restaurant on Davie Street. Her husband loved his Greek food. Sometimes, he'd spend his time fantasizing about the bill of fare he'd offer if he owned a restaurant.

As his wife unloaded the children from the van, Charalambous presented her a dozen roses. Then, according to Shelley, her husband told her that he had met Brian West in Stanley Park and had given him some more money. "Brian looks very different," she recalled her husband telling her. "I almost didn't recognize him. He's shaved off his beard and dyed his hair red."

Her husband's friend, Shelley heard, had assumed a different identity. According to the doctor, he had an Indian Affairs card and a driver's license in someone else's name. "It's sad," she recalled her husband telling her, "that two people that are like brothers can't even acknowledge knowing each other." Shelley recalled her husband also telling her that his friend was going to leave town. "He's going to go across Canada. His end destination is Amsterdam. He's got a friend there that he knows he can stay with."

All the talk about foreign travel seemed suddenly to remind Dr. Charalambous that his own documents had expired, and he called the next day at the Foreign Affairs Department in Surrey to renew his passport. If anyone questioned him about it, he would say that he had an uncle in Cyprus who'd died on February 24, and that he was merely planning to go home for a holiday.

Shelley heard a different story, however. "I'm thinking of leaving Canada and going back to Cyprus." he told her. "There's too much heat around me." Her husband, she recalled, speculated whether or not there was an extradition treaty between Canada and Cyprus, but another possibility, he suggested, was that he might go to one of the Greek islands.

Charalambous gave his wife signing authority on his business account. "If I have to leave suddenly," he told her, "you can continue running the practise with a locum."

He would send for her and the children at a later date, he explained, after she had the practise running with a replacement doctor. Although Shelley and the children didn't have passports of their own, Charalambous thought it possible the family might nonetheless have to emigrate with him. "Otherwise," he told Shelley, "the police might use you as a pawn to bring me back into the country."

Charalambous didn't know it, but Gary Straughan and his team had already decided they'd arrest him if he attempted to cross the U.S. border or to leave the country by any other means. There was no extradition treaty between Canada and Cyprus. The police, however, still lacked key evidence against him, and decided to try unnerving him by putting some pressure on his wife.

Two days after the Stanley Park incident, Comrie and Trekofski were on their way to Robinson Street. They drove up to the dark and foreboding Charalambous bungalow in an unmarked car. Comrie knocked on the front door. It was 9:45 on the morning of March 23, and Comrie and Trekofski wanted to have a word with Shelley while her husband was at work.

Although the police officers could hear people inside the house, there was no answer. A young child peered at them through the window as they stood on the front step, but still no one opened the door.

Comrie slipped one of his business cards through the mail slot. He and Trekofski got back into their car and drove to the nearby Burquitlam Shopping Center in search of a pay phone.

Shelley answered as Comrie identified himself. "I just left my card there," said the corporal. "We'd like to talk to you." Declining to elaborate on the reason for his call, Comrie arranged to return to the house at eleven o'clock to discuss the matter in person.

This time the tall, lean, young woman came to the door, sweeping aside her long hair with her hand as Comrie opened the conversation. The two policemen told Shelley they were concerned that she and her husband were making "concerted efforts" to locate the patient who'd accused Charalambous of exploiting her by giving drugs to her father.

Shelley knew her husband had been charged in the affair the previous month and listened politely as Comrie warned her not to interfere with a potential witness. She refused, however, to answer any of the policeman's questions. "I don't have any information," she said.

"Look," said Comrie, more urgently, "we don't think you're involved but we also want to talk to you about the murder of Sian
Simmonds."

Shelley said she had no information that she could give him on that
matter either. But she looked at the policeman with big, brown pleading
eyes. Surely he could see her predicament? Apparently not. "Give us a
call any time if you do want to speak to us about it," said Comrie.

23   Emergency

When the doctor returned home from work, Shelley told him the police had visited the house. She nervously reconstructed the questions Comrie had asked, and showed her husband the card that the tall policeman had left behind. After the beating she'd received for talking to the police seven years ago, she knew better than to do it again.

Apparently, Shelley recalled, her husband realized that Comrie was one of the police officers who'd called at his office five days ago. He also noticed that the address on Comrie's card was for the RCMP headquarters on Heather Street in Vancouver. "I'm going to drive round there and see if I can recognize some of the cars that have been following us," Charalambous told his wife.

The doctor, she knew, considered himself much smarter than the police. Also, she felt, there was no way he'd ever surrender to them without a fight. He'd already told her how he could kill someone without a trace with the insulin-filled syringe that he kept in the console of his Trans-Am. Also, he confided, he'd been having fantasies about ambushing police officers on their coffee breaks.

In one scenario, Shelley recalled, he dreamed of gunning down several policemen as they gathered for coffee at the Tim Horton's donut shop, near his office, while another fun-filled spree had him riding his mountain bike down a hill at Confederation Park and shooting police officers in the picnic area, before continuing to pedal downhill to make his escape in a waiting car.

But thoughts of outgunning the Royal Canadian Mounted Police amounted to little more than daydreams. If anyone were being bombarded, it was Charalambous. Police eyes and ears were everywhere. Such a plethora of electronic bugs and wiretaps were now arrayed against him that sometimes, when he took a shower or bath, he must have wondered whether he should carefully check his body, in case there were bugs there too.

Nonetheless, Gary Straughan and his team were concerned that things were beginning to drag. Charalambous was being extremely careful. Clearly, he knew great efforts were being made to find evidence against him.

Occasionally, while driving with one of his Greek friends, the doctor would speak in his native tongue. Translated for Straughan and his team by Constable Papagiannis, a Greek speaking Mountie in Campbell River, the conversations turned out to be amusing but not especially incriminating.

"Sometimes they try to fucking stick you if they don't like you," the doctor told his friend. "The police, they are fucking idiots."

As far as Straughan was concerned, the feeling was mutual. Like a lot of criminals, thought Straughan, the doctor often showed a naivete bordering on the absurd.

Despite all the bugs, however, the doctor still hadn't slipped up. Straughan and the other investigators continued to meet each day in the police boardroom but there hadn't been any promising new developments for several weeks.

Straughan and his colleagues wondered if it might be possible to goad the doctor into another meeting with whoever had hired Schlender—only this time with police recording the conversation from a distance with parabolic microphones. As a security team member at the 1976 Olympics, Straughan had experimented with such equipment, trying to monitor conversations between suspicious targets in the Montreal Stadium. He'd been disappointed with the results, but imagined there'd been technological improvements since that time.

Investigators were kicking the idea around at a file briefing when Sergeant Don Rinn came up with a definite plan. "How about if we have a couple of undercover operators go to the doctor's office," proposed Rinn, "under the pretext of collecting money for Schlender to keep his mouth shut?"

Everyone liked the idea. It was well known that Schlender had been

217

arrested but there was no reason yet for those on the outside to suspect that he had already talked. If nothing happened soon, Straughan and his team would consider acting on Rinn's suggestion.

"Things were starting to grind and drag on us," recalled Straughan. "We were at a very frustrating stage in the investigation. We had nothing to lose at that point."

The task force decided the type of undercover operator that would best suit their scenario would be a male between thirty and thirty-five, a person who looked like a biker with a good knowledge of street level criminals and penal institutions.

Eventually, RCMP headquarters in Vancouver supplied not one, but two undercover policemen—and they were everything that Straughan and his colleagues could have wished for. "For the role they were playing, they walked the walk and talked the talk," smiled Straughan.

The file coordinator informed the undercover men of the plan. "We want you to attend at Charalambous' office near closing time," Straughan explained, "and tell the doctor that Schlender wants $10,000 to keep his mouth shut."

The undercover operators went into action at 5:10 on the cloudy afternoon of Tuesday, April 27. After climbing the stairs to the doctor's second floor office, they presented themselves to Charalambous' receptionist.

"Do you have an appointment?" asked the young woman.

"No we're friends of his," said one of the undercovermen.

"He's in with patients," said the receptionist. She cast a dubious look at the rough looking men, before bidding them to be seated in the waiting room. After a few minutes, Charalambous emerged to speak with his receptionist, who directed his attention to the two visitors.

Charalambous eyed them curiously, watching with revulsion as the undercovermen approached him. "Have you got a minute?" one of them asked. "I've got to talk to you.

"Yes," said Charalambous, hesitantly.

The men followed the doctor towards his private office down the hall. Once inside, they closed the door, both of them facing Charalambous as the shorter of the two opened up. "Just so you know, Joe, I'm not fucking around here...."

"What is it?" Charalambous interrupted.

The shorter man with the leather jacket and biker boots continued: "David told me to come here."

"What?" the doctor squinted.

"Never mind, just sit down!" said the undercoverman.

"No!" exclaimed Joe.

Hurrying out of the room, Charalambous told his receptionist to call 911, then decided to call the emergency number himself.

"You're wasting your time," growled the undercoverman. "We'll be gone before the cops get here. You should listen to what I'm saying."

As Charalambous began talking with the 911 operator, the two undercovermen prepared to leave the office. The call seemed to ward them off, but Charalambous quickly discovered that an emergency operator could be almost as tough to deal with.

According to Straughan, the operator had not been informed of the undercover operation but seemed to know from experience that the caller was being less than candid.

The call came in at 5:20 P.M., the emergency equipment displaying not only the incoming phone number but also the address of the building in which the phone itself was located, and the conversation went as follows:

Dr. C: Okay, this is ahh, this is Dr. Charalambous.

Operator: Yes.

Dr. C: I need the police, please.

Operator: What's the problem.

Dr. C: Ahh, I've got two, two men in my office....

Operator: Okay.

Dr. C: Okay, its number 206....

Operator: Yes, I have the address here. What's the problem with the men?

Dr. C: Well the men are—seem to be threatening me here.

Operator: About what? What are they threatening you over?

Dr. C: Yeah, well I'm not sure but I—you know, I don't like the look of them and I don't know them and I don't want them in my office.

Operator: Is your office closed for business now or—?

Dr. C: Well it's almost closed for business and I don't want them here.

Operator: Okay, well how—what did, what do they want, sir?

Dr. C: (Okay, go ahead and leave. I don't want to talk. I don't want to talk to you, I don't know you. No I don't want to talk to you, okay.)

219

Operator: You don't know these people at all?

Dr. C.: I don't know these people and they're here and they seem to be threatening me.

Operator: Well, what do you mean, they seem to be? What threats are they saying?

Dr. C: Okay....

Operator: Sir?

Dr. C: Well listen, I think you should get the police over here.

Operator: No, no, you tell me what's going on there? Okay, why—what are—?

Dr. C: Well, I'm not sure what's going on.

Operator: You—

Dr. C: They keep insisting they want to talk to me and I don't know them.

Operator: Okay, what—did you ask them what they want to talk to you about?

Dr. C: Well, they're not telling me. They want me to go in a room with them and I'm not going to do that.

Operator: Okay, what kind of threats are they making?

Dr. C: Well they're—it's just that they're big guys and I'm a little bit afraid of them. Will you send the police over?

Operator: I'll send someone over.

Dr. C: Okay....

Operator: Yeah.

Dr. C: It's number 206....

Operator: Yes, I have the address, sir.

Dr. C: 206, 9808 King George Highway.

Operator: I have the address.

Dr. C: What's your name?

Operator: It's Operator Number Nine.

Dr. C: Operator Number Nine?

Operator: Yeah.

Dr. C: Well, I think you should get the police here, okay?

Operator: Sir....

Dr. C: Yes.

Operator: What you're going to have to do is, when the officer gets there, you're going to have to explain this story a little better than what you're telling me.

Dr. C: Okay, I'll explain the story.

Operator: All right.
Dr. C: Okay.
Operator: Bye.
Dr. C: All right, yeah.

Like the 911 operator, Constable Steve Fullerton knew nothing of the ruse either. He had simply been driving his police car in the area when he had received word by radio to attend an emergency call at the doctor's office.

Fullerton was a slightly built, clean cut young man with fair hair, who spoke slowly in a slurred, laid-back sort of way. He had a disarming smile, which tended to make people forget they were dealing with an astute investigator, but at the moment the joke was on him.

The undercovermen tried not to smile as Fullerton arrived and parked his police car almost beside their vehicle, outside the medical building. Without noticing them, Fullerton hurried up to the doctor's second floor office, where he asked Charalambous to explain what had happened.

"Well this one guy came down the hall with his arms close to his body saying, 'Come here, come here,'" reported an agitated Charalambous. "He said someone else is going to come and talk to me."

It was all very mysterious but the doctor was able to supply quite good descriptions, which Fullerton wrote down in his notebook:

Caucasian male, five-foot-eight to five-foot-nine, 200 pounds, black leather jacket with wings on the back, sunglasses, beard, wearing yellow, snakeskin boots. The second male was bigger: Six-foot-three, 230 pounds, wearing an Australian style trench coat and black Daytons, long, wavy light brown hair.

Fullerton still didn't know he was being used. He'd heard that Charalambous was a suspect in the Sian Simmonds' murder investigation but didn't know if the incident might have something to do with that.

The constable began making inquiries at other offices in the building. The receptionist at the doctor's office below reported that two men of similar description had called twice in the past two weeks, insisting on getting a form signed, and she'd had to advise them in no uncertain terms that her employer wasn't taking any new patients. They had left in a huff, very reluctantly after she had referred them to a nearby walk-in medical clinic on King George Highway.

Thinking he'd stumbled across some good information, Fullerton returned upstairs, but Charalambous seemed irritated when the constable came back with his findings. The doctor raised his voice, as he repeated what had happened, causing an apologetic Fullerton to offer to make further inquiries.

As they watched Fullerton leave, the undercovermen decided to make a phone call to the doctor's office. At 6:15 P.M., the shorter of the two picked up the receiver of a pay phone, having first established it was one of the few coin operated telephones that could still take incoming calls.

Charalambous, however, realized who was calling and hung up immediately, but the undercoverman wasn't about to be dissuaded. Calling again, he got the doctor's answering machine and left Charalambous a message.

"This is the biggest emergency you'll ever have in your life," he said. "David wasn't paid enough, $1,000 won't cut it. There's Colleen and the kids, and David wants them looked after. Ten thousand will save you a lot of hassle. David will bide his time for now, but he won't be happy when I tell him what happened here. If you want to call me, I'm at a pay phone and you can call me back."

But the undercovermen waited in vain. Shortly after the phone call, Charalambous emerged from the office building, spotting them and writing down the license number of their car before heading north on King George Highway.

Fullerton meanwhile didn't know what to make of the strange incident, but Sergeant Rinn put him out of his misery as soon as the constable got back to the police station. The young policeman was flabbergasted, but smiled as the sergeant told him to act as if the doctor's call were a genuine complaint and to follow up with his "investigation" the next day.

Fullerton again attended at the doctor's office at 4:50 the next afternoon, only to find it was Charalambous' regular day off. Obtaining the doctor's home number from the receptionist, Fullerton called Charalambous but got no answer. On the second call at 10:20 P.M., the doctor picked up his phone.

"Is Dr. Charalambous there?" asked Fullerton.

"Yeah, speaking," said Charalambous.

"It's Constable Fullerton of the Surrey RCMP."

The doctor seemed disinterested. "Did I talk to you before?" he asked.

"Yes," said Fullerton. "Yesterday."

"Oh yeah," recalled Charalambous. He paused for a moment. "Forget about those guys," he said. "We have to pray for those guys. Good-bye."

Fullerton's role in the investigation had come to an end but the undercovermen were far from finished.

At 7:00 the next morning, the shorter one left a message on the doctor's answering machine yet again. "If you're smart," he said, "you'll listen and know this is for real.

"David wants $10,000 for Colleen and the kids. He'll do his time but to get only $1,000 for what he did was a fuckin' joke. You'll get one more chance. If you fuck up, David will be forced to get money someplace else. He told me to tell you he's got other options, the cops, the newspapers or somebody that wants to write a book."

Events were now moving quickly. Just a week after he'd made the 911 call, Charalambous heard on May 4 that David Walter Schlender had pleaded "Guilty" to a reduced charge of second degree murder. The doctor angrily discussed the matter with Shelley, saying Schlender had clearly bungled the murder and had obviously struck a bargain with the police. "It's just a waiting game now," said Charalambous, handing his wife the newspaper. "We have to wait until Schlender is sentenced and put in the general population. We can't get to him in protective custody."

In the long term, her husband continued, Schlender's whole family would be dealt with. "Rats are rats," the doctor told his wife, "and they have to be taken care of too."

Charalambous had been told by one of his lawyers that the threatening phone calls on his answering machine more than likely were the work of undercover police officers. After he'd spotted the biker types outside his office, the doctor had given their license plate number to his lawyer, who in turn had passed it on to a private investigator. The private eye was a former policeman. Finding that the vehicle was one of several registered in the same mysterious way, the investigator had checked further and concluded that it probably was a police vehicle. Charalambous was advised of this in a telephone call to his house which was monitored by the police.

The RCMP subsequently made changes to the way they registered their undercover vehicles, but decided in the meantime there was nothing to lose by keeping up the pressure. On May 13, the undercoverman made another call, this one to the doctor's receptionist. "Everybody's time is running out," he said. "Tell him he can page me."

Then, at lunchtime the following day, the undercoverman left still another communication on the doctor's answering machine. The calls had become frequent and taunting: "You ain't taking this thing for real!" said the undercoverman. "David is only looking after Colleen and the kids, nothing more. You know time is on his side. When he finds out how much he's stuck with, he won't care who helps him. You have to look after your own. You can control them. Page me!"

But the doctor ignored the call as usual.

Shortly afterwards, Gary Straughan and his colleagues gathered in the parking lot at the prestigious Vancouver Golf Club in Coquitlam and rolled a Harley Davidson down a ramp from the back of an unmarked van.

Golfers clicking across the blacktop watched in astonishment as a rough looking biker, who was actually another undercover RCMP officer, straddled the machine, before thundering out of the golf club grounds.

Tailpipes rattling, the biker circled the Charalambous residence on Robinson Street, making a couple of noisy passes before pulling into the driveway. The biker then dismounted and stuck a note under one of the windshield wipers of the Charalambous family van.

The note, written on the inside of an empty cigarette package, said, "David has taken the first step to deal with the problem of his family. He's being sentenced later and knows that is when his time is starting. His family is out everything and he is going to see they are looked after. As you were told, you're his first and hopefully his last. Before you end up reading your name in the paper, you had better page me and hear your ways out."

A Special O surveillance team watched Charalambous return home from work that night. They saw him park his Trans-Am, take the empty cigarette package liner from the windshield of the van and walk into the house.

Unknown to the police, the pressure tactics were working. The Charalambous household was about to blow apart.

24   An Affair with a Cop

S helley Charalambous was her husband's greatest risk. She was desperate to get out of her marriage, but was afraid if she left that her husband would come after her to ensure that she didn't talk. The doctor hadn't bothered to conceal things from her. *Why bother?* presumably he thought. He was sure Shelley would be too afraid to say anything.

Little did he know what his wife was thinking. What Shelley really wanted to know was whether she'd be blamed if she stuck a knife in him.

But he felt he could trust her. The doctor had told his friends—and even Shelley's own doctor—he'd got his wife at such a young age that he'd been able to train her to be exactly what he wanted. "You're like a little puppy that I adopted from the SPCA," he told Shelley. "I gave you a life. If I hadn't adopted you, then you would have got put down."

Shelley had become accustomed to abuse for nearly eight years. Now, though, things would never be normal again. Her husband complained about strangers sitting too close in restaurants, and the surveillance was becoming unbearable.

The doctor was beginning to crack under the heat, and was already in a bad mood when he asked her on one of his days off to accompany him downtown to purchase equipment for his karate club. Shelley dreaded what might happen next. The couple's three-year-old son had begun to misbehave, and her husband would get even angrier, she thought, if she spent more time with him. "I'll go get the equipment tomorrow," she offered.

It wasn't a good suggestion, she discovered. Her husband "freaked out," slapping her twice in the mouth. She was used to that, but she was surprised when her husband also slapped their son's face. The stress really must be getting to him, she thought. He didn't usually slap the kids.

"We're going down to Mikado's to buy the equipment," Charalambous insisted, "and we're going now." Dutifully, Shelley buckled the children into the van, but the doctor was still angry as they pulled out of the driveway. "You've ruined my life," he began. "The last eight years of my life, from the day I met you have been ruined."

Shelley cringed as the harangue continued all the way downtown. "You're no good," Charalambous told his wife. "You're worse than a hooker. You're worse than a heroin addict. You don't deserve to have a family. You don't deserve to have children. You don't deserve to have me. You don't deserve to live in a nice house. You don't deserve to be driving a nice vehicle."

As the van pulled up outside Mikado's, Charalambous spoke more calmly. "Now, go in and buy the karate equipment," he said. Tearfully, Shelley went into the store. She picked up the items her husband wanted. When she brought the equipment out to the van, the tirade continued. "Why did you go in there?" her husband demanded.

"Because you told me to," Shelley sobbed.

"Now the people in the store will know that we had a fight," Charalambous yelled. "They'll know you've been crying!"

The doctor slapped his wife in the face and head as the family drove home. Eventually, he dropped his wife and children off at the house. "Now you've ruined my day," he said. "You got me all stressed out so when I go to the racetrack and I bet on the horses, I'm going to lose; so tonight I won't be able to sleep; so tomorrow I won't be able to see patients; you are going to ruin my day, which means tomorrow night I won't be able to teach karate."

Shelley sat frozen, saying nothing as her husband repeated how the Mikado's incident had ruined the following week of his life. Finally, after he'd departed, Shelley went to a pay phone. Glad to see the back of her husband, she called her father at work, crying so hard she could barely talk.

"Your Dad's not in the office," said a sympathetic secretary.

"It's an emergency," said Shelley. "I need him paged."

Shortly, Shelley's father called back. "Dad," she sobbed, "I need you to take the day off work and bring your truck and help me move out. I have to get out tomorrow morning."

"Are you okay?" her father asked.

"I'm fine," said Shelley. "Just come at 9:30 in the morning."

Shelley didn't have enough money for a house of her own and she began to wonder if there were any place where she and her children could stay. Because she'd had the kids when she was very young, she hadn't finished high school or obtained any career skills. She couldn't stay with her closest friend Gail Pikker. With their asthma, Shelley and her children would be allergic to Gail's housepets.

And no matter where she went, Shelley knew, Joe would probably be there kicking in the door. When a previous girlfriend had left him, she recalled, he'd gone over to her parents' house and done $1,000 worth of damage.

Lost in her thoughts, Shelley pondered her options. She couldn't call her mother. After not speaking to her for almost eight years, that wasn't even a consideration. But by the time her husband returned that evening, he had calmed down. He brought her a bottle of wine and gifts for the children. "Things are going to be okay," he said. "I'm going to the racetrack."

Shelley made another call to her father. "Dad," she said, after ensuring her husband had left, "I still don't have any money. I have nowhere to go. I'm leaving him but it won't be tomorrow. So don't come tomorrow."

Despite the temporary truce, Shelley was becoming increasingly afraid for her life, feeling sure her days were numbered when her husband proposed a Mother's Day trip to a remote place called Silver Lake. There, she and the children could have a picnic, her husband suggested, while he went target shooting with one of his friends.

Shelley didn't know if her husband's friend might be in on any plan to harm her, but she wouldn't put it past them. In Shelley's mind, "they were Greek gambling buddies and they seemed to stick together pretty closely."

The young woman phoned Gail Pikker to discuss her fears about the trip. She told Gail she had visited the same spot before and that it was far from the main highway, accessible only via a dirt road through extremely isolated bushland. "I might get shot while he's target shooting," said Shelley. "I don't know by going with him if I'm going to make it back from that trip...I truly don't know."

"Don't go!" Gail sobbed, agreeing neither she nor Shelley knew what the doctor's next step might be. "I'm begging you not to go."

"It's one of the very few outings we've planned," Shelley replied. "I don't know how to get out of it."

Gail reminded the doctor's wife about "Lily"—the emergency password the two women had devised in case Shelley ever needed help. Lily had been one of Gail's cats. It had died the year before, but Gail knew just how desperate the situation had become. If Shelley ever mentioned the cat's name, Gail would immediately dial 911. The password was also known to Gail's son and to one of her friends, who would also send help if Shelley mentioned the name.

Shelley spent more time talking with Gail than anyone else. The doctor's wife didn't have to explain things to her. Instinctively, Gail knew her concerns and the danger she was in.

Despite her fears that she or the children might be murdered, Shelley went on the trip to Silver Lake. But the day passed without incident, Shelley calling on her cellular phone several times to assure Gail that everything was all right. She and the children, she reported, were enjoying their picnic beside the lake. Nothing untoward was happening.

Then, something did happen that seemed to leap out right out of the pages of fiction. It was strange timing indeed while her husband was the prime suspect in a murder investigation, but Shelley Charalambous was about to fall in love with another man.

And even stranger, by coincidence, was the fact that her new lover was an off-duty cop.

Like Shelley, Scott Leslie* was slim and five feet nine. He was a constable with the RCMP in Richmond, south of Vancouver. At twenty-seven, he was much closer in age to Shelley than her husband was—and also much kinder.

The doctor's wife had met the clean shaven, dark-haired young man while the two of them were at a playground with their children, and Scott had seemed to sense her unhappiness the first time their eyes met.

Shelley had kept her distance from him at first, partly because Scott was married. But she found him "very understanding" from the outset. "He picked out things that I didn't," Shelley recalled. "I'm not sure how...but he knew how afraid I was of my husband...just through friendly conversations.

"I liked his understanding, his compassion. Scott understood what I was going through."

Shelley kept running into the off-duty policeman over the next few weeks as the two of them dropped off their children at kindergarten. She considered him to be her best friend, and dreamed of the two of them getting out of their respective marriages, starting a new life together in some other location.

After almost eight years of being starved for emotion, she was ready to take the risk. While her husband went off to the races, Shelley hired a babysitter and went to the mall. There, she bought herself a brand new pair of jeans, checking how she looked in the dressing room mirror before heading off in her van for her first ever real date with a man close to her own age. With Scott beside her, she watched the movie *Indecent Proposal* at Richmond Square, fairly exploding with passion in his arms afterwards as her van rocked back and forth in the parking lot. At that point, she didn't even care if the van was bugged or not.

"We talked about marriage," she recalled, "but we were both married at the time so it was silly."

Eventually, Scott phoned Shelley to say that his wife Carmen had found out about the affair. Heartbroken, Scott's wife had driven out to Chilliwack and had phoned her husband at 1:30 in the morning to give him a piece of her mind.

The off duty policeman apparently had no clue that his clandestine telephone calls to the Charalambous residence were being monitored by his own bosses. He told Shelley on the phone how upset his wife had been. "She started smoking again," he said. "Right on, all sorts of neat stuff."

"Oh, that's good," joked Shelley. "Maybe she'll die faster and we can get all the kids."

"Yeah, really," Scott laughed.

"Sorry to be so insensitive," said Shelley. "You are married to her but I don't hold a lot of sympathy for her."

In another call, Shelley suggested that Scott might forget about his wife. "When I'm finished with you," she crooned, "you'll forget that you knew her, but I haven't started yet."

"When do you start?" Scott asked. "When you leave?"

"Uh-hmm," said Shelley.

"That needs to happen though," said Scott. "You know that."

"What?"

"That needs to happen before you can come on to me," Scott repeated.

"Does it?" teased Shelley.

"Well...."

"Yeah," Shelley concurred. "Uh-hmm."

"It's got to be legitimate," said Scott.

"Uh-hmm."

In another taped conversation, Shelley told her lover she had been sitting on the couch with Joe the night before. "I just sat there," she began, "and stared at him like I wanted to talk to him but I can't."

"Yeah," Scott interjected.

"So," Shelley continued, "he looks at me and he goes, 'Is there something you want to tell me?' And like a wimp I go, 'No.' He goes, 'Are you thinking about leaving me?' I says, 'Yes.'"

It was one thing to say she was thinking about leaving, she explained. But it would have been quite another to tell her husband she was actually going to. That would be too risky.

"Can you imagine if we got married?" Scott asked. "Five kids. That would be so cool."

"Would Carmen ever let you have them?" Shelley asked.

"No," replied Scott.

"Would she be reasonable though?"

"Yes."

"And yours?"

"Mine, oh I'd have mine," said Shelley. "I'd leave the country before I'd give mine up. I'd get mine. That's it, period."

"Would you stay in the Lower Mainland?"

"Would I?"

"Yeah, even though he might stalk you."

"He's not going to do that," said Shelley. "He wouldn't do that."

"Uhm," said Scott. "Personality says different."

The affair continued. Carmen, when she found out it was still going on, was furious. In one conversation, she called Shelley a "slut." She decided to go to the Charalambous residence to confront her husband's mistress once and for all.

After hearing of Carmen's plans, Scott and Shelley discussed the matter on the phone. "Are you alone?" asked Scott.

"Yeah," said Shelley. "Your wife just phoned me."

"We need to talk," said Scott. "I can't go into it on the phone."

"I am afraid of your fucking wife," said Shelley.

"Okay, what did she say on the phone?" Scott wanted to know.

"What? You won't tell me?"

"Doesn't matter. It was nothing. It's pretty veiled. She's going to kill me."

"No she's not," said Scott. "If you get out of there before she leaves...."

"Do you think she'll come over here?" Shelley asked.

"Oh, she might," replied Scott. "But, if you're not there, then she's not going to drop by. Right?"

"Right, and where do you want to meet?" asked Shelley. She realized as she spoke, however, that a meeting with Scott just now would be too dangerous. "She's going to kill me," Shelley repeated.

"Fuck no, she's not going to kill you," Scott insisted.

"Yes she will," said Shelley.

"Purple belt in karate," said Scott. "You could kick the living...."

"Yeah, and I haven't done karate for two years," said Shelley.

"No. Don't worry about it," Scott insisted. "She's not going to."

"Do you have any weapons in your house?" Shelley asked. "I better leave now before your fucking wife gets here."

But it was too late. Joe got home before Carmen knocked on the door. Carmen was so angry that Shelley thought Scott's wife was going to hit her. "How would I have dealt with Carmen hitting me on one side and Joe beating me on the other?" Shelley thought later.

"What was all that about?" Joe asked, after hearing the ruckus at the door.

"She just accused me of having an affair with her husband," Shelley said, turning into the house. Desperate for a way out, Shelley hoped that confessing the affair to her husband would bring a very quick end to the marriage. That way, she thought, either she would have been murdered or severely beaten.

But her husband thought the scene was hilarious and started laughing. "Isn't that silly," he said. "You would never do such a thing."

Shelley was dumbstruck. If her husband had asked her, she'd intended to confront him with the truth. But he didn't ask. He continued laughing hysterically. "Isn't that foolish," he added. "Like why would she think that? She looks crazy."

Charalambous knew his wife was afraid of him. He was convinced she'd never do such a thing, but his hyena-like laughter had caught Shelley completely off guard. She hadn't expected that reaction. It was a lost moment. It would have taken a lot of courage to have told him, she consoled herself. She knew what his reaction would have been to that.

After Scott heard about the incident, he informed Carmen she should never have gone to the house because Shelley's husband had a very violent temper. Both he and Carmen called Shelley from a pay phone.

"I'm sorry," said Carmen, sarcastically. "I didn't realize I was causing you that much trouble."

"No, it's okay, I'm fine," said Shelley.

"Take the kids and just get out of the house," said Scott. "As long as you're out of the house, even if you're in the front yard, he can't touch you."

Soon afterwards, Carmen phoned again. "Please stay away from Scott," she begged Shelley. "You are going to be sorry 'cause you don't know anything about him. Please don't talk to him."

Carmen and Scott had separated but were still trying to patch up their relationship. The two women made a pact. Shelley agreed she wouldn't see Scott any more and Carmen agreed she wouldn't call Joe.

The relationship seemed to have ended almost as suddenly as it had begun. Shelley felt a bit sheepish over the whole affair. Perhaps she'd made a mistake. But then, ten days later, something else happened, and Shelley's marriage to the man she'd known since she was twelve years old was about to come to a dramatic end.

25 Desertion

Shelley wished there was some way she could end the marriage, at times wondering if she might have to take her own life before Charalambous could take it for her. She thought of leaving anonymous tips with "Crimestoppers," but then realized her husband was already the prime suspect anyway. She had been so young and foolish when the police had come to rescue her almost eight years ago. If only they could rescue her now, she would never go back to the doctor again.

When it came to the messages on his answering machine, Charalambous wasn't taking the bait. The doctor continued to ignore the undercover operators and still wasn't saying anything within earshot of any of the electronic surveillance devices. If he were communicating with his underworld associates, police suspected, it was probably by pay phone.

It had been three and a half months since Sian Simmonds' murder and he was still a free man. Surely, if they had anything on him, they would have arrested him by now. It was beginning to look as though he might be in the clear.

Despite feeling he was under a microscope, the doctor had continued to consort with hookers downtown, but on the evening of May 14 he felt like staying home and having sex with his wife—which wouldn't have been noteworthy except that Shelley responded by doing something unthinkable.

She refused him.

Charalambous left the house in a huff, but Shelley knew that wouldn't be the end of it. He always got his way. Turning him down was dangerous, but she had deliberately taken a calculated risk.

As she lay in bed, Shelley was scared to fall asleep in case her husband might come back and inject her with insulin, so she was still awake an hour later when he stormed back in, ripping off the freezer door and throwing water and ice cubes at her.

"You've got two weeks to leave the house!" he yelled. "If you're still here on June the first, I'll load my shotgun and shoot you, not once but a hundred times."

The doctor sat on Shelley's stomach, pulling her hair and punching her in the head as he raged on. In their bedrooms, the children had been asleep but now, hearing their mother's screams, they woke up crying.

Charalambous went back into the kitchen, where the police listening device was located, ripping off a cupboard door as he began smashing cups and dishes. As they sat in their cars outside monitoring the commotion, Special O officers desperately feared for Shelley's life, agonizing over whether or not to blow their cover and storm into the house.

From time to time, the surveillance members thought Shelley was about to be murdered. They considered the possibility of calling uniformed officers on the pretext that someone had overheard a domestic dispute, but decided against it. They'd intervene themselves if they had to, but only at the very last minute. In the meantime, they listened in frustration as the disturbance continued for the next two hours.

Shelley felt herself being punched in the stomach and thrown about the room as her husband continued his rampage. Then he pointed to a hammer that he kept beside the bed in case any burglars broke in. "This fight's nothing," he told Shelley. "If we have another fight, I'll take that hammer and hit you over the head with it until there's nothing left."

Suddenly, as an afterthought, the doctor seemed concerned what his wife might do if she did get out as he'd been insisting: "If you ever go to the police, I will find you," he added. "I can be in jail...I can have one foot in the grave and I can still get to you. I know people that I won't even admit that I know."

When Shelley woke up the next day, her husband was out. It was a Saturday. He had gone to work as usual. Shelley looked in the bathroom mirror but her vision was blurred. Then she noticed the lacerations on her body where the ice cubes had hit her the night before.

Shelley was angry. No matter the consequences, the doctor had beaten up his wife one too many times. Shelley had spent her last night with Dr. Charalambous. She was about to walk out on him, never to return. Even puppies run away from home sometimes. She may have licked the hand of her master in the past, but now she was more like a pit bull.

The young woman realized, however, that it wouldn't be easy finding a place to stay. Catering to the demands of her husband for the past eight years, she'd made very few friends of her own. Whom could she call for help? She phoned her father and Gail Pikker, but neither of them answered.

Shelley hadn't talked to Scott Leslie for the past ten days. Perhaps he could help, now that she was finally leaving. She phoned him, breathing a huge sigh of relief as he confirmed that he was off duty and would be able to see her. They would meet at McDonald's Restaurant at Cassiar and Hastings Street in Vancouver, where they could talk while the children had somewhere to play.

Shelley gathered up some of her things, packed the children's clothes and loaded the children into her van. From the moment she pulled out of the driveway, she knew she'd never go back. At long last, could it be that the nightmare was coming to an end?

By the time her husband got home, his wife and children were gone. He hadn't really meant it, he said later, when he'd told Shelley to leave, but obviously she'd taken him seriously. Dr. Josephakis Charalambous, for once in his life, wasn't in control. He didn't like that. "But maybe it wasn't too late," he thought. Maybe he could still get her back.

The Charalambous children played boisterously at the McDonald's playground while Shelley asked Scott Leslie if he thought the police would be able to protect her. "I really don't know if I have anything important enough to tell them," she said.

"Don't you want the bad people to go to jail?" Scott prodded. "Let the cops decide if you have anything. Just go talk to them." The two of them took the children to Whytecliff Park in West Vancouver, then drove to Richmond, where Shelley temporarily was able to find refuge at a women's shelter.

Charalambous, meanwhile, thought for some reason that his wife might have gone to Kamloops, or have rented a place somewhere else in Coquitlam. From one of her friends, Shelley learned of her husband's frantic efforts to find her. The doctor had phoned Gail Pikker, but she had pretended she didn't know what was going on.

Then, her husband had placed a newspaper advertisement offering a reward for anybody who could tell him where she was staying. He had phoned landlords of advertised rental homes to ask if they'd seen anyone by her description.

And finally, Shelley learned, he'd bought a CB and was radioing truckers to ask if they'd seen his wife's distinctive van on the highway.

Shelley was already aware her husband would stop at nothing once he was obsessed like that, and his actions came as no surprise. She had lacked self-confidence while she was with him but now, with Scott's encouragement, she was gaining strength.

She would go to the police after all, Shelley resolved. Although she was afraid for her life, she also knew her husband had arranged Sian's murder. And she wasn't prepared just to let that happen. She wanted justice for Sian Simmonds.

"With the way he talked, I knew that he would do it again," she said later. "He's a very, very dangerous individual."

She had memorized Doug Comrie's name after he had visited her in March—and on May 18 she left the number of the Richmond shelter on the police officer's pager.

Comrie picked up the phone at 1:20 in the afternoon to call the Richmond phone number. "It's Corporal Comrie of the RCMP," he said. "I've got a message to call this number."

"It's Shelley Charalambous!" said at an urgent voice at the other end of the line. "I want to talk to you. Can you meet me here in Richmond?"

"Okay," said Comrie, taking a deep breath. "Is it okay if Sergeant Trekofski comes along? We can be there about three o'clock."

"No," said Shelley. "I don't want to see anybody else. I just want to talk to you."

Comrie could feel the rush of adrenaline as he headed south across the Fraser River into the flat, low-lying municipality of Richmond, the location of Vancouver International Airport. Observing a passenger jet as it climbed overhead, Comrie was acutely aware of the importance of his task. There was so much at stake, and his mind raced as he attempted to rehearse the questions he needed to ask. "Don't put a put a lot of pressure on her," he told himself. "Stroke her. Handle this right, and Charalambous won't be taking off for Cyprus or anywhere else."

When he arrived at the women's shelter, Comrie was met by two people. They identified themselves as Gail Pikker and Scott Leslie. The off-duty policeman had persuaded Shelley that Comrie could be trusted. Gail Pikker offered to leave the room. "Thank you," said Comrie, "I'd prefer that you did."

Shelley then appeared on the scene, Comrie sensing her distress as she told him of the beating her husband had inflicted four nights ago. The young woman displayed her bruises to the policeman as she spoke. "Do you want to lay charges?" asked Comrie.

"No."

"No?" Comrie repeated. "Okay."

He felt sympathetic towards the young woman across from him. She was very nervous, tentative and upset. To Comrie, it seemed clear from the outset that she had nothing to do with Sian Simmonds' murder.

Her husband hated the police so much, said Shelley. She wasn't sure if the police could protect her. If not, she said, once she talked to them, she was as good as dead. She wasn't sure how seriously the police would take what she had to say.

Comrie spoke reassuringly to the young woman for one hour and fifteen minutes, finally arranging to meet her the next day for a tape-recorded interview. He made no arrangements for her safety for now. For the time being at least, she appeared to feel secure.

Comrie drove to the RCMP detachment in Surrey, where he and the task force spent the rest of the day celebrating the sudden turn of events, and covering the questions they wanted him to ask Shelley the next time he talked with her.

Corporal Comrie met with the doctor's wife the next day as arranged. He had been talking with Shelley for a few minutes when he realized the tape recorder was running but not recording their conversation.

Then they started again. "Yeah, I tell you Shelley, I have some grave concerns, like I've said before," Comrie repeated. "I feel very, very strongly that Joe's involved and was part of setting up the death of Sian Simmonds. I have no doubt in my mind whatsoever."

"He knows that you're investigating him," Shelley agreed.

"Oh," said Comrie. "I'm sure he does."

"He says, 'They've got a big bulletin board...your picture's here and my picture's here...it's like a puzzle and they put all the pieces together.'"

Shelley told the policeman she felt sure her husband had arranged Sian's murder. She described how upset he'd been about the complaint to the college and how he had threatened to kill Katie too. Then, she described the aftermath.

"The next day I was listening to the radio in my truck and it said that Sian Simmonds had been murdered and I was like shocked...my first reaction was weird, like, you know, he had said that might happen."

"Uh-huh."

"And now it's happened and then I went...'No way, it couldn't have, like he wouldn't do that.' And the other thing is, when you live with somebody you see the good side and the bad side."

"Uh-huh."

"And you keep thinking of the good, kind side that's a doctor that would never do anything like that and you kind of go back and forth, like he might have done it, 'Well, no, I don't really think he'd ever do something like that.'"

"Uh-huh."

"And there's a big difference between like I mean...how many people threaten somebody in their lives...just saying it."

"Yeah."

"But they...don't mean it. So there's a big difference between threatening somebody or talking about somebody and actually going and doing it, and I never thought that he would actually carry something like that out."

Comrie could sense that Shelley didn't completely trust him yet with just how much she had known about her husband's murderous plans. "Did he at any time ever say to you point blank anything that would lead you to believe that he was responsible or had anything to do with Sian's murder?" the policeman asked.

"No," said Shelley.

"Okay, has he ever talked about Sian Simmonds or her family or anything since Sian's death?"

"He just said that he really, really liked her Dad and that it really let him down that his daughters would complain...."

"Did Joe ever say to you, 'Well...it's done now. Everything can sort of resume as normal?'"

"No, he did say things like, that Katie would never testify." Comrie was right. Shelley was afraid to admit outright that Joe had told her he

238

had planned the murder. Obviously, it was still too traumatic. She hadn't believed he would carry it out. She had to go through a process to admit that it was a "horrible, horrible thing."

"Now that I've told you I may as well be dead," Shelley sighed.

"You and the children are in grave danger," Comrie agreed, as he arranged for Shelley and the three children to be moved to another location. "I want you to make sure you don't tell anyone where you're residing," he said. "And don't frequent areas where you may come into contact with your husband or anybody that may pass the information on to him...."

Comrie also persuaded Shelley to give up her distinctive white Ford van, arranging for it to be parked securely out of sight in the basement of RCMP headquarters in Surrey.

The policeman arranged two more interviews with Shelley for the following week, and made temporary arrangements to cover her hotel and living expenses.

As he sat down with her again, Comrie wanted to know more about the doctor's friendship with Brian West. "How many times did Joe have anything to do with West?" he asked.

"There was the time when...he was trying to get revenge on my Mom...he talked about just having her beat up.... My Mom is very manipulative.... She's a bitch."

Comrie listened with astonishment. Shelley's husband, evidently, had brainwashed her to hate her own mother. But there was something in the young woman's tone that sounded ambivalent, unconvincing.

"I'm glad that I don't talk to her," Shelley continued. "Joe's...the one who's forbidden me to talk to her (but) even without Joe, I don't think I'll talk to her anyways.... She's very manipulative and I think...she agreed to let Joe see me because she likes him a little bit and...thought that he was one more person that she could add to her collection."

Comrie was right. In the back of her mind, Shelley missed her mother. No matter what had happened, she was still an important person and her daughter knew she should have stayed in touch.

"And then also he was in contact with Brian," Shelley continued. "I just remember this, Brian had beaten up his girlfriend or his wife. Joe wrote a letter for Brian saying that Joe has known him for so many years and that he helped out with the karate clubs...kind of a reference let-

239

ter...so there was a contact there too. And then he did contact Brian again in November or December of 1992.... Brian did phone him back."

"Was this at the time that Sian had laid the charge against him?" asked Comrie.

"Yeah...around the same time...probably around the time when he actually realized there was going to be a formal hearing."

"Uh-huh. What was his state of mind at that time?"

"Stressed out and hyper, but it was always stressed out and hyper. If it's not one thing, it's something else."

Comrie asked Shelley if the meeting her husband told her he'd had with West in Stanley Park had been prearranged.

"Well no, he hadn't told me that but then, when he came back, he said that he had seen Brian there and...he almost didn't recognize him 'cause he'd changed his appearance. And he talked about how sad it was that two people that were really close can't even admit that they know each other and...can hardly acknowledge each other. So he didn't tell me that he was going to meet Brian, but once he got back he told me that he had seen Brian and at that point he had given him more money, but I don't have any idea how much."

Shelley told Comrie about the cellular phone call in which she and her husband had arranged to meet at the Greek restaurant. The policeman already knew about the conversation from intercepted transcripts. "This young woman is telling me the truth," thought Comrie. "She's corroborating what we already know."

Comrie also wanted to know if the doctor had made any large cash withdrawals after Sian's death. "Have you ever...known Joe to withdraw any money from...his bank accounts other than his gambling debts and pay anybody any money?" he asked.

"No," said Shelley. "Lots of times, he'll tell me 'Go get me $3,000' and I take it to him and then he goes out and I assume he's gone to the casino or to the racetrack."

"Uh-huh."

"So on those occasions...I don't know...maybe he took the money and gave it to somebody." It wouldn't be possible, Shelley added, to pinpoint a specific withdrawal that was unusual.

The interview was drawing to a close and Shelley wanted to know where she stood with Scott Leslie so far as the RCMP were concerned. "I guess my question is, can I still see him?" she asked.

"I can't answer that for you," said Comrie.

Shelley looked at the policeman with big pleading eyes. "But again, without his support and without his encouragement, I don't know if I—he's really important to me and it was him that made me see that this was the right thing to do. He is basically one of the main reasons that I came forward. I really want to be with him—especially right now."

"Uh-huh."

"He's really supportive of me."

"Yep," said Comrie, "I appreciate that.... I'll bring that all up."

The tall policeman didn't think it was up to him to approve of the relationship. It might be fraught with problems.

26   Arrest

"Okay," said Gary Straughan, "Let's go!"

The file coordinator was speaking in the police boardroom. It had been exactly four months since Sian's murder. Since then, Straughan had accumulated mountains of files detailing every aspect of the investigation, and now he was ready for some action. Government prosecutors and Staff Sergeant Briske agreed with him. At last, the task force had enough evidence. Both Charalambous and West would be arrested tomorrow—Friday, May 28, 1995—and charged with first-degree murder.

The takedown, they decided, would begin at 8:00 A.M., when the doctor would arrive for work at his office. West would be arrested later in the morning, as he left his home in Coquitlam.

Comrie and Trekofski were dispatched to arrest the doctor, backed up by two uniformed officers and Constables Deanna Kohlsmith and Gordon Black.

It was a cloudy morning as Comrie and Trekofski waited in an unmarked gray Dodge, outside the doctor's office. A marked police car was parked beside them, while Black and Kohlsmith in a light blue Chevrolet Corsica cruised nearby in the rush hour traffic, along King George Highway.

Tension built as fifteen, twenty, twenty-five minutes ticked by, and the officers began to wonder if their man was coming. But then word reached them that Charalambous had gone directly to the hospital, two blocks away, to tend to a pregnant woman.

Finally, on the half hour, Kohlsmith and Black spotted Charalambous in his black sports car. The doctor was returning from the hospital and signalling to make a right turn into his office parking lot. As he spotted the police cars, he canceled his traffic signal and continued northbound on the six-lane, divided highway.

Kohlsmith and Black followed the Trans-Am for approximately one mile, before the policewoman glanced in her rearview mirror and noticed the two marked police cars behind her. "Deanna!" a voice barked over the radio. "Get out of the way!"

Kohlsmith moved her vehicle over to the far left lane. Turning on their flashing lights and sirens, two police cars sped past her, pulling in behind and alongside the black sports car. For a split second, it seemed to Deanna that Charalambous was considering accelerating away. Smartly, she maneuvered her vehicle in front of the Trans-Am, cutting it off and bringing it to a stop. "I think by then," Deanna said later, "he knew the gig was up."

With Charalambous boxed in by three police cars in the morning rush hour traffic, two uniformed officers jumped out with guns drawn. The doctor, they knew, was in a high-stress situation. They didn't know how he might react. But knowing he kept potentially lethal needles and insulin in the console of his car, they were taking no chances.

Comrie leaped out of the Dodge, shouting at Charalambous through the Trans-Am's partially open window. "Put your hands on the dash where I can see them," said Comrie. "Step out of your car when I open the door."

As he glanced at the uniformed policemen leveling their guns at his head, Charalambous appeared to lose the color from his face. "Settle down," he said nervously.

Surrounded by the police officers, Charalambous appeared smaller than ever as Comrie spun him around, cuffing his hands behind his back as he placed the doctor against the rear, left fender of the Trans-Am.

Sergeant Trekofski read the suspect his rights. "I'm arresting you," he began, "for the first-degree murder of Sian Simmonds. It is my duty to inform you that you have the right to retain and instruct counsel without delay...."

At a nearby bus stop, three chatting men scarcely bothered to turn their heads as Trekofski continued with his lengthy reading of the prisoner's rights. Arrests in this part of town were not uncommon. "You may call any lawyer you want," the sergeant continued in a monotone. "Do you want to call a lawyer? You are not obliged to say anything, but anything you do say may be given in evidence."

The doctor said nothing. Unceremoniously, he was placed in the back of one of the marked cars and taken to the police station. There he was escorted to the same booking area where Schlender had been interrogated four months earlier, and thence to his cell.

Among his effects, which he'd been carrying in a fanny pack around his waist, were his passport and $2,237 in American currency. Police also seized $444 in Canadian money, a Rolex wristwatch, a gold ring, a comb and a pen.

Straughan breathed a sigh of relief. As he received the news, a police dispatcher was already radioing word of the doctor's arrest to the officers who had been assigned to apprehend West.

The bearded man, after leaving home in his station wagon, was to be pulled over by a marked police car during a supposed routine check. The marked police unit however, got caught up in traffic, leaving it to officers in unmarked units to do the takedown.

Shortly before noon, West exited his house at 715 Hailey Street and climbed into the full-size station wagon. He had traveled about one and a half miles from his home when three unmarked cars suddenly swooped on him from all directions. The station wagon was forced to a halt at a busy intersection. Constable Tom Robertson opened the driver's door. As he reached in to grab the bearded suspect, West resisted, perhaps wondering if the plainclothesmen were really police officers.

Constable John Gould, the same officer who had arrested Schlender four months earlier, and who had broken news of Sian's murder to her parents, noticed that West, like a fine upstanding citizen, was wearing his seatbelt.

Gould reached into the station wagon to assist Robertson. Both policemen grappled with West as they pulled him out of the vehicle and onto the ground. But the station wagon was still in drive. It moved forward, running over Robertson's leg and crashing into one of the police cars.

After his leg swelled up, Robertson had it x-rayed but there were no fractures, only bruises.

Usually, the doctor examined other people, but now in the police cells he was about to be examined himself. During his years with the RCMP, Trekofski had seen prisoners conceal all manner of weapons—a razor blade taped under long hair, bits of wire hidden in different parts of the body. "Drop your pants," he told the doctor, as he put on a pair of rubber gloves. "I'm going to do a skin search."

"You guys are going a little overboard," said Charalambous, as he complied with the sergeant's request.

It was the first indication to Trekofski that the doctor was even so much as flustered. He'd seemed extremely calm—unemotional to the point that even the veteran police officer was quite surprised. In the past, Trekofski recalled, whenever he'd arrested anyone for murder, he'd always got some kind of response. Not this time though, not even a denial.

The sergeant checked the soles of the doctor's feet as he finished his search. Then Charalambous discovered that perhaps Trekofski wasn't such a bad guy after all. Under normal circumstances, the prisoner would only have been allowed one phone call to his lawyer, but the sergeant allowed the doctor to call his office to ensure somebody could look after his patients.

After he was photographed, Charalambous pointed out he'd already given his fingerprints when he was arrested by Constable Justason, back in February. Trekofski patiently explained that new prints were required whenever there were new charges.

At 9:50 that morning, Comrie and Trekofski sat down with the suspect in Interview Room 5. "You're still under arrest," said Comrie. "Have you got anything to say?"

Charalambous made no response to the question. Instead, he stared straight ahead and looked at his watch. "Can I go back to my cell?" he asked.

Lawyer George Angelomatis visited Charalambous but told Comrie and Trekofski he was only acting for the doctor on financial matters regarding the medical practise.

Shortly before lunch, Charalambous was escorted back to the interview room, but the interview was brief and one-sided. Comrie advised the doctor that Shelley had made several statements to the police and that surveillance teams had twice observed him visiting the home of Brian West.

"I'm outta here," said Charalambous. "Take me to my cell." There

245

were still no telltale signs of anger or remorse, no reaction one way or the other. The doctor appeared totally emotionless. He asked for his glasses. Trekofski fetched them for him. In the doctor's cell, Comrie sat briefly with the prisoner on the end of his bed, but still couldn't get him to talk.

After lunch, Comrie and other officers armed with a search warrant went to the Charalambous residence in Coquitlam, looking for items that might corroborate what Shelley had told them.

In the kitchen cupboard, they found her birth certificates as expected. Comrie looked at the forged documents and scratched his head. They weren't even especially well done.

In another cupboard, one of the officers found a hand-held tape recorder, containing a cassette which still had a recording on it. Comrie smiled as he played it back. It was a recording of the undercover operator asking the doctor to come up with more money for the Schlenders.

The officers also seized a 12-gauge, semiautomatic shotgun from a bedroom closet, and found a hammer on the bedroom floor beside a basket of dirty laundry. In the doctor's briefcase near the TV, they found the medical files of Sian and Katie Simmonds.

Comrie returned to the cellblock that evening with a justice of the peace, a red-haired, short, chubby woman who formally read the charge to Charalambous, before advising him that his first appearance in court had been scheduled for 1:30 P.M. the next day.

Corporal Comrie picked up the phone the next morning to inform Shelley that her husband had been arrested and was in police custody. Shelley had signed the necessary documents to receive financial assistance under the RCMP's witness protection program and had now been relocated. She was relieved but shocked that a traumatic eight-year episode had finally come to an end.

Comrie and Trekofski met again with the doctor at 10:51 A.M. The taller policeman wanted to have a word with Charalambous about the devastation he'd caused in so many people's lives. Although interrogation procedures ruled out threats or inducements, there was nothing to stop Comrie from giving the doctor a piece of his mind.

"Don't you realize the impact this has had on the Simmonds family?" said Comrie. "Her mother, father and sister are having a great deal of difficulty dealing with this situation."

Charalambous again showed absolutely no reaction, apparently not even listening as he meditated in a karatelike trance.

It began to dawn on Comrie that he was wasting his breath, but he continued with his monologue, hoping that turning up the heat might elicit some kind of response. "You call yourself a doctor," he berated. "Why do you have to have a chaperon present when you see your female patients?"

When there still was no response, Comrie asked the prisoner if he could explain why a doctor would consort with prostitutes and associate with known criminals. The police knew his every move, said Comrie. They'd watched him gambling, and cruising the red-light district for the past four months.

Although the doctor maintained his silence, he scoffed when Comrie asked if it were true that he'd had someone beaten up for outbidding him in the purchase of a Greek restaurant. If he spoke at all, it was only to ask to be taken back to his cell.

Comrie and Trekofski had one remaining item of business. At eleven o'clock the next day—a Sunday morning—they went to see the doctor's mother at her home in Burnaby. Harry Charalambous was also present when they arrived.

Harry explained that he hadn't had much contact with his brother for several years. "He's too much like my Dad," said Harry, giving the policemen the impression that he had a poor opinion of his late father.

The doctor's mother seemed anxious to cooperate. She was a dark haired, extremely short woman with old country ways, struggling to retain her dignity as she wept for her son. She didn't have any knowledge that Joe had physically abused his wife. Since Shelley had left, Joe's mother had been over to the house to do her son's laundry.

Back at the police station, Sergeant Trekofski called on Charalambous in Cell F-2 to advise the prisoner that he and Comrie had just been to see his mother and his brother. "My lawyer has told me not to say anything or speak to anyone but him," Charalambous said.

Now that the doctor was in custody, there was no longer any need to keep his wife's van in the basement. Police arranged for it to be towed back to Robinson Street. Someone had discovered that Charalambous was behind on his payments and tipped off the creditors. The next day, the van was repossessed.

27   Angela Street

Angela Street lit a cigarette and sat down at home to read the Sunday newspaper. Since complaining to the College of Physicians and Surgeons six years ago, she had abandoned a career in hairdressing in favor of becoming a registered professional counselor, and she was savoring a day off with absolutely nothing to do having recently completed her studies.

While reading the top story, however, she felt herself going numb and her face draining of color. "Doctor Facing Murder Charge," said the headlines, "Teenager Killed After Complaining To College of Physicians."

Angela suddenly felt terrified as she saw the name Charalambous and realized it was the same doctor who had abused her. According to the May 30 article in *The Province*, Charalambous had been charged two days ago with the first-degree murder of a patient by the name of Sian Simmonds.

Angela had never heard of the victim, but a recent graduation photo showed that she was a beautiful girl. There were also smaller pictures of Dr. Charalambous and two men he'd allegedly hired to have his patient killed.

Struggling to see through tears, Angela read how Charalambous had also been charged only three months previously with the sexual exploitation of another patient. "A doctor accused of trading drugs for sex with one teenage girl," said reporter Greg Middleton's story, "has been charged with the first-degree murder of another."

"Rick!" Angela called out to her boyfriend, pointing to the newspaper. "Look at this! This is that doctor I was telling you about."

Up until that point, Angela Street had not been following the story of Sian Simmonds' murder. She had, however, by no means forgotten about Dr. Josephakis Charalambous. Though she had long since replaced him as her personal physician, Charalambous had been uppermost in her mind even as recently as the previous month.

As a newly qualified counselor, Angela had anticipated that some of her future clients might be referred to her by the medical community and she had sent out her new brochure to most of the doctors in the area. She had held back, however, from sending a brochure to Dr. Charalambous. The appointments she'd had with the doctor six years ago still troubled her. Finally, she had woken up late one night and determined to send Charalambous a brochure after all. "Fuck you, Charalambous," she said out loud at the time. "I know what you did to me."

Now, as she read and reread the Sunday newspaper article, Angela felt consumed by guilt. "Maybe," she told her boyfriend, "if I had gone further with the college, this girl wouldn't be dead."

That night, Angela saw an interview with Chris Simmonds on the local television news, listing the family's telephone number at the bottom of the screen. Angela wondered if it was too late to call but, with a shaking hand, she picked up the phone.

It was just before midnight. Chris Simmonds was not yet in bed. Since the January 27 murder of his daughter, sleep had been difficult to come by. In his family room, he picked up the ringing telephone, surprised by the late call.

"Hello, Mr. Simmonds," the young woman began. "My name is Angela Street. I just wanted to let you know how sorry I am...." Again fighting to hold back tears, Angela informed Sian's father how she had complained about Charalambous to the College of Physicians and Surgeons in December 1986.

"You've got to talk to the police," urged Sian's father.

The next morning Angela Street climbed into her family wagon and drove to the Simmonds' house. She felt extremely nervous as she found the long driveway leading up to the once happy split-level home, but Chris Simmonds invited her in and put her at ease. "I feel so guilty," she told Sian's parents. "If I'd stuck with my complaint maybe none of this would have happened."

"Angela," Chris Simmonds told her, "you can't blame yourself. Sue and I are glad you came forward. We wonder how many others there might be."

Susan Simmonds made tea, but Angela was inconsolable. She picked up a framed photograph of Sian from the family room mantelpiece. Tears streamed down her face as she gazed at the picture and said: "Sian, I am so sorry. Maybe I could have saved your life. I feel so guilty."

As Angela got into her wagon at the conclusion of her visit, she turned to look at Chris Simmonds. "I just bawled and bawled, thinking it's all my fault," she recalled. "I still go through that."

When she got home, Angela gave the first of more than two dozen media interviews. She also gave a three hour statement to Constable John Gould. Unlike the abrupt manner of the medical college, she immediately liked the dark, curly haired officer from the serious crimes section, finding him "sensitive and understanding."

"If only I had followed through with the college, maybe this girl would still be alive," she told Gould. "I feel so guilty."

"Yes," Gould sympathized, "but, if you had, maybe you'd be the one six feet under."

Although the College of Physicians and Surgeons had failed to follow up on Angela's previous accusations, the police believed them valid enough, even after six years, to go ahead and press charges. As a result of Gould's investigation, Charalambous was charged with six counts of sexual assault against patients, three of them arising from the information of Angela Street.

With her three children, Shelley Charalambous had sat quietly in a McDonalds' restaurant while customers all around her discussed the case after reading about it in that weekend's newspapers. The news that a doctor had been charged with the first degree murder of one of his patients produced a maelstrom of public criticism and demands for government action. Sian's murder also generated inquiries from news organizations around the world, and was the topic of a ten-minute segment on the New York-based tabloid TV show *Inside Edition*.

"A doctor is someone to be trusted," Chris Simmonds told reporter Craig Rivera. "We bring our children up to believe that. For me to realize now that I may have made a terrible mistake is something I will have to live with the rest of my life."

Sitting beside her father, Katie Simmonds reiterated how she had dissuaded Sian from dropping the complaint, despite the length of time it was taking. The murder, Katie added, had made her a very hard person. "I have to watch what I say, that I don't snap at people because I'm so angry. I feel like I've lost half of me. I loved her so much."

Rivera asked the College of Physicians and Surgeons why it had taken so long to hear Sian's complaint. Dr. Paul Bratty, a gray-bearded neurologist and president of the college, told him that the hearing had been postponed at the request of the doctor's lawyer. "We cannot suspend or erase somebody without going through due process," Bratty said, "that is to say without giving the individual the chance to explain his actions and defend himself." The college president conceded, however, that the college should have followed up on the complaint of Angela Street.

Facing the glare of television lights, the soft-spoken doctor said the college was hiring two new investigators, including a woman, in efforts to speed up its procedures. He defended the college's right, however, to continue as a self-regulating body. "Keeping the discipline in the hands of a professional body means you have professional experts involved," he told reporters. "We know what the doctors should be doing and we know how seriously they went wrong. I don't think a lay body can know that."

Bratty added: "I believe the college deals effectively and expeditiously with complaints that proceed to a hearing. As any system can withstand improvements, the college is continually monitoring its ability to protect the public by holding hearings as quickly as possible." He pointed out that the college had studied the subject of sexual misconduct by physicians in detail, and was waiting for the government to act on numerous recommendations it had made only the year before in its *Crossing the Boundaries* report.

In addition to canvassing the public, the committee had polled almost 1,500 physicians, fifty of whom (3.5 percent) had admitted to sexual contact with a person who was a patient at the time. The number doubled when it came to former patients.

The essence of sexual misconduct between physician and patient, the report found, was the exploitation of the relationship. "A physician who engages in sexual activity with a patient is putting his or her own

251

wants and needs before the patient's interests," said the report. "We concluded that in most cases...the patient's consent will not be genuine but will be tainted by the imbalance of power in the relationship....

"Even though we could envision relationships which are consensual...we concluded that these cases will be rare and it is better to absolutely prohibit all sexual contact between physicians and patients."

(While not illegal in Canada, fourteen of the United States including California, Florida, and Texas, have made it a criminal offense for doctors to have sex with their patients. In Texas, a second offense can result in imprisonment for up to twenty years. In some states, doctors can never have sex with their patients or former patients, while in others there is a cooling off period of several years.)

Despite its efforts, however, the college faced continuing criticism. Gerry Stevenson, a woman who started the Patients' Rights Association in 1993, said a complaint she made to the college a decade previously had never been dealt with. "The college doesn't do anything," she complained. "They cover up."

Other members of Stevenson's group urged patients to bypass the college entirely. Instead of going to the college, they suggested, patients who had been sexually abused by a doctor should go directly to the police. A woman who claimed she'd been a sex slave of her psychiatrist accused the college of making it too difficult for patients to file complaints by, among other requirements, insisting that doctors be informed of the complainant's name. "One woman got a death threat two weeks after she filed the complaint," she said.

Neither, it seemed, were the problems limited to the sexual exploitation of women. In late July, the local newspapers carried stories about a retired Vancouver psychiatrist, facing two charges of sexual assault against males. One of the complainants was a forty-one-year-old man who thought masturbating himself in the doctor's office, and having the psychiatrist hug and French kiss him were all part of the treatment. "I thought it was very sophisticated bodywork therapy," he told Justice Kirsti Gill. "He was helping me to like myself, I thought." The psychiatrist was acquitted for insufficient evidence, but outside the courtroom, a patient who had consulted him about anxiety attacks remembered that the doctor had been irritable and sarcastic when the patient had disagreed with his immediate diagnosis that such medical problems always stemmed from a weak father image.

Later in 1993, yet another doctor in the college jurisdiction was found guilty of sexual assault. Dr. Brian Thomson was sentenced to two years in jail after being found guilty of having intercourse with a woman whom he'd drugged during a house call, though he later won a new trial.

With the controversy continuing to pick up momentum, and accusations and counter charges flying back and forth, the politicians moved with almost unprecedented dispatch. Less than six months after Sian's murder, a series of new laws were enacted by the provincial government specifically to regulate the roles of various medical colleges.

"Professional colleges are sometimes criticized for acting in the interests of the profession rather than in the public interest," said the provincial health minister. "We are making changes to clarify what the government expects of a college regulating a health profession."

The changes, said the health minister, addressed previous concerns that medical practitioners facing even the most serious of complaints could not necessarily be suspended prior to a hearing. Under the government changes announced July 6, 1993, medical colleges were given immediate power to suspend any practitioner whom they deemed to be a threat to patients.

The medical colleges were also ordered to establish programs to prevent professional misconduct of a sexual nature. In addition, lay representation was increased on college boards, so that one-third of their memberships in future would have to come from the general public.

Covering fourteen health professions including doctors, dentists, nurses, psychologists, optometrists, chiropractors and naturopaths, the legislation reaffirmed through a new "duty and objects" clause that the primary objective of medical colleges would be to serve the public interest.

The death of Sian Simmonds had not gone unnoticed.

28

The Hireling

A part from his own fate, David Walter Schlender was about to learn the terrible impact that his actions had had on members of the Simmonds family. He'd already pleaded guilty to second degree murder, prior to the arrests of Charalambous and West—and now that all three alleged conspirators were in custody, he was being brought back into court to be sentenced.

Still wearing his bushy ponytail, Schlender sat with his back to the family and other spectators as the British Columbia Supreme Court hearing got under way on June 2, 1993, in New Westminster. Staff Sergeant Briske and Corporal Straughan were among those present, hoping to see justice for the Simmonds family.

It was just over four months since the pretty teenager had been murdered, and many observers in the emotion-filled courtroom wished that the wheels of justice could always turn so quickly. The original courthouse in the historic city had been replaced by a four-storey edifice of concrete and glass, less attractive than the old, but more functional and secure.

Schlender bowed his head, his mind numb to the proceedings as he slumped in the glass-enclosed prisoner's box unable to face the solemn, accusatory glances behind him.

His lawyer, he knew, had been "pissed off" with him for having pleaded guilty, but he wanted to get it over with. Pleading that the murder had been second degree and unpremeditated would still get him a life term, but he might get eligibility for parole as early as ten years rather than the supposedly mandatory twenty-five for a first-degree conviction.

(Part of the Canadian justice debate triggered by this case and others centered on the fact that the twenty-five-year minimum for first degree murder had been eroded by the infamous "faint hope" clause allowing parole hearings after fifteen years, a window that many critics wanted closed.)

Appearing before Justice John Rowan, Schlender faced two charges: the murder of Sian Simmonds and the attempted murder by shooting of Manjjyet Nareg. After everyone sat down, prosecutor Sean Madigan rose to outline the circumstances, describing how Schlender had firstly shot his drug dealer only to be granted bail the next day on his own recognizance.

"Despite his release, unfortunately, six months later on January 27, 1993, Mr. Schlender was active again," the prosecutor intoned. "Now we come to the count of second-degree murder of Sian Simmonds. Sian Simmonds, the young woman, who on that day, was one day shy of reaching the age of twenty years. Her birthday was January 28, 1993."

After filing Schlender's criminal record, Madigan said: "We cannot forget there are two counts although one seems to overwhelm the other.

"We're dealing with a man who on June 15 tried to kill a drug trafficker. He had a weapon with a silencer on it. He was released on bail with a condition that he not possess any more weapons. So the first thing we know about him is that he did possess another weapon, amazingly enough a weapon that seems to be a twin of the first one, a revolver with a big silencer on it.

"The second thing we know about him, is despite his actions against the drug trafficker Nareg, he agrees to commit another crime ... that he himself says is an extraordinarily serious crime, that he was to go for money—he's a *hireling*—to the house of a young woman and in essence threaten her with death."

Madigan said Schlender didn't even know his victim. "He's a mercenary of the worst order," said the prosecutor. "His instructions come from this fellow West, and even though he did refuse to burn the house down, that request alone should have brought home to any human being the vicious attitude of West to these unfortunate people because West was going to provide him with gasoline just to burn them up.

"Though Schlender refused to do that, his conscience obviously

255

was barely aroused because within a short time he is agreeing to take a gun to this unfortunate girl and threaten her. These were his instructions from this wonderful West and he agreed to do this."

Madigan added: "One would have thought for such a wonderful planner that if the girl screamed he could have run away if his intentions were so good. He didn't. He beat her to death with this big gun and in so doing he has deprived a family of their daughter and a young woman of her life and that's what he's pled guilty to here.

"I'd like to file...a number of victim impact statements. The trial is in receipt of a considerable number of them, showing the attitude and the reaction of the community to this savage killing, but I think it's sufficient that we bring to the court's attention the reactions of her own family, that's her mother Susan Simmonds, her father Chris Simmonds and her roommate and sister Katie Simmonds.

"I think it could safely be said that the cry of this family, the loss of their daughter and sister, is the cry of the community. A young woman has been killed because she was going to do something she felt had to be done, and that's to testify. It wasn't a court case, but in its own way was just as important and for that she was killed."

Madigan then read the family's statements, beginning with the letter from Sian's mother, which read as follows:

"My name is Susan Simmonds and I am the mother of Sian. I remember every day the pain of her birth and then the joy that she brought, then I remember the pain of her death and I think to myself, there is no pain at birth, just joy and love. This is the pain I feel now, an emptiness inside of me.

"I feel the hate and anger for the man that killed her. She was a beautiful person. It was so senseless, so tragic, he just went in and took her away from me and I don't know why, or what to do....

"People ask me: 'How are you?' They wouldn't ask if they had lost a child in such a brutal way. There is no answer for me to give them as to how I feel because I am half dead. How do you explain how half dead feels? So I say nothing.

"I tried to commit suicide two weeks ago. I feel ashamed of myself but I just wanted to be with my Sian. I can't see life without her lovely smiling face.

"What angers me the most is that this man was out on bail for attempted murder. Why are we and our families not being protected by our justice system? The criminal is. He has all the rights.

256

"There wasn't a day went by that Sian and I weren't together or talking on the phone. I phoned her from work the morning she was murdered.... That was the last time I talked to her...it would have been her twentieth birthday had she lived.

"I hope and pray whoever reads this never ever has to experience what we are going through. All I know in my heart is that no one will ever hurt her again, but I also know that I will never see her and hold her and tell her how much I love her again as long as I live....

"Some of the statements submitted from Sian's friends...will give you a better idea of what a lovely human being she was...she is and always will be so terribly missed."

Next to be read into the record was the victim impact statement of Chris Simmonds:

"It is now the ninth week since my daughter's death and I am still off work and will be for the next three or four weeks due to the emotional effect this sudden and terrible loss to me and my family has had on me.

"As head of the family, I feel very much the stress and trauma that my wife and daughter Katie are going through. 'I can't cope. I can't go on without her.' This phrase was and is often expressed to me by my wife and I think it sums up the awful feeling of despair we are experiencing.

"This despicable act of murder has cost us dearly in the loss of our beloved daughter Sian....

"I suffer with the plight and agony of our older daughter—not only has she lost her only sibling, but her best friend, and her home because Sian had only just moved in with Katie two months prior to her death.... She has moved back with her mother and me, but feels so lost and despondent as she tries to put her life back together and start over.

"Added to the pain is the fear for my wife's well-being...although out of hospital, (she) still expresses her feelings of emptiness in her depressed times.

"I have no desire to work in my garden, a source of great pleasure for me in the past. It has so many memories of my daughter who spent a great deal of time in it with us.

"Not only have we lost so much, but so has society. She was so looking forward to the summer as she was going to be engaged to be married. Her mother and I were very happy for her and for ourselves. We were looking forward to grandchildren, all part of our family growing about us and fulfilling our lives.

"Sian was a very special child. She had to check in with her Mom every day after she moved out to make sure she was doing well, and would always put time aside to see us both each day if only for ten or fifteen minutes on her way to work or school. She loved us dearly.

"Because of the violent nature of this senseless act, I have become somewhat withdrawn from family and close friends, certainly a personality change in me. My wife has reacted even more so. Definitely a great deal of fear and apprehension to a knock on the door, especially from my wife and daughter.

"Although we do not know the exact goings on of what actually happened as our daughter was being murdered, what we do know will be a torture to our minds and souls for the rest of our lives.

"I would like the court to know of my anger, easily understood by a father who has lost a dearly loved child in this way. My anger is directed to the whole world as I stand at her grave and shout at the heavens, feeling the most pain and suffering I have ever experienced in my forty-six years. These feelings of anger and frustration are only natural after such traumatic loss, so say the grief counselors and consolers. But I should not have to feel this way, not now or ever. This should never have happened. We are good people, God-loving and law-abiding. We did, and she did nothing to deserve this.

"Katie, our daughter, knows she is the key to our future. Living her life for us, even having a family of her own for us, instead of living for herself. This is a burden that she should not have to bear, but is further victimized by her sister's murder.

"Perhaps my anger and pain can be eased somewhat when I see justice done in this matter."

The next equally touching victim impact statement was from Katie Simmonds. She began by explaining that she was eighteen months older than her murdered sister and then described growing up with Sian in the quiet community of Willoughby:

"I have procrastinated in writing this letter to you because I usually am not sure if you will even be able to feel anything for us, unless of course the very same thing with the exact circumstances has happened to you.

"Please listen to my words for they are very painful. I love Sian so much...from the time I was sixteen until the day she died, we somehow grew even closer....

"I moved out at the age of nineteen to my Mom and Dad's rental home. My Dad bought the house so that they would feel safer, knowing what shape my accommodations were in. Sian moved in two years later with me to help out.

"I worked full time. We wanted new jeeps so that's how we could afford it. In November of 1992 we drove home two identical jeeps.

"I guess my point in writing you this letter is to try to make you understand how close we were. Losing her is like losing half of myself. I don't want to live here on this place we call Earth any more. I want to go where she is now.

"I live now for my parents because I know I am all they have left. I am a strong person...and will live to my fullest potential because I know it's the right thing to do. My boyfriend and I are talking about getting married soon so I know I have a future.

"But I am so sad I can't stand it. I think she will come home some day.

"Sian was murdered in our little home just short of three months of being there with me. I came home from work the day before her birthday to find my house taped off with yellow ribbon, police were everywhere, so was the media. I ran from my car leaving my purse and her birthday present on the seat.

"I feel so badly for my Mom and Dad. They are and always have been excellent, loving and giving, unconditional parents. Sian and I loved and admired them all through our lives."

By now, there was barely a dry eye in the courtroom. Corporal Straughan, who had forgotten to bring a handkerchief, was sniffing so loudly he was worried about disrupting the proceedings. Several veteran newsmen were in tears.

Madigan paused.

"These," he said, "are the victim impact statements." He reminded the court that the punishment for second-degree murder could range from not less than ten years, to not more than twenty-five years, without eligibility for parole.

The court, he added, could take into account the character of the accused, his record, nature of the offense, and surrounding circumstances, public opinion, deterrent to others and denunciation of the crime itself.

The murder of Sian Simmonds, said Madigan, was a horrible crime. "You see a deliberate effort by a man who ought to know better because he does have a record, because six months before he did something very similar. You see a deliberate effort to interfere with the testimony of a witness.

"You see cooperation for money to assist others in destroying a person, culminating in the destruction of that person, that is their death in a violent and grisly fashion."

Madigan discounted Schlender's proclaimed remorse. "I know you've received letters from Mr. Schlender where he says he's sorry, but I think we really have to cast our minds back to Mr. Brian McCann, because, after all this is over, when the witnesses are looking at the police running around the place and putting up their yellow tape, and Mrs. Phelps is finding her niece dead in the basement, Mr. Schlender goes for a drink at the Biltmore with Mr. McCann, and that night from his biker-type friend Mr. West, receives another $700 blood money. That's what this crime is about. This is why it must be denounced.

"It's from crimes of this nature the public must be protected. It's from crimes of this nature that young women must be protected. The children must be protected.

"If hirelings are allowed to go around killing people without the courts taking the strongest measures, then society itself isn't safe."

Madigan asked the court to sentence Schlender to a minimum of twenty years before eligibility for parole. Twenty years, said Madigan, would send a message that crimes of such a nature would never ever be tolerated, that anyone who commited such crimes, no matter how they felt afterwards, would suffer a very severe penalty. "Now there is no doubt that this man was simply a tool of somebody else—that somebody else will be dealt with in due course—but he's not an ignorant tool.

"He's a man who has a record—not a great record—but more importantly has within six months before committed and now pled guilty to an attempted murder of another person—whatever we think about the other person—in which he used a gun with a silencer.

"He's a man who was let out on bail. His counsel made representations on his behalf and he was let out.

"One of the conditions was 'You just don't have another gun.' I presume when he signed that bail, as he would have to, he agreed to that, and here he is dealing with this fellow West...and he knows West is a vicious creature because he himself has said West wanted to burn the place down, and all this gas and fuse to do it, so he's not deluded, he's not fooled.

"He doesn't think this is a lark or something minor. He knows this is a very serious matter and he doesn't even agree to the first part, according to him, but days later...he agrees to carry a gun to this poor, young woman, and he does do that and she dies.

"There's a calculation to this case. There's money. It's mercenary...the karate instructor is in danger from this woman testifying against him. So he knows that West's motives are biased. His motive is to undermine some system, in this case a hearing under the medical act, but he continues with it.

"I'm not saying it's a first-degree murder, but this case is a first cousin to first-degree murder. It reaches the highest stages of second-degree murder."

The public and the court, Madigan concluded, should demand that Schlender be given close to the maximum sentence.

It was just before midmorning as the bespectacled prosecutor wound up his case. Schlender would have to wait a bit longer to learn his fate. The court recessed for the morning break.

261

29 Schlender Looks at Life

George Wool was a homespun, quick-thinking sort of defense attorney whose words sometimes came out in impatient splutters and, as he got up to address the court, nobody could have envied him the difficult task of defending the man who had just been described by Prosecutor Sean Madigan as a "hireling."

Schlender was still denying premeditated murder but his best hope now, Wool decided, was the fact that his client had at least admitted the killing and had expressed remorse.

"What I am about to say as counsel for Mr. Schlender is not justification or an excuse for the crimes that he has committed and pled guilty to," Wool began. "The best that sometimes a man can do when faced with such serious crimes is to simply...offer his explanation of why an otherwise nonviolent family man would unpredictably commit crimes of this kind.

"That they're not serious crimes is an understatement. These are, and my client concedes this, horrible, terrible acts that he committed, and again I say here is his side of the story for the record.

"David Schlender was not always a killer or a violent person. In fact, prior to June 15, 1992, his record had no violence to it, either to his family or to the community...."

Wool gave the judge details of Schlender's family, asking that the information be kept sealed. "There is some concern for his safety and

262

the members of his family," said Wool. "These are the names of his wife, his daughters, his family and people of that nature."

Wool referred to Schlender's escalating use of drugs. "Now I don't know—and I don't think anybody in the medical profession or even in this courtroom will know—what will make one person an addict and what will make another person a nonaddict. The best I can say...is that by March, 1991, David Schlender was beginning to inject and freebase crack cocaine. His...consumption ranged from one to four grams per day.

"Now when you accelerate your use of cocaine, you come into contact with people who are cocaine suppliers and one of these suppliers was...Mr. Manjjyet Nareg....

"Now I don't want to interpret this as some sort of sympathy towards Mr. Schlender, except to this extent: Manjjyet Nareg was a supplier of cocaine. He was not a user of cocaine...never used the substance at all, but he sold it and his practise—he admitted this also—it was solely greed and money that he wanted—his practise was to buff cocaine.

"Now by buffing cocaine, as you cut the amounts, so you put some pollutants in it so you can get more money, and what he did to Mr. Schlender was that he had buffed some cocaine and Mr. Schlender felt that he had been ripped off.

"Now that's the mind of a cocaine addict who had come to the point where he wanted the cocaine, but he didn't have the money to pay for it.

"What he expected would happen is that Mr. Nareg would hand him a bag of cocaine and then he would simply rip off Mr. Nareg in exchange.

"Now what we know is that by that time he had come in contact with a man by the name of Brian West. It was through Mr. West that Mr. Schlender obtained a gun with a silencer.

"The plan was that he would go and, in effect, use the gun as his trump card, not planning to necessarily kill Mr. Nareg, but if there was going to be a problem, well, he had the gun with him."

According to Wool, Schlender pulled out the gun and Nareg backed the car up over him. "In other words," said Wool, "he had...tire marks over his body where the car had run at him; then he took a shot.

"In any case, my client fired the bullets, he accepts responsibility for it, it's clearly attempted murder and he's pled guilty to it."

Wool reiterated that Schlender had phoned the police when he got home and subsequently cooperated with them. "The one area that he did not tell the truth...is that he had the gun, not Mr. Nareg, so when it came time for his bail application, the court had before it a man with no history of violence, a man who had called the police himself, had given them a statement, taken them to where the gun was.

"The person he shot was not as portrayed in the news media flashes of the day; that a couple were driving along when they were picked up by a man with a gun. Of course, if hindsight was something, we would all have said, 'No, Mr. Schlender shouldn't have been released,' but that wasn't what was known at the time.

"If we could turn back the clock, if we had known what Mr. Schlender was really up to, of course he wouldn't be released. Those are things that none of us knew. The court can't know, psychologists can't know, and neither can the police. I'm sure if the police had known about Mr. Schlender's involvement, there would have been a stronger objection to his release.

"Mr. Schlender went back, went back to the same friends, went back to the deadly association that he had with a man called West, and...throughout...to the time of the Simmonds tragedy...Mr. Schlender was accumulating a substantial drug debt...in the range of $7,000.

"For those citizens in the community that don't understand how drug dealers collect debts, I'm simply going to say that the drug collection business is one where threats, violence, and killings are not uncommon.

"In the mind of Mr. Schlender he had a vice...he believed that Mr. West would harm him or his family because Mr. West knew where Schlender lived and the drug debt was getting very big."

It wasn't Schlender's idea to burn down the house, said Wool. "He didn't even know who the Simmonds were, what the relationship was between her and her doctor."

But, Wool added, Schlender was a "prime candidate to carry out the rotten work of the cocaine trade and that is, '...You will burn or threaten this young girl.'"

The fact that Schlender had used a borrowed car, according to Wool, showed his client had intended only to warn the victim, not to kill her. Schlender's inquiry about the jeep at Mrs. Phelps' door, said Wool, was not consistent with a planned murder because Schlender had shown his face at the scene of the crime.

"None of us really know what happened as except Mr. Schlender and Miss Simmonds, but this is what he says happened.

"He says he gave her the registration, and incidentally the registration was found in the house, so he didn't have any intention of killing her at that point. He says she was across the room, says 'I was standing there, I pulled out the gun, I showed it to her and I said, "Don't move."'

"She came across the room at him, this is his side of the story...he panicked, he says 'I had the gun, I saw her coming, I hit her, the gun went off. I tried to keep her quiet...she struggled...I fell to the ground with her, she fought....'

"Now at that point he would have been on cocaine...it's not an excuse...but the man was strung out on cocaine. As he says to me in his language 'I was totally whacked out.'

"You have the registration left in the house. It wasn't long before the police were able to find him. He makes his phone call to a lawyer...I took the call, (it) sounded serious and I went to the police station....

"From the time that I had left my office until I arrived...Mr. Schlender's pubic hairs...were in the possession of the police. They had removed these after he had voiced his desire to talk to counsel and there are some things I am going to have to set straight on the record today, and not leave it to some parole board years from now to speculate about."

Schlender, said Wool, wanted to make it clear he was not a sexual pervert. "In the first days, nobody really understood, there was no motive. He was approached by fellow prisoners, story waved in his face, 'We don't want no pervert on our ward' and he's since been in protective custody.

"What I want to put on the record very forcefully today is that my client did not kill for sexual gratification.... After this sentencing, I may come before the court to have the pubic hairs...returned or destroyed so that there can be no misinterpretation. A person who goes into custody...suspected of sexual misconduct serves hard time...and while there may be those members of the gallery who would...like it, I want to tell them that...Mr. Schlender...in his letter quite frankly invites the death penalty...."

Wool, was interrupted by a voice from the gallery: "Hear ye! Hear ye! Asshole!"

Wool stiffened at the interruption, but continued: "So he is a dead man...as he says in his letter, 'I am marked.' David Walter Schlender didn't stick around and calculate how he could best come out of this situation by putting the family, the court system, or the public through the agony and expense of long trials.

"He chose early...to tell it all...that was his decision." Soon after Schlender was charged with Sian's murder, said Wool, the accused man's father had died of a heart attack. "Medically, I know I can't support it but to David Schlender, for what he'd done, his father died of a heart attack. In Mr. Schlender's words it was a broken heart for what his son had done."

Wool produced a copy of a letter from Schlender to the Simmonds' family. "The family doesn't have to read it," the lawyer said. "The family probably has good reason not to even give it a bit of thought (but) Mr. Schlender took at least that amount of courage to put what he did on paper to the family."

Schlender's letter, on prison stationery, read as follows:

"I stand before you today knowing that I am facing a life sentence. In my heart and soul, I realize that I deserve it. Only God can forgive me for what I've done, the taking of a human life.

"I've had four months to try to figure out where to look for forgiveness. In that time it has become quite clear to me that it can't and won't be given, it must be earned and it will be a long time coming.

"After I was able to realize that, I am now able to begin to heal, which has enabled me to see the real destruction I've done to the Simmonds' family....

"I will for the rest of my life be a marked man. I'll try to tell you how I feel inside. At this point in time, I'm so disgusted with what I've done that I no longer can think of anything besides pain.

"When I listen to the radio, the songs I used to like no more have the same feeling. When I try to watch television, all I see is hate and I cannot focus on anything except pain. I've asked for help, but the orderlies here can't help until you're sentenced, so all they can do is put you on medication.

"I don't want to be a lost soul, not ever.... I have to be able to deal with my actions. The remorse I feel is unbearable at times, it will not leave me day or night.

"The knowing and living the pain and anger I am putting the Simmonds' family through is so clear to me and I want you to believe me Justice Rowan.

266

"I have two daughters of my own and, when I think of losing one of them, it became so clear the loss I've put on their family. When I think of them never hearing their daughter's voice again, to have to go to bed at night knowing she's gone. She'll never get married and give them the grandchildren they dreamed of. The constant reminder of their loss at family gatherings, how empty they will be without her. Their lives will never be the same, then what they will feel in your courtroom, their anger and hate as it is all right there in front of their eyes.

"So I beg you...to see that I do feel. I am not an animal. I do have a family. I will have a reason to rebuild my life. And I want to pay for my sin. I must for the people that love me, and the Simmonds.

"I also know that your sentence will never take the Simmonds' family pain and anger away but it will help me to move on. The day I pled 'Guilty' to you Justice Rowan was the only day that I was able to start to see a hope, a chance for forgiveness. Up until that day there was only total disgust."

The letter was signed David Schlender with a P.S.: "Your sentence, Justice Rowan, will probably turn out to be a death sentence, and I am also ready to die for my sin."

Pausing after reading the letter, Wool continued: "That is what Mr. Schlender has said.... It's not an excuse, it's not justification, it's simply a man saying what he has in his mind."

Wool cited other second-degree murder cases as he fought for a lesser sentence than the twenty years proposed by Madigan. "The starting point really is ten years," Wool contended. "After ten years, the man is not released, but simply it is his first opportunity for parole.

"The best that can be said for David Schlender is remorse. I can't possibly offer some prediction of what a man will do after ten years of imprisonment of hard time, of being marked.

"He has at least come clean.... There are many times in these courts where we go through agonizing long trials and people deny, deny, deny and finally after a long jury trial...they're found guilty and they slowly accept the fact that what they've done is wrong.

"This man from the beginning recognized what he'd done and at least came forward, not to grovel in front of the court, but to say that 'I've committed a crime and I'm here to pay for it.'

"It's my recommendation that it's open from ten years on

267

and...judging (by) the cases that are before the Court of Appeal and the ones that I've cited, I think that it's open to say twelve.

"There comes a point when the parole board can look at him and assess him for release or some contribution to society.

"Now, my friend has made a correct statement in saying that the public may be outraged at what this man did, and my client says he is outraged himself at what he has done. If it assists...he told me something the other day that he wants you to know. He says, 'I have a hard time looking in the mirror in the morning.'

"He's not here to be felt sorry for. He's not here to say, 'Oh, don't punish me, I'm a poor cocaine addict.' He is saying, 'I deserve punishment, I deserve a sentence.' The only matter in his favor...is one of remorse and hopefully pointing out why he committed these crimes."

Wool had done the best he could. He sat down. Madigan waived his opportunity to reply and Justice Rowan adjourned the proceedings for lunch.

When the court reconvened at 1:30 P.M. Justice Rowan reviewed the evidence against Schlender. "He has a criminal record that extends back to 1973," the judge began. "However, nothing in the criminal record would lead one to expect him to commit the outrageous crimes which have happened and for which he is now standing before the court for sentence."

Referring firstly to the attempted murder of Manjjyet Nareg, the judge speculated that the drug trafficker was probably still alive only because the Browning pistol had malfunctioned.

The judge questioned Wool's contention that Schlender had not intended to kill Sian Simmonds, only to threaten her. "One might pause to ask," remarked the judge, "why then the silencer? The case has all the hallmarks of an execution, but I will judge the case on the charge before me, that is second-degree murder."

The judge added that the circumstances of Sian's murder were so shocking that he had no difficulty in acceding to Madigan's request that the accused serve twenty years without parole. "I can only think that a twenty-year minimum sentence should be imposed, that is just twenty years' minimum incarceration on a sentence of life imprisonment and I so order.

"I sentence the accused to life imprisonment and for...the count of attempted murder, I sentence the accused to fifteen years to be served concurrently with the life term."

The clerk announced the proceedings were adjourned. It was four months since Sian Simmonds had been shot and beaten to death. As the convicted murderer was led from the courtroom, Katie Simmonds exploded with some carefully chosen words on behalf of her sister. "Burn in hell, Schlender!" she screamed.

30 Interlude

Whatsoever you shall see or hear of the lives of people which is
not fitting to be spoken, you will keep inviolably secret....

The Simmonds family left the courthouse and went for a round of
drinks at the new Guildford Sheraton Hotel in Surrey. Although the
sentence had been the best they could expect, they still wondered if
anyone would ever confirm their suspicions that the murder had been a
deliberate act from the outset.

Afterwards, Katie departed from the hotel by herself, not telling her
parents or anyone else that she had decided to drop back at the house on
160 Street. Her mind racing from the effects of the alcohol combined
with the stress of the court proceedings, Katie intended to give her aunt
a piece of her mind.

As she arrived outside her aunt's house, she drove her jeep into the
lane where she'd always parked before. She burst unannounced into the
kitchen, but Gill wasn't home. Her aunt's boyfriend Colin, an electrician in his early forties, was startled by the sudden intrusion. "Hi
Katie," the curly-haired man said nervously. "Gill's gone shopping."

Katie ignored him. She descended purposefully to the basement—
where only four months earlier her sister had been so brutally mur-

dered—and was shocked by what she saw. Sian's bedroom was full of toys. Aunt Gill had transformed it into a playroom for her young son! Katie stood there for a moment, shaking with anger as she stared at the toys on the floor. No one in the family should even be living here, she thought, let alone playing in this shrine as though nothing had ever happened.

As Katie went into the bathroom, retching, overwhelming grief was finally catching up with her. She ripped the top off the toilet tank, returned to the bedroom and rammed the heavy ceramic lid through the bedroom window. Then, for good measure, she broke another window and smashed the wicker furniture that she and Sian had left behind. As Katie got back into her vehicle, an alarmed and frightened Colin called the police. Still shaking, Katie drove home in a blur.

The police took no action against Katie, but it was made clear to her that she would have to pay for the damage. Reluctantly, she wrote her father a cheque for $220, but neither he nor anyone else ever cashed it.

All through the summer, Katie continued to feel as though none of it were real. It would be much later before she could really cry. When the tears did come, they seldom stopped. Often, Katie attempted a brave smile, but her eyes were blurred by mascara. She and Sian had been so close. Part of her had been ripped off.

The confession that the family had been hoping for was finally made by Schlender on June 16, 1993, two weeks after he was sentenced. It still wasn't the entire truth, even though he made his statement to Sergeant Rinn and Corporal Straughan under oath before a justice of the peace, but Schlender finally changed his story to admit that the murder had been premeditated.

The confession contemplated what the police and the victim's family had always suspected. Up until then, Schlender had repeatedly told the police that West had "screwed up his life" and that he "wasn't going to go down by himself"—but that the killing had been an accident.

Schlender was still concerned for his safety and that of his family. He had been reluctant to make the videotaped confession, fearing that once they had him on video, the police would drop him "like a hot potato." But finally he was ready to admit that he'd lied.

At one point in the interview, Rinn asked him if West had specifically told him: "You take that fuckin' gun, then you go in there and kill that poor girl?"

"He never said, 'poor girl,'" Schlender corrected.

"Did he use the phrase 'kill'?" asked Rinn.

"Yes sir," said Schlender. "Yes I have to admit he did.... I tried to fuck him.... I just wanted to tell her not to fuckin' testify.... It just got all fucked up, Don. I know I can't prove it.... I lost it, here I am, oh God."

Schlender said he had taken it for granted that West would erase his drug debt. "I just naturally assumed that was fuckin' wiped out," said Schlender. "It wasn't.... He's a very...bad motherfucker.

"He used me...maybe he was getting $50,000 from the doctor, I don't fuckin' know Don and that's the honest-to-God truth." The statement ran twenty-five pages and concluded at 3:45 P.M.

Still in custody awaiting his trial for murder, Charalambous appeared once more in Surrey Provincial Court on September 7 to face the charges that he'd prescribed drugs in exchange for sex with the teenage daughter of one of his patients.

At a preliminary hearing to determine if there was sufficient evidence for him to stand trial, onlookers filled the two rows of public seating to hear details of the scandal. Among the spectators, several of them wearing shorts in the late summer heat wave, was Angela Street.

Nattily dressed in a dark blue suit and red tie, Charalambous had grown a neatly trimmed gray mustache and beard, and showed a hint of a smile as he glanced at the assembled spectators. "Order in court, all rise," the clerk intoned as the thoughtful looking Judge Howard Thomas took his place on the bench.

The doctor's co-accused, another man with a ponytail, had allegedly procured his own daughter to become a prostitute, while Charalambous faced three charges:

Count 1 that he breached his position of trust or authority towards a young person for a sexual purpose, "by inviting, counseling or inciting her to touch his penis with her hands and mouth" contrary to Section 153 of the Criminal Code;

Count 2 that he obtained for consideration the sexual services of a person under eighteen contrary to Section 212(4);

Count 3 that he committed sexual assault in contravention of Section 271.

Both Charalambous and the girl's father pleaded "Not Guilty" to all counts. Prosecutor Terry Schultes, a dark-haired, mustachioed young man who liked to play soccer, called his star witness to relate how her father had betrayed her. The witness broke down in tears, but friends of the Simmonds family rallied to her side during a recess and she was able to complete her testimony the following day.

At the conclusion of the hearing, Richard Peck persuaded the judge to throw out Count 2 against his client for lack of evidence, but both defendants were committed for trial on the remainder of the charges. The girl's father was granted bail on condition that he would have no contact with his daughter in the meantime. Charalambous made no such request, apparently aware it would be futile while he was separately charged with a contract killing.

No sooner had the proceedings been adjourned, it seemed, when Schultes dropped a new bombshell. The prosecution, he announced, would be laying six additional charges against Charalambous, all alleging sexual assault against three female patients during an eight-year period beginning on or about November 2, 1984. The doctor was now being called upon to face his accusers. After more than eight years of rumors, complaints, and ineffective sanctions, someone—at last it seemed—was throwing the book at him.

Chris and Sue Simmonds meanwhile reached out to the families of other murder victims and helped organize a "Voices on Violence" forum held one evening at a local college. As one of the panelists, Chris Simmonds explained how his daughter's killer had received a life sentence, but complained that the fifteen year sentence for the attempted murder of drug dealer Nareg had been a "freebie" because Schlender was to serve it concurrently.

He referred to the pain and suffering his family had endured since Sian's murder. "It is the most severe pain a parent can experience in a lifetime," he said. "To say that the public is frustrated is putting it mildly. There is no question that violent crime is on the increase and that the justice system is not coping. There is no longer any need for the experts. I know for sure they haven't got it right. It doesn't work. It's time for a change."

Members of his family, however, held out little hope for compensation. They had been told that they had not actually witnessed the crime or been injured by it personally. "I have applied through my lawyer," he said. "I have been told it's a waste of time but you have to go through the process and I intend to do so, but to tell me that I never witnessed her death is an insult. I see her die every night."

There was an emotionally charged response from a woman nearby in the audience. "It's terrible," she whispered. (Later, the provincial government introduced a new Victims of Crime Act specifically providing compensation for the families of anyone murdered since January 1991.)

As Sian's father sat down to loud applause, moderator George Garrett commended him. "I have been a reporter covering the crime beat for forty years," said Garrett. "It's just remarkable the way Chris is able to express his anger and frustration."

Sian's father said later, however, he could no longer derive much enjoyment from his pastimes, such as playing darts, and he generally found himself feeling depressed. Charalambous, he claimed, had planned to kill not only Sian. "He also planned to kill Katie and, if necessary, to take out the whole family. Dr. Death, I call him."

He explained how Charalambous had continued to be the family doctor. "When you have an appointment with a doctor, he is always asking you how you feel. You don't ask much about him. You are very much the focus, not him. He's been put forward by the College of Physicians and Surgeons as someone who is okay to be in practise. Why should you think there is anything wrong with him?

"A doctor in our society is someone whose name has been put forward as someone who is okay and who can be trusted. We instill in our children that it's okay for them to tell this person exactly how they feel, that it's okay if this man wants you to take your clothes off, because Mommy and Daddy have put him on a pedestal—this is something that we have brought them up to believe. This man has taken all the privileges that our society has to offer and exploited them for his own evil ends."

Charalambous was in custody, but he continued to practise his karate and steadfastly maintained his innocence. "I'm a doctor," he told a guard at the Vancouver pre-trial center. "I had a very successful practise. I'll be back within two years."

"Don't tell me you haven't been inside before," the guard replied skeptically. "You fit right in."

Meanwhile, the legal maneuvering got under way, defense lawyers successfully arguing that Charalambous and West were entitled to separate trials, as well as a change of venue because of detrimental publicity. Though West stuck to this arrangement, the doctor eventually changed

274

his mind, and opted to be tried by a judge without a jury, allowing the trial to revert to the local jurisdiction of New Westminster.

In the meantime, the doctor was back in Surrey Provincial Court on May 2, 1994 at the preliminary hearing to determine if there was sufficient evidence to try him on the six sexual assault charges. While three of the counts involved the allegations of Angela Street, two other women had come forward regarding assaults alleged to have occurred during examinations in the doctor's office between 1984 and 1992. The doctor had shaved off his beard and had regained the weight he'd lost after his arrest, looking well as he sat in an open-necked shirt in the prisoner's box.

Jacqueline Jongkind at last showed up among the spectators. She hadn't yet been able to reestablish her relationship with Shelley, and stared frostily at her accused "son-in-law," just two years younger than her. Shelley's mother was smartly dressed in a black outfit and black accessories that seemed somehow appropriate for the occasion. Even her earrings were black. Charalambous seemed to avoid her gaze.

Outside the courtroom, Angela Street waited to give her evidence. The anticipation for the past several months of having to testify had been stressful. Her latest relationship had ended under the strain and she had succumbed to the habit she'd quit six months ago, smoking several cigarettes as she waited to be called to the witness stand. Soon, she hoped, she might drop out of the limelight and resume a normal life.

The prosecutors, however, were winning on all counts. Charalambous was committed to stand trial on all six charges and David Schlender, it was learned in the meantime, had dropped the appeal he had launched in hopes of getting a lighter sentence.

Spring was in the air and Katie Simmonds got married to her boyfriend Dean. She had known the slim, clean-shaven young man since Grade 2 and he had told her on the night of Sian's murder that he thought it was time for them to get married. They would leave afterwards for a Hawaiian honeymoon on the island of Maui.

In a bittersweet ceremony, it was painfully apparent that Sian was absent as Katie's bridesmaid, and the wedding was also spoiled somewhat by the continuing rift between the family and Aunt Gillian. For appearances' sake, Gill attended the wedding, but the family would always be critical that she had not responded sooner to the commotion in Sian's suite. Gill's friends, however, were amazed that *she* was still alive. "She got such a perfectly good look at Schlender when he came to her door," said one of them. "She still can't believe he didn't come upstairs and kill her too."

In the fall, Angela Street, who had been divorced for several years, also got married. Just as the Charalambous trial was finally scheduled to get under way, Angela flew to the Caribbean with her police-officer fiance for a wedding on the beach at St. Thomas, far away from the gloom that Charalambous had caused her and all the others.

31   See You in Hell

After so many delays, it seemed hard to believe that the Charalambous murder trial was to begin at last, with no one actually standing in the way asking for another adjournment. The proceedings before Justice Ronald McKinnon began on October 24, 1994, in the New Westminster courthouse, which was approximately midway between downtown Vancouver and the Surrey location where Sian had been murdered.

Spectators, including Jacqueline Jongkind, her daughter Shawna, Edna Neighbour, the doctor's mother and members of Sian's family, were required to empty their purses and pockets as they passed through a metal detector prior to entering the security courtroom.

Dave Sella also came for the first day of the trial, but several others were turned away by sheriffs after the early arrivals and the large media contingent took every available seat. Charalambous sat in the prisoner's box, his back to the public gallery. He was protected on three sides by bullet proof glass.

He was asked by the court clerk to stand for the arraignment: Josephakis Charalambous stands charged, Count 1, that he, on or about January 27, 1993, at or near Surrey, in the Province of British Columbia, together with Brian Gerald West and David Walter Schlender, did commit first-degree murder on the person of Sian Simmonds, contrary to Section 235 of the Criminal Code of Canada;

Count 2, that he together with Brian Gerald West and David Walter

Schlender, between October 1, 1992, and January 20, 1993, at or near Surrey and Port Coquitlam in the Province of British Columbia, did conspire together to cause Sian Simmonds to be murdered contrary to Section 465(1a) and Section 235 (1) of the Criminal Code.

Charalambous entered his plea after hearing each of the charges. "Not Guilty, My Lord," he responded to both.

The air was thick with tension and anticipation. Members of the family had been told that the prosecution was cautiously optimistic, but Sean Madigan knew the Crown would have to prove that Charalambous had intended to kill the victim. And proving intent, Madigan knew, would not be easy.

"For the record, My Lord," Madigan said, "all agree this will be a trial without a jury.... Mr. Schultes will open, My Lord, and give you an idea what this case is all about."

Schultes began: "The Crown alleges in this case," he said, "that the accused Josephakis Charalambous, a medical doctor, committed the first-degree murder of Sian Simmonds, a former patient, by arranging to have her killed, in order to prevent her from giving evidence against him at a hearing before the College of Physicians and Surgeons of British Columbia...."

Schultes succinctly outlined the Crown's case before calling his first witness. Corporal Gene Krecsy, wearing a gray suit and a brushcut hairstyle, took the stand carrying a briefcase full of files. He had gone to the murder scene, he explained, at 2:15 in the afternoon of January 27, 1993, to take photographs and measurements as a member of the RCMP's identification section.

Krecsy showed the court a sketch he'd made of the crime scene, as well as several photos including one of a revolver with a silencer and another showing a scratch on the side of Sian Simmonds' jeep.

In the prisoner's box, the accused shifted uncomfortably as the witness also produced a photograph of some car insurance documents that Krecsy had observed on a wicker desk in the victim's suite. (Closer inspection of the insurance documents showed that they had actually expired four weeks before the murder took place.)

Krecsy agreed in response to a question from defense counsel Richard Peck that the door to the basement suite had been ajar upon his arrival at the scene.

The next witness, Dr. Sheila Carlyle, testified how she'd seen Sian lying in the foyer in a pool of blood. The pathologist, wearing a tweed jacket and skirt, had conducted the autopsy the following day and had found that loss of blood had been the most immediate cause of death.

Madigan showed her a photo of the alleged murder weapon. "Would this type of an object be the object that could have caused these particular injuries?" he asked.

"Yes," said the pathologist. "I have had an opportunity to inspect this instrument, and in fact, the patterned injury that I have referred to as being evident on the side of the face appears to correspond to that area of the firearm above the handle at the base of the firing mechanism." The injuries, said Dr. Carlyle, were consistent with someone having wielded the gun by the silencer as a blunt instrument.

"Used as a club?" asked the judge.

"Yes," said the doctor.

Constable Deanna Kohlsmith was the next witness. She carried a large box into the courtroom and, after being sworn in, explained that she was the person who had been in charge of collecting the exhibits. In addition to the weapon, she handed in several items that had been seized under search warrant from the home of the accused after his arrest.

These included the victim's medical files found in the doctor's home in a briefcase and an obituary notice of Sian's death contained in one of several newspapers stashed beside the Charalambous fireplace.

Later, said Kohlsmith, Sergeant Rinn had given her an audio cassette, that he had received from the doctor's wife, of a telephone call between Dr. Charalambous and Katie Simmonds. Shelley had retrieved the tape from her husband's desk while cleaning out the family home after his arrest.

The witness also tendered birth certificates belonging to the doctor's wife, a karate club license that had been found in the back of the doctor's car, and a letter to Sian Simmonds from the College of Physicians and Surgeons, notifying her of the date of a hearing into her complaint against Dr. Charalambous.

The second day of the trial had been awaited with even greater anticipation than the first, the next witness being none other than David Walter Schlender.

The public, however, would have to wait a little while longer to hear what the killer had to say.

The lawyer for Brian Gerald West had come to court to request a ban on the publication of Schlender's evidence, or at least on parts of it concerning West not specifically related to the murder of Sian Simmonds.

If published, Brian Jackson petitioned the judge, Schlender's testimony would make it extremely difficult for West to get a fair trial. There had already been "excessive pre-trial publicity," said the lawyer, adding that a judge in the future would be hard pressed not to grant his client a mistrial if certain parts of Schlender's evidence were reported in the media.

Rumblings of discontent rippled through the media contingent. The public had been waiting for twenty-two months to hear what Schlender had to say, and now, it appeared there would be a ban. But no sooner had Justice McKinnon begun speaking reluctantly of acceding to Jackson's request when *BCTV* reporter John Daly stood up in the public gallery to interrupt him. The startled judge allowed the audacious newsman to make his point.

"My only position would be that we the press...." said Daly "ought to have had notice respecting the ban. I respectfully submit...we could appear at 1:30 P.M. with counsel." Justice McKinnon said he would impose the ban for the time being but agreed to hear from *BCTV*'s lawyer prior to the afternoon session.

Flanked by two sheriffs, Schlender entered the courtroom wearing an open-necked shirt with a blue blazer and gray slacks, his ponytail even fuller than before. As soon as he'd been sworn in, he twisted his large frame in the witness box so that his back was almost fully turned to the public gallery. He bowed his head as he began to answer questions from Terry Schultes.

"Mr. Schlender," the assistant prosecutor began, "did you kill Sian Simmonds?"

"Yes sir, I did," said Schlender. "...I was in a predicament at that time. I felt there was no way out and that I had to do it."

Schlender spoke of his longstanding cocaine addiction, before the prosecutor asked his next question. "Now, do you know Joseph Charalambous, the accused in this matter, the man sitting in the prisoner's docket?"

"Never met him before in my life," said Schlender. "Never seen him before today."

The witness said West had never told him that it was a doctor who wanted the Simmonds residence burned to the ground. "He said a karate instructor.... I must have asked him ten times, 'Why, why?' I asked him was it over drugs...he would not collaborate (sic). Just that they were testifying against his long time friend, a karate expert."

"When you say—you use the word *collaborate*—do you mean *explain further?*" asked Schultes.

"Yeah," said Schlender. "That's the one."

"...Did West tell you, in terms of the equipment that was there, how physically the burning of the house was going to be carried out?"

"This is absolutely insane," replied the witness. "Through the front entrance of the house.... They didn't even realize that another relative lived up there. They were going to dump it through the mail slot and put this end of the fuse through—through in there—and then the other garbage can on the porch was going to be full of gas, and somehow they were going to light it; and God knows how it was going to end up."

"You have told us that West said his friend wanted it burned down with the people in it because someone in there was testifying against him?"

"That's correct, sir. And he—in the tone of voice, it was absolutely essential.... It was just insane. It had to be done. It was almost like Brian was being forced."

"...Now, after going home, did you hear from Mr. West again on this topic?"

"Yes," said Schlender. "Within a week he was over again.... I don't know if it was the first time or the second time, but then it was beyond burning of the house.... Both those girls were to be killed."

The witness appeared to choke on his words as he described how the plot was narrowed down in further meetings to killing Sian Simmonds alone.

"Would you like a drink?" asked Schultes.

"No," said Schlender. "I can't drink nothing."

"I'd like you to tell the court, if you could, what West said to you the last meeting before (the murder)?"

"He told me, 'You are to go in there and kill Sian Simmonds.' Not threaten her, kill her. She's testifying against his best friend in a court of law, for what reason I don't know, and she has to die.... He said, 'I'm under pressure.... There's no more time on this. It has to be done. You are going to do it or else.'"

The witness said he drank and used cocaine on the morning of the murder, finally carrying through with his plan to scratch the victim's jeep.

"Why did you do that?" asked Schultes.

"'Cause I wanted to make sure it was—that I knew who Sian Simmonds was."

In the gallery, several of Sian's friends sobbed as Schlender described how he had killed her. "I pulled out the gun and held it to the back of her head and I couldn't do it.

"And she turned around and it just—she went absolutely crazy and the next thing you know the gun—she got shot. And then she screamed and I freaked out, went nuts and beat her over the head with the gun and killed her.

"And that's exactly what happened. And then I left. I went home and I drank some more and then I took the car back to Brian McCann.... Before I went home, I hid the gun."

After the murder, said the witness, West was "very, very happy."

The defense began its questioning of Schlender after the morning break, Richard Peck at his adversarial best as he grilled the witness over inconsistencies in his statements, sometimes taunting him during a riveting cross-examination frequently marked by testy exchanges.

"About the time that you caused the death of Sian Simmonds you were no stranger to crime?" asked Peck.

"That's true," said Schlender.

"You were no stranger to violent crime, were you?"

"Yes," agreed Schlender. "I had one other violent crime before that." He denied Peck's suggestions, however, that he had been a drug-world enforcer.

"Had you ever threatened anyone in the past?" asked Peck.

"No," said Schlender.

"You weren't into that...(when) you met with Mr. Manjjyet Nareg?"

"That was a totally different circumstance."

"Okay," said Peck, enjoying the challenge, as though playing a fish on a line. "So you didn't really do anything wrong with Mr. Nareg, is that what you're telling us?"

"Oh yes," said Schlender. "I pled guilty like I pled guilty to (murdering) Sian Simmonds."

"But you said to us that you pled guilty because after you go down for murder what is the point."

"Well, what is the point?" asked Schlender.

"Well you tell me," said Peck.

"There is no point," said Schlender. "I'm guilty."

The lawyer asked Schlender about statements he had made concerning how people react when threatened to pay up their debts. "What have you observed to take place?" asked Peck.

"They usually find ways and means of coming up with the money," said Schlender.

"What do they do when they're threatened, these ones you have observed but not participated in?"

"What do they do?" Schlender repeated. "They get the money."

"I see," said Peck. "They fall to the ground and tremble and that type of thing?"

"They usually make phone calls, sell their cars, their stereos, pawn things off."

"Witness," said Peck, changing his attack, "in your first two statements...you denied anything to do with the offense of the killing of Sian Simmonds, is that correct?"

"That's correct."

"You looked the police officers in the eye and said, 'I didn't do it.'"

"...Yes, I did."

"...You had resolved to tell the truth, is that correct?"

"No, that's not correct."

"...So you were still lying to the police, were you?"

"Lying to myself.... To make things shorter for you, I lied right up until I came into this courtroom (referring to his sentencing the previous June) and confessed in front of the judge and the world that I had done it."

Schlender added that his own lawyer had misunderstood him on several points, making representations for example that he had been using cocaine on a recreational basis.

"He just made that up out of thin air, did he?" asked Peck.

"That's what he did," said Schlender. "That's what lawyers do I guess."

"The point is that your lawyer told the court...that you had gone to this house for the purpose of threatening," said Peck. "You were aware that your lawyer was going to say that?"

"No," said Schlender. "You are wrong there.... I was here but I wasn't. I wasn't thinking. I had one thing and one thing in mind only....

283

Confess to murder so there wouldn't be a long trial and the Simmonds family wouldn't have to be dragged through all this and deal with it."

Peck asked the witness about his discussions with the police after he had asked them to turn off the tape recorder. "You secured a hope of some kind of benefit for yourself, your family...in exchange for giving the police information in your possession, isn't that true?"

"I received nothing, my family did...." said Schlender. "There was no bargain."

"I thought we already agreed there was a bargain of sorts?"

"You can say whatever you want.... You call it a bargain.... I am saying nothing there."

"There had been no bargain up to this point?" asked Peck. "No offer of protection for your family, no agreement when the tape was turned off....?"

"Yeah," said Schlender. "There was protection for the family. I asked for absolutely nothing and got absolutely nothing except protection for my family."

Schlender said he wished it had been true that he been sent only to threaten the victim. He said his denial was based on his "weird state of mind" while he was in the interrogation room. "Your mind is going a mile a minute," he added. "I wish it was the truth. I wish it was just to frighten her. It wasn't, was it?"

When the court reconvened after lunch, lawyers for *BCTV* and the *Vancouver Sun* persuaded Justice McKinnon to modify his news blackout. "Publicity is the soul of all justice," argued *BCTV* lawyer Dan Burnett. After hearing their representations, the judge agreed that Schlender's evidence could be reported, except any parts of it that might implicate West in matters having nothing to do with the present trial. Media representatives heaved a collective sigh of relief. Schlender would make the six o'clock news after all.

Peck's gruelling cross-examination continued.

Schlender agreed he had been high on alcohol and cocaine at the time of the murder. "That's not an excuse though," he added.

"Did I offer it as an excuse, Mr. Schlender?" asked Peck.

"Well," retorted Schlender, "whatever you are trying to do, then."

The following day, Peck got Schlender to admit that West hadn't actually shown him how to fire the murder weapon as he'd previously alleged. "He showed me how to load a gun a long time ago.... This gun he never showed me...all handguns are the same."

Peck asked still more questions about what Schlender had originally told the police. At first, said Schlender, the police were trying to see if they could make a case against West. "At that point," he added, "they had no idea that this so-called doctor was involved."

Schlender was wrong on this point. Police already suspected that the karate expert was the victim's doctor, but the answer would do for now. *So-called doctor.* It had a nice ring to it, a good quote for the headline writers.

The witness said he finally told the RCMP the truth just before he left the remand center on May 2, 1993, to plead guilty to second degree murder. He agreed with Peck that he had been relocated to a jail outside the province for his own safety. "I'm not protected," he added however. "I'm doing life imprisonment, maximum security institution."

Schlender said the police at first had suspected a sexual assault, and had suggested he might get a ten-year sentence for rape. He had quickly wanted to set them straight that there was no sexual assault involved. Later, he told Sergeant Rinn that Constable Fleming had "ripped my fuckin' hairs off my fuckin' head and my balls" believing that the murder had been a crime of passion.

"Did he rip the hair off your balls?" asked Peck.

"Made me give it to him or else they would have took them themselves, yes.... They have their ways, believe me."

Schlender reiterated that he had been sent to the crime scene to commit murder. "I was sent there to kill her," he said. "No threatening. I received a life sentence. What the hell do you want?"

"I want to know the truth, Mr. Schlender."

"...You're getting on my nerves. What the hell do you want?" Schlender agreed having told the police that West had ruined his life and that he wasn't going to do down for the murder by himself. He admitted he was still lying to the police, even two weeks after he was sentenced.

"Tell us why you lied on this day of coming clean?" asked Peck.

"...I don't know," said Schlender. "You tell me how the mind works."

"I have no idea how your mind works.... Tell us why you lied."

"I don't know why," said Schlender. "There's no answer for it. Denial that you actually did it. Whatever you want."

"...If you would not agree to arson," asked Peck, "why would you so readily agree to commit murder?"

"Because," said Schlender, "it just went on for weeks, and the threats and all the bullshit that led up to it, and I just couldn't handle it any more, okay?"

"But why were threats made?"

"I don't know, go ask him."

"I'm asking you," said Peck, refusing to let go. "Threats relating to a drug debt?"

"Yes."

"But you'd owed him money on many, many occasions?"

"That's right," Schlender groaned. "Can't you understand he was under pressure from this doctor. This thing was insane, man. Get it through your head."

"I want to get into your head, Mr. Schlender," countered Peck. "I want to know—"

"I'm done with, buddy," said Schlender. "I'm done, okay. You can't change my mind!"

Justice McKinnon intervened, urging the witness to calm down. Peck then asked Schlender about the silencer-equipped gun. "Did it go off accidentally?" the lawyer inquired.

"No," replied Schlender. "I wish it had. I wish I wasn't there."

The witness said he hadn't bothered to disguise his appearance before knocking on the door because "the state of mind I was in, I was beyond caring about anything. I just wanted to get the job done. I was completely gone."

Schlender agreed that police had picked up his family and moved them away. He knew his wife was receiving financial help from the police but denied knowing the amounts.

Peck produced documents showing payments to the family of $1,000 per month for accommodation and utilities, $300 per week living expenses for up to six months, payment of airfare to a new location, payment of medical premiums, and an allowance of up to $1,000 to pay for psychological counseling.

"Ever discuss this with your wife?" asked Peck.

"No," said Schlender, adding he knew that his wife had been receiving financial assistance from the police but that he was unaware of the amounts or other details. "To this day I don't know exactly where she lives."

The witness admitted the RCMP had asked prison authorities to give him a transfer, but he'd had to sign an acknowledgment that the police didn't accept responsibility for his security. Peck suggested once again that Schlender was only supposed to have threatened the victim, and that he had killed her because she had resisted him.

"No," said Schlender. "That's a good suggestion on your part but you weren't there.... You don't know nothing about it."

"I'm suggesting to you...." said Peck.

"Suggest all you want," Schlender snapped.

"I'm suggesting to you that you're a person who will lie to suit whatever purpose is important to you at any given time; you agree with that?"

"No," said Schlender, "I don't agree with that."

Schlender had finished his two-day ordeal. As he was being led away, he suddenly stopped, rearing up like a grizzly bear in the direction of Charalambous. Although there were sheriffs on each side of him, spectators wondered what Schlender was about to do. Schlender paused for a moment, before addressing Charalambous in a loud voice:

"See you in hell, doc!" he snarled.

The doctor said nothing as Schlender was escorted from the court-room. An articling student on the defense team offered Charalambous a glass of water, but the doctor declined.

Gillian Phelps testified the following day how Schlender had knocked on the door of her house on the morning of the murder. The dark-haired, bespectacled witness, wearing a lavender sweater and olive green slacks, hadn't thought the stranger was under the influence of alcohol or drugs. Had she realized this, she told defense lawyer Peter Wilson, she would have been reluctant to direct him to her niece down-stairs.

Her evidence was followed by that of the neighbors. Darlene Kennedy was asked by the prosecution to draw a series of stick figures, showing the relative positions of the killer and the victim, as they had circled the jeep before entering the basement suite. The sketches were marked as trial exhibits.

The next witness was Sian's friend Kimberley Jones, a pretty but nervous, long haired teenager who had been on the phone talking to the victim immediately prior to the murder. She had known Sian since kindergarten, she testified, and the two of them had been discussing their plans together for the weekend when she'd heard Sian suddenly scream.

"There was a ruffling sound," said the witness, "like somebody had started to come in unexpectedly."

In the gallery, an older woman remarked: "Poor thing, she should have known there was something wrong right then."

Afterwards, postman Todd Martin and Constable Pokorny told what they had seen.

The first week of the trial ended the next day—Friday, October 28—with the evidence of half a dozen members of Special O. Outside the courtroom, another twenty or so officers from the surveillance division chatted in a waiting room in case their testimony might be needed too.

Overnight, there'd been rumors circulating that Charalambous might try to escape. Possibly, it was suggested, he was going to do some kind of flying karate leap and make a run for it. If so—with all the police officers milling about—obviously he'd picked the wrong day.

32   Implacable Discord

The second week of the Charalambous murder trial began on Halloween Monday, October 31, 1994. Firecrackers would be going off tonight all over the continent, but those in court today would witness a fireworks display all of their own.

It was a day when Justice McKinnon would hear not only from Katie Simmonds but also from Shelley Charalambous—two women whose lives for all time had been affected by this case beyond measure.

But the first witness to be called was the victim's father. Chris Simmonds usually preferred wearing casual clothes, though he always seemed to dress formally when the occasion demanded. He appeared in court today in a dark suit and tie, touching the Bible to his heart as he took the oath.

The witness remained calm as he gave his evidence, looking only occasionally at the accused without revealing his emotions. He agreed with Terry Schultes that he had been aware of the doctor's six-month suspension. He understood at the time that Charalambous had married a former patient, that the doctor and his wife were in love, and he had felt that there was no reason to stop seeing him.

The witness confirmed for the prosecutor that his younger daughter Sian had been approximately five-foot-eight with blonde hair, which she wore slightly below the shoulder. He was aware that Charalambous had phoned Katie on being notified of the college hearing and he had expressed his concern over this to Daryl Beere.

He described how his daughters had purchased their jeeps. "Katie's was black," he confirmed. "Sian's was red, with a white canvas top." Although Sian had moved in with Katie, she was still working in Langley and visited her mother whenever she could fit it in. "We have two garages," said the witness, "but Sian parked in the driveway which was visible from the road."

Katie Simmonds was equally composed as she took the stand, wearing a sweater, white blouse, and mid-length skirt. She identified photos of the basement suite and confirmed that Charalambous had been her doctor for about ten years.

"And he's this man here in that box?" asked Sean Madigan.

"Yes he is," said Katie, staring defiantly at the accused.

The witness said she and her sister were notified in November, 1992, that their complaints against Charalambous were to be heard the following March. "She was supposed to go on March 4 and I was supposed to go on March 5," said Katie.

Madigan then picked up a stereo ghetto blaster from the floor at the side of the room and placed it on the bench beside the judge. With no TV cameras or media tape recorders allowed in the courtroom, the ghetto blaster looked curiously out of place.

Katie Simmonds watched from the witness stand as Madigan fumbled for a moment with the dials and switches, figuring how to insert the cassette tape he held in his hand. "Now Katie," he said, when he was ready at last. "I'd like you to listen to, and see if you can recognize the voices on it."

Madigan pressed the play button, and everyone listened entranced as Exhibit 19—the November 11 conversation between Dr. Charalambous and Katie Simmonds—was recreated in the courtroom, clear as a bell, for all to hear. While it was playing, some of the spectators whispered their amazement that Charalambous had kept a tape of the conversation at all. But the doctor, it seemed, apparently regarded the tape as vindicating rather than incriminating his position.

Katie confirmed that the voices on the tape were those of herself and of the accused. She confirmed that she had called the college lawyer David Martin, soon after the conversation. "I told him Dr. Charalambous had called me at home and I didn't appreciate it," she testified. "I didn't want to be bothered at home."

Katie had appeared so strong on the stand, so stoic in confronting the accused face to face, that several observers felt she must have been on some form of sedation. That was not the case. The man in the prisoner's box, the man supposedly interested in safeguarding her health, had allegedly schemed to take her life but, more importantly than anything else, Katie, right now, had to put on the bravest of all faces. She wanted justice for her sister. Incredibly, she was able to keep her own emotions under control.

The next witness was Dr. Thomas Handley, a clean-shaven man with thinning, curly hair, who agreed with Madigan that his job as registrar of the College of Physicians and Surgeons meant in essence that he was chief executive officer of that organization.

Looking at records through his gold-rimmed, half-moon glasses, Handley confirmed that the accused had been suspended from medical practise for six months, beginning on January 1, 1989. The complaint of Sian and Katie Simmonds, he added, was received in September 1991.

"At that time," said Handley, "the college council passed a resolution under Section 50 (4) of the Medical Practitioners Act that the conduct of Dr. Charalambous be investigated."

The registrar testified that Daryl Beere had looked into the complaints and that the college had submitted the investigator's findings to its legal counsel for an opinion.

He said Beere went to the office of the accused the following March to convey to Charalambous the substance of the complaints. All of the materials, said Handley, were sent to the college's lawyer in April and Charalambous was advised in two, double registered letters sent to him in November that the college had set aside two days the following March for each of the hearings.

The prosecution was now ready to call its star witness.

Shelley Charalambous had hidden under a coat as she was whisked by car up to the courthouse. Now that she was in the witness protection program, authorities didn't want any photographs taken of her, and courtroom artists were asked by the judge not to publish any sketches that might tend to identify her. Concerned that the attendance of relatives might inhibit Shelley's testimony, police had asked Jacqueline and Shawna to stay away for the next three days.

Shelley entered the courtroom. She was escorted by two sheriffs as she walked directly behind the accused on her way to the witness stand. She hadn't seen her husband for eighteen months, and had been unable to sleep overnight thinking of the confrontation. But as she permitted

291

herself a glance at him, sitting there in the prisoner's box, he suddenly looked so feeble and pathetic. She had always been terrified of him— until now. All of a sudden, *she* was in control. The doctor watched Shelley intently as she took the oath. The tall, slender woman wore an olive green suit and hair down to her waist. Her differences with the accused, she testified, were irreconcilable and she intended to divorce him.

Until only three years previously, legal tradition had held that a woman could not testify for or against her husband. The English legal authority Lord Coke had explained the reasoning for this as long ago as 1628. "It might be a cause of implacable discord and dissension between the husband and the wife, and a meane of great inconvenience," his lordship wrote.

The law, however, had been changed in 1991 by the Supreme Court of Canada in a landmark case known as *Salituro v. The Queen.* Citing contemporary values in the Canadian Charter of Rights and Freedoms, the Supreme Court had ruled that irreconcilably separated spouses could testify against each other as though they were already divorced, there no longer being any marital harmony in such cases to be preserved.

The witness testified that she had been twelve years old when she had first met her husband. She was now twenty-four and had three children by him aged six, five and three.

Occasionally pausing to sip on a glass of water, the fresh-faced young woman was articulate and clear spoken as she described to Sean Madigan how her husband frequently spoke of killing the Simmonds sisters to stop them from testifying.

"...After being notified that the college was going to hold a hearing to investigate the complaints, he started trying to contact Brian West," said Shelley. "He called him solid.... Joe said that Brian had always been there for him and that if either of them had ever needed any favors done that they had always pulled through for each other."

The witness testified she hadn't really believed her husband's threats. "I trusted him a lot and I didn't think he was capable of doing it," she said.

Charalambous had spent the night of the murder, she testified, flipping through TV channels. Afterwards, her husband told her that the killer had also been involved in a similar murder in Port Coquitlam, in which a man had been shot while he was shaving by someone claiming accidentally to have damaged his wife's car.

"Did your then husband ever talk to you about the killing of Sian Simmonds itself, how it happened?" asked Madigan.

"He said that Schlender had scratched Sian's vehicle and then had gone to her house kind of apologizing.... He said Sian was very mad that the vehicle had been scratched...he shot her...but that she was very tough and she kicked him in the groin, and that she scratched him and that Schlender was a mess because she fought back very hard...."

"Did you husband tell you where he got this information?" asked Madigan.

"That West had—that Schlender had told West and that West had relayed it to Joe."

"Did he ever discuss with you whether he had given any money to West?"

"He said that one night he had gone over to Brian West's house and that he had given Brian all the money that he had on him, except for $50 and that they had put it in a sink and filled it with water, trying to get all the fingerprints off the money."

Later, the witness said, her husband talked of having given West more money in Stanley Park and told her that West had changed his appearance and had talked of leaving town.

Soon afterwards, Shelley added, her husband renewed his passport and told her he was thinking of going back to Cyprus or one of the Greek islands. "He said that there was too much heat around him and he speculated whether...there was an extradition treaty between Canada and Cyprus."

In her last year with him, said Shelley, her husband earned $450,000. She, however, had no money when she left him on May 15, 1993. She went to the police a few days later. And shortly afterwards, the RCMP gave her an agreement for the protection of herself and her children.

Although Richard Peck had conducted the cross-examination of Schlender, the defense had decided that Peter Wilson would handle the questioning of Shelley Charalambous.

The thin, sandy-haired lawyer, with his mustache and glasses, was the diametric opposite of his legal colleague. While Peck was flamboyant and colorful, Wilson spoke in plodding monotones, seldom showing any facial expression.

He was also meticulously patient, frequently allowing the witness to give long, uninterrupted answers as he sought to portray her as a person biased against her husband and prone to exaggeration.

The court heard for the first time perhaps why Sian had been singled out as the victim. "He knew that Sian Simmonds owned the red jeep," said Shelley. "He never did pinpoint which vehicle Katie drove."

Shelley testified that her husband had seemed quite satisfied and happy as he had watched televised reports of the victim's funeral. Up until the time of the murder, she had not believed the accused would actually carry out his threats.

"...Then I became terribly afraid because he had confided in me.... He had told me all these things which therefore put my life in danger.... He took great confidence in me because he knew, if I did anything he didn't like, he'd beat the shit out of me."

When the witness again took the stand the following morning, Wilson asked what had prompted her to go to the police after she had left her husband.

"...I knew at this point," said Shelley, "that he had carried out Sian Simmonds' murder and that wasn't something that I was prepared to just let happen or let pass by....

"I knew especially once he'd done that—with the way he talked—I knew that he would do it again.... I knew he was a very, very dangerous individual....

"I wanted justice for Sian Simmonds' murder and I wanted safety for myself."

Shelley said she hadn't been able to go to her father, because his safety would have been jeopardized if he'd helped her get away from her husband. "...Joe knew where my dad lived and I was very reluctant to go to family members or friends.... I knew that by asking them to help me that I was...possibly jeopardizing their well-being...."

And she had lost touch with her mother, having been forbidden by her husband from speaking with her for the past nine years. Finally, now that she was on the stand, Shelley retracted her earlier statements to the police that she been glad not to speak to her mother because of past differences. "I had differences with her, no doubt, but...not so great so as to cut myself off from my infant brothers—one who hadn't been born yet—and from my sister.

"I wasn't glad that I didn't talk to her, no. What fifteen- or sixteen- or twenty-year-old doesn't want contact with her mother, regardless? Every teenager has differences with her mother. I don't know a teenager that's fifteen, sixteen, or seventeen years old that doesn't have some type of difference with their mother, but they don't go to that extreme.

"Throughout those years, he told me what a bad person she was, and that I wasn't to have contact with her. He blamed her to a great deal for all the problems that he was having like gambling and for losing the house because she originally complained to the college, she screwed up, basically screwed up his life.

"And after hearing it for so many years, at that point I probably felt glad that I didn't talk to her, because, after listening to him for those many years telling me how evil she was, and how she had ruined his career, at that point I probably didn't feel like talking to her very much; but originally, when I stopped the contact with her, it was because he had forbidden me to talk to her; and if it was on my own, I would never have stopped.

"I may have had differences with her—and I may have even argued or fought with her—but it wasn't...so drastic as to warrant cutting her off....

"My brothers were three and five when I left home and when I just saw them recently now, they're eleven and thirteen, and I met a brother that I didn't know I had—sorry, I knew I had him but I had never met him—and he's eight years old. I wouldn't have missed that."

In the public gallery, a radio reporter suppressed a smile as Shelley testified how her husband had thought it hilarious when it had been suggested to him that his wife might be having an affair. "Sure," said the reporter, speaking from the back of his hand. "Why would anyone have an affair when they've got Super Studley?"

Shelley agreed with Wilson that her husband had wanted to go on holiday to Cyprus as long as she'd known him, but after the murder, she insisted, he began talking about it in the context of whether Canada and Cyprus had an extradition treaty.

"He knew that his time for working in Canada was limited," said Shelley. "He knew that he was under surveillance and he knew that he was the main suspect in Sian Simmonds' murder."

By that time, she suggested, he had abandoned long-held plans to expand his office and was more interested in fleeing the country.

"I'm suggesting," said Wilson, "...that he talked to the bank about securing a loan to fund renovations for his office."

"Yes," replied the witness, "but that loan wasn't for actually renovating the office. It was for his own personal use.... They wouldn't give him a loan if he asked for it for gambling. They would have said, 'No.'"

Shelley agreed she was office manager of the practise, but implied the title had been primarily designed as a spousal tax deferral.

"So you knew about his finances?" asked Wilson.

"I knew some of them, yes," said Shelley. "I knew how much money he made. I didn't know how much money he owed or how much money he spent—the same way I didn't know he was sexually assaulting patients or seeing hookers on his lunch break."

Wilson seemed to let the answer go, but then returned to it. "You threw that in to make him look bad, didn't you?" asked the lawyer.

"Maybe," said Shelley.

"Maybe?"

"Yeah, maybe I did."

"Maybe you did?"

"It ain't that hard."

Shelley glared at the accused in the prisoner's box. Her physical confrontations with her husband had been very violent, she said. "It wasn't just a slap across the face," Shelley added. "They were hard slaps, and punches and a few times, kicks from someone who had done martial arts for more than twenty years."

The doctor's wife was answering yet more questions when the attention of all in the courtroom was suddenly diverted to the public gallery. Sian's maternal grandmother Kate Davis, sitting in the second row, was having some kind of seizure.

Katie Simmonds was the first to notice. She and her sister had sung a duet at their grandmother's eightieth birthday and they loved her dearly. Katie leapt over a seat to rush to her grandmother's side as the eighty-three-year-old woman fell unconscious. While a concerned Katie attended to her grandmother, one of the sheriffs ordered spectators to clear the courtroom.

As they filed outside, the spectators were praying that surely in the midst of the trial, another member of the family would not be stricken down.

"There's no pulse, we're losing her," someone said. During the panic, someone had asked for a doctor, prompting the accused to turn around in the prisoner's box to see what was going on. Not *him*, the spectators thought. Not even if he were the last doctor in the world.

33   Without Conscience

Shelley Charalambous testified she hadn't believed her husband would actually carry out the murder, even though he had threatened it. "I didn't want to believe that it had happened or that he had been responsible for it," she said.

"He was the father of my children. He was my husband for eight years. He was a doctor. Doctors don't do that kind of thing and I didn't want to believe that he had done it."

As Shelley continued to give her evidence, Peter Wilson drew attention to the fact that the police never had been able to pinpoint any specific bank withdrawal indicating that Charalambous had paid West or anyone else for arranging Sian's murder.

The witness countered it wouldn't have been possible to point to one specific transaction because her husband was continually withdrawing large amounts of money for gambling.

But still, Wilson persisted, shouldn't there be a record if Charalambous had taken money out of the bank to pay $3,000 to $4,000 to Brian West as the witness had alleged?

Madigan objected. "The evidence was that he gave the money to West, not the source of the money," said the prosecutor. "...He's a gambler. He can win it at the track."

Justice McKinnon seemed to cast doubt on the suggestion, but his response had the connotations of a double entendre. "It doesn't sound like he was winning at anything from what I've heard," said the judge.

Shelley continued that she had been "very, very afraid" to mention West's name to the police because her husband's friend had always been described to her as a biker type.

"He was not a Hell's Angel but...he did associate with them and I was deathly afraid of mentioning someone's name who was associated with the Hell's Angels.

"My life was in jeopardy—just by talking to the police—from Joe, but now it would be doubly so in mentioning the name of an almost Hell's Angel."

Her life at home was never the same after the murder, Shelley said. "I mean, what was normal after something like this had happened and we were being followed by the police and numerous different surveillance things? Nothing ever did return to normal."

Just how much had Shelley known before she went to the police?

Wilson elicited some of the answers with a series of careful questions. Shelley had been reluctant at first to tell the police everything, even though Scott Leslie had told her that the police could be trusted. She'd been reticent because the police had been asking her to describe events that were "extremely traumatic."

"I wanted to talk to them, but it was a process I had to go through to be able to admit that, because that's an absolutely horrible, horrible thing.

"It took a great deal of emotional sorting out and there was a lot of conflict there because Joe had told me that he was going to murder Sian and I didn't believe him and I didn't act on it."

"You trusted Scott?" asked Wilson.

Shelley replied argumentatively. "Joe told me I could trust *him*," she said. " 'Trust me, I'm a doctor.' "

Scott Leslie had not been the only influence on her, she added. "All Scott did was encourage me. He was very supportive and encouraged me to tell the truth. 'Let the cops decide' were his exact words."

Wilson asked about the protection Shelley had been receiving from the RCMP. The witness agreed she had been given a name change as well as a new location, $900 a month for accommodation and utilities, and $350 a week living allowance, as well as the cost of medical premiums. "And I take it that's how you've been supporting yourself, basically?" he asked.

"Basically," said Shelley, "I have worked."

"One of the conditions was that you had to seek gainful employment, right?"

"Yes."

"But you get that in addition to whatever income you derive at work?"

"Yes."

"When you left you started a divorce action and you wanted full custody of the children, right?"

"Yes."

"And you asked for $6,000 a month....?"

"Yes," said Shelley, "and for the income that he was bringing in, that was reasonable."

Wilson wanted to hear Shelley's version of what had happened to the medical practise after her husband's arrest. Shelley confirmed she had gone to the office to pick up some personal items, such as photographs of her children, as well as some cheques. She had cashed the cheques and used the remainder of the money herself.

She couldn't remember the amounts but told Wilson they were of no great significance.

"Well," Wilson disagreed, "I am going to suggest to you, Mrs. Charalambous, that you scooped a very significant number of your husband's assets when you left; do you agree with me or not?"

Shelley agreed with Wilson that she had kept some jewelry and some pocket watches from a safety deposit box, including items that her mother-in-law had given her over the years.

When Shelley described the necklace as being worth about $5,000, the doctor's mother muttered in the public gallery that the actual value was $7,000. Bringing with her a brown-bag lunch, Betty Charalambous had come to the trial virtually every day, ignoring the media and walking away in silence when anyone attempted to ask her a question. But she told other people she felt Shelley should have stuck by her husband. She may have been a gold digger, but she was still the mother of his children.

Shelley continued with her evidence. She agreed she had received a $58,000 cheque that her husband had been carrying at the time of his arrest. He had conveyed explicit instructions through his lawyer, George Angelomatis, that she was to deposit the cheque the following day and withdraw the money from the account "before all of this hits the papers." She had used some of the money to pay pharmacy bills, as well as wages, and holiday pay for the receptionists. "He (Joe) wanted to make sure his receptionists got paid."

The witness explained that the practise was run for a short time by another doctor, but agreed she hadn't personally made any efforts to find an office manager or replacement doctor. Financially, it would have been in her best interests to keep the practise running, Shelley confirmed, but she'd had to move, and managing the practise wouldn't have been geographically possible.

Wilson asked her if she had made any inquiries about selling the practise.

"There was nothing to sell," said Shelley. "If no patients are willing to come to you, you don't have a practise.... I could have started selling medical equipment, I suppose, but with having headlines that 'Doctor murders patient,' there is no practise.... You can have a person's chart there but that doesn't mean they're going to come in to visit you."

"You just wanted to get out?" asked Wilson.

"Yes," said the witness.

After paying bills with the money from her husband, Shelley agreed she had used the balance of the money for herself and her family. "We didn't have a house at that time...so that was the only way I was going to get any money.... Usually when you divorce, the house sells and you get part of the money. That was the only money that was available...for the kids, for their future education costs, or for any of their costs."

"So actually," said Wilson, "it turns out that when you left Joe, not only didn't he murder you, but he started giving you cheques for $50,000?"

Shelley wasn't about to concede that her husband had good motives for anything. He was trying to lure her back, she said, by paying off her credit card. "...He didn't murder me or harm me because from the minute I left there, he never ever found me." Afterwards, she added, she never used the same credit card again. Through his lawyer, her husband had also given her the cash he had on him at the time of his arrest, as well as his $12,000 wristwatch. "The Rolex he had promised to my son...when he turned eighteen."

"I suggest to you, Mrs. Charalambous, that you have a tendency to exaggerate when it suits you," said Wilson.

"No I don't," Shelley countered.

After Wilson finished his cross-examination, prosecutor Madigan wanted to know if Shelley was aware that another doctor had continued to run the practise until early July when "that wonderful organization Revenue Canada came in and seized everything?"

She wasn't aware of that, said Shelley. Nor did she know that the replacement doctor was getting only 50 percent and that the other 50 percent was going to pay her mother-in-law's mortgage.

Wilson objected. "My friend is not only cross-examining his own witness," said the lawyer. "He is giving the evidence for her. Maybe he should get in the box and just tell us about it."

"I will if you like," smiled Madigan.

At last, the ordeal of two and a half days on the witness stand was over. Shelley still was not ready to meet with her own mother, but she had asked the prosecutors to allow her to meet with Chris Simmonds to express her condolences.

The private meeting between the witness and Sian's father took place as the court recessed for lunch. Shelley had been dry-eyed throughout as she had given her testimony, but she cried behind closed doors as Chris Simmonds took her hand.

She felt very badly for the family, she said, and was so very sorry she hadn't been able to do anything sooner. She had been so genuinely afraid for her own safety, Shelley explained.

Meeting her for the first time since the murder, Sian's father forgave her. Until they'd seen her on the stand, he explained, neither he nor his family had realized the extent of the physical and emotional abuse she'd been through. "I feel a lot of compassion for you," Sian's father told her. "We didn't realize you were just a victim too."

As Shelley came out of the private room, Corporal Doug Comrie who had arranged the meeting saw the tears in her eyes. Then, the big strong policeman of whom she had first been so scared, broke down too—and wept on her shoulder like a child.

Meanwhile, there was heartwarming news from another front. Kate Davis, Sian's grandmother, was resting comfortably at home. After succumbing to heat and stress the day before, she had been taken from the crowded courtroom by ambulance, but she'd been seen chatting cheerfully with the paramedics even as they had wheeled her away. Kate Davis wasn't the type of person who could be kept down for long. If she'd had her way, she would have continued to attend the trial, but doctors and family members insisted she stay in bed.

The prosecution still had a few more witnesses to call, but speculation after Shelley's testimony now centered on whether Charalambous himself would be likely to take the stand.

As the accused, he was under no obligation to do so, but the betting seemed to be that he would, partly at least to rebut some of the more incriminating evidence put forward by his wife.

Constable Tom Robertson, the next witness, testified how he had found Charles Kirton dead from gunshot wounds in his bathroom on April 24, 1992. The dark-haired policeman, wearing a mustache and a gray sports coat, told how "Crimestoppers" had deliberately misrepresented that Kirton had been shot while reading a newspaper in his kitchen.

Corporal Al Kautzman, wearing a beige shirt and brown suit, told of his investigation into the shooting of Manjjyet Nareg.

His evidence was followed by that of Brian McCann, who appeared in black jeans and a leather jacket, to relate how he had lent his car to Schlender the day before the murder. McCann also related how the heavyset man named Brian had visited Schlender on the evening of the murder. McCann said he had seen the same bearded, tattooed man at the Schlender residence previously. After seeing Schlender with a roll of cash in his shirt pocket, the witness testified how he'd stayed at the residence overnight before phoning police the next morning.

Corporal Doug Comrie took the stand to tell of his interviews with Shelley Charalambous. "Originally when I first met her in Richmond she was very nervous and very cautious," he said, "...But because I had contact with her two or three times a week until the end of June our conversations became easier...."

The last witness for the prosecution was the policeman who had been responsible for coordinating the entire file, Corporal Gary Straughan. Looking smart in a dark blue suit, Straughan took the stand only to present a catalog of the audio listening devices and telephone intercepts that had been arrayed against Charalambous throughout the investigation. It was a simple task after the huge amount of work Straughan had done throughout the investigation.

"Call Dr. Joseph Charalambous to the witness stand," said Peter Wilson.

Each day that he had come into court, Charalambous had pushed the microphone away from himself in the prisoner's box, but now he was about to speak up with his side of the story and he was escorted by a sheriff across the courtroom floor to the witness stand.

After swearing on the Bible to tell the truth, the accused looked straight ahead as he gave his evidence, avoiding eye contact with members of the Simmonds family in the public gallery.

He confirmed having come to Canada from Cyprus, aged eight, and having begun his medical practise in 1982. Questioned by Wilson, he denied having been concerned that Sian's complaint might have cost him his license. "My view was that the outcome would be very positive and that we would win the case," he said. If not, he added, he thought he might have been suspended for six months at most.

Charalambous admitted he had driven past the Simmonds' residences in Langley and Surrey, explaining he had been trying unsuccessfully to find the nerve to speak to the girls or to their father. Finally, he said, he had asked Brian West to approach either of the girls to say something to them. "I just wanted him to say, 'I don't want you to lie about any of my friends.'"

"Did you intend any harm to Sian Simmonds?" asked Wilson. "No," said Charalambous. "Absolutely not."

The accused admitted he had probably made threats against the sisters in front of his wife. "In our family—the way we were brought up—there was a lot of emotional, loose talk," he said. "Everyone just talked that way."

Charalambous testified he'd felt a "bit relieved" when he had heard that Schlender had been charged with the murder, but then his wife Shelley had told him that she was being followed. Thereafter, he said, it became very obvious to him that he and his wife were the objects of a major police investigation.

And it was because of that he'd gone to see Brian West to ask him if he knew what was going on. "I wanted to know if he had been followed and if he had any knowledge of David Schlender."

After West confirmed to him that he did know Schlender, the accused had asked him to consider speaking to a lawyer. Charalambous denied, however, that he had met West in Stanley Park or that he had ever given him any money.

The witness testified he had renewed his passport in anticipation of a holiday. When he was arrested, Charalambous explained, he had been in the midst of plans to renovate his practise.

And there it was. The defense. It seemed a bit glib but did it have any merit? Court recessed for lunch, most observers feeling that the doctor's version of events was a bit feeble to say the least. Insanity, some of them thought, might have been a better defense.

Sean Madigan appeared cautiously optimistic. In the past, prosecutors had been able to win murder cases if they could prove that death had occurred during the commission of another crime. But changes since the Charter of Rights meant it was no longer that easy.

Charalambous may have admitted that he wanted to scare the victim—that much, at least, was open to interpretation—but the admission standing alone wouldn't likely be good enough to obtain a conviction. Legal changes in 1987 meant Madigan had to prove not only that Charalambous had sent someone to do something to Sian Simmonds, but that specifically he had sent that person to kill her.

It was a tall order, but one thing was certain. The prosecutor had already decided that this man supposedly concerned with the art of healing was in fact without conscience. Madigan resolved to do the best he could to bring this out on cross-examination.

34 Cross Examination

After giving her evidence, Shelley Charalambous was spirited back into hiding, thereby missing the highlight of the trial—the scintillating and enchanting cross examination of her husband by prosecutor Sean Madigan. A legendary figure of the Canadian courts, Madigan was born in Limerick, Ireland in 1936, the son of a railway accounts clerk. He was the youngest of five children, and had no idea as he grew up in the agricultural market town on the banks of the Shannon River that one day he would become a famous lawyer. He had trained first, in fact, to become a teacher.

Madigan had traded in his classroom after emigrating to Canada in 1958. He graduated from the University of British Columbia law school five years later and had been a prosecutor virtually ever since, passing up many opportunities to make more money in private practise because quite simply, as he put it, he liked the work. Throughout those years, Madigan had prosecuted a veritable rogue's gallery of criminals but the present case struck him as oddly unique. "Here we have one supposedly ordinary citizen reaching out to cause the death of another ordinary citizen," he said.

Madigan's confidence stemmed from his legal knowledge and quick wit, both of which were well respected by his adversaries. With his rich Irish brogue and wealth of courtroom experience, the sandy-haired, bespectacled and sometimes curt prosecutor seemed just the man for the job. Madigan had seemed a bit subdued throughout much of the trial, leaving a good part of the sparkle and drama to his capable and energetic young assistant Terry Schultes, but now that he could sink his teeth into the adversarial role, the ruddy-faced prosecutor, like a wily old fox, was ready to begin his riveting cross-examination of the villain.

Madigan rose to his feet and adjusted his black, lawyer's gown. He had been soft and gentle with Shelley, but his demeanor now was that of someone about to tuck into his dinner with relish. "I want to find out something about you doctor," he began. "You're a medical doctor?"

"Yes, that's correct," said the accused, brightly.

"Your name is Josephakis Charalambous?" Madigan inquired, speaking with his finest Churchillian lisp.

Charalambous corrected him. "Usually, since I've been in Canada," he said, "they call me Joe or Joseph."

Madigan ignored the correction, turning to his next question. "You are and have been described as an expert in karate?"

"Yes, that's correct."

"What size are you?" Madigan asked.

"I'm sorry?"

"What size are you?"

"About five four and a half," the accused replied.

"And your weight?"

"About 165 pounds, I believe now."

Madigan showed the accused a photo exhibit of Brian West, asking the doctor to give the court a description of his friend. Charalambous estimated West to be five feet eight and 180 or more pounds.

"He's a big man for that height?" the prosecutor inquired.

"Yes, he is," Charalambous said, agreeing with Madigan that West also had visible tattoos.

The prosecutor turned up the heat. "One could call him a fearsome looking fellow to the average person?" he asked.

"Yes, he looks rather intimidating," the doctor admitted.

"You knew that West had at least two assaults to his credit for which he was convicted?"

"That's correct."

Charalambous agreed with Madigan that one of West's convictions had been for an assault on West's wife Tami in 1990. The other, he thought, was prior to 1970 for which West had served time in jail.

Madigan asked Charalambous to describe Sian and Katie Simmonds. Charalambous readily obliged. Sian, the doctor said, was about five-foot-eight and 135 pounds. Katie was smaller at five-foot-two and 115 pounds.

"And you've known Sian and Katie since they were quite small kids?"

"That's correct."

Madigan asked some questions about the doctor's relationship with Chris Simmonds, then changed his attack. "Now, you're a medical doctor I think, are you?"

"Yes, that's correct."

"You also read newspapers?"

"Yes."

"I presume you have some kind of training in how young people react to things?"

"Yes, that's true."

"Wouldn't you agree with me that young females are particularly affected by threats from strangers?"

"Yes, that's probably correct."

"And they've got that constant fear of assault and/or rape?"

"I don't know if it's constant," said the doctor, "but I'm sure there might be a few more in women than men."

Madigan continued: "This is well known as kind of a folklore of anybody, not to mention the medical practitioners, isn't that right?"

"What is?"

"That young girls are afraid of being assaulted by strangers and they're afraid of being attacked, is that right?"

"To a certain extent, yes."

Madigan switched to the subject of Charalambous's six-month suspension in 1989, getting the doctor to agree that he had mortgaged his house on Foster Avenue in anticipation of his lost income.

"So it was a very expensive time for you?"

"Only from the point of view that I used most of that money to gamble. If I...."

Madigan cut in: "You lost a lot of money staying off work for six months?"

"I lost—I lost money staying off work, yes."

Madigan questioned Charalambous about the course he had taken in bio-ethics at Georgetown University, then the prosecutor paused for a moment, suddenly changing his tone to one of incredulity.

"Why did you, a medical practitioner, send a creature like Brian West to see two of your young patients? Why did you do that?"

"I'm sorry?" said Charalambous, surprised or unable to hear the question.

"Why did you send him to see them," Madigan repeated.

"I sent him there because I had known him for over twenty years, and I felt comfortable talking to him about the problem I had with Sian and Katie Simmonds.... I felt that I could trust him and I sent him there basically to say a few words to them.... I picked him because he did look intimidating."

Madigan still looked incredulous. "So you're telling this court that you deliberately, not mistakenly, but deliberately sent this fellow who looked like a gorilla to two of your young female patients to intimidate them from testifying against you; is that what you said?"

The gorilla reference drew muffled laughter from the gallery. "Yes, that's correct," the witness replied.

Madigan appeared as though he could scarcely believe how readily the doctor would incriminate himself. The man really is conscienceless, the prosecutor mused.

"What did you think you were accomplishing?"

"Well, I was hoping to dissuade them."

"Through fear?"

"Yes."

"Is that part of your medical training?" Madigan asked.

"No, it isn't," Charalambous conceded.

"Are there articles on fear of patients in the *New England Journal of Medicine*?"

"Not to my knowledge."

Charalambous added he had been "very upset and anxious" about the complaints from the Simmonds sisters and believed the girls were lying about him.

"Why didn't you consult your lawyer?" asked Madigan. "You said your lawyer told you you're home free."

"Well no, I didn't say that."

"What did he tell you?"

"Basically, he told me not to contact Sian and Katie Simmonds."

Charalambous added that the Simmonds family were no longer patients; he hadn't spoken to Chris Simmonds about the complaints because his lawyer had instructed him to have no contact with the family; the complaint hadn't affected him at first and he hadn't thought the college would act on it.

"It only worried you," said Madigan, "when the college put a bullet in their gun, as it were, and decided to hold a hearing, isn't that right?"

"That's correct."

"Because you had gone through a similar hearing with Shelley?" Madigan pressed.

"That's correct."

"Which had turned out to be quite expensive for you?"

"Relatively speaking, not to me, but it was expensive, but it depends on how you look at money, I mean...."

"It cost you a buck, didn't it?" the prosecutor asked rhetorically.

"It cost me a few dollars, yes."

"It could have cost you your medical practise, couldn't it?" asked Madigan, his voice rising.

"It's possible."

"So you were aware, in other words, you had fallen at a jump already and now another jump was coming up, wasn't it?"

"That's correct."

"Yes," said Madigan. "And until the college, who aren't speedy in this matter, moved and told you that they were going to hold...a hearing you thought, 'Oh well, who cares?' Is that right?"

"I thought that if they examined the charts correctly and conducted the interviews in the proper manner, that they would find that the complaints were frivolous and baseless...."

The court recessed for lunch. After the break, Madigan asked Charalambous if it were true that he had been angry with Jacqueline Jongkind for making the first complaint against him in 1985.

"My recollections of those events are that actually my wife was much angrier than I was."

"Does that mean you were not angry or you were angry?" asked Madigan, a trace of irritation in his voice.

"Oh, I was angry too."

"That's all I'm asking you," confirmed the prosecutor. But it wasn't all. Far from it. Madigan was still chasing down his quarry. "You also said in chief that you're inclined to make intemperate remarks, is that right?"

"That's correct."

Madigan asked if it was correct that the doctor's "intemperate remark" at the time was that Shelley's mother should be killed.

"I might have said that," the doctor replied. "I don't remember." This was trademark Charalambous, the type of reply that by now had spectators shaking their heads.

Charalambous stuck to his defense that he believed that Katie, more than Sian, was the instigator of the complaint to the college.

"When I spoke to West, I asked him to speak to one of the girls," the doctor explained.

"I see," said Madigan, skeptically. "Not the girl with the red jeep?"

"I described both young women to him and both vehicles that I felt they were driving," said Charalambous, adding: "I wasn't even sure what they were driving."

"I see," said Madigan. "Katie isn't blonde, is she?"

"No, she's got kind of maybe dirty-brown, blonde or light brown hair," said the doctor.

"Schlender heard the girl with the red jeep with the long blonde hair...that's Sian isn't it?"

"That's Sian, but I didn't tell him that."

Charalambous agreed with the prosecutor that he had phoned Katie Simmonds and recorded the conversation because he felt it might be helpful to his case.

"But she told you on the tape...that she intended to go ahead.... How did you react to that?"

"I was—I was upset."

"Your wife remembers the phrase, 'Rats will be rats'. Would you have said a thing like that about them?"

"No, I didn't say that.... I believe I said something about they really believe what they're saying...they were just lying...I don't know where she got that phrase from."

"This wouldn't be one of your intemperate remarks you tend to make, you and your family?"

"No."

Charalambous agreed with Madigan that he felt his 1989 suspension had been unjustified.

"You thought that society was out to get you because of who you were?" asked Madigan.

Charalambous forced a chuckle. "I might have said that," he conceded, "but that's not true."

"And now, not too many years later...two other girls...are making allegations about you of a somewhat similar nature."

"No," said Charalambous. "I think they're completely different....With Shelley, we were living together, we had gotten married, we had a child, and the college, with her mother's urging, persisted and gave me what I felt was an unfair penalty."

"But the second one," Madigan pressed on, "you knew with that track record, that you were a good candidate if they found you guilty of this unprofessional conduct that they might strike you from the register?"

"No, that was never a consideration," said Charalambous, adding his lawyer had speculated the harshest college penalty might have been a suspension as long as one year.

"You got six (months) the last time," said Madigan.

"I know," Charalambous concurred. "But that was a completely different thing. I was cohabiting, living together, with my wife at the time...and the college perceived...that she was still my patient....That's a much more serious charge."

"You were somewhat panic stricken?" Madigan inquired.

"To a certain extent, yes," said Charalambous.

"You started needing sleeping pills...and you upped your consumption of Grand Marnier?"

"Not to the extent that my wife describes, no, absolutely not."

"And you spoke of killing the girls, didn't you?"

Madigan, like everyone else in the court, knew by now what to expect.

"I might have said that, yes," Charalambous said unflinchingly.

The accused agreed with Madigan that he'd then started to leave messages for Brian West with West's mother, but claimed his efforts to locate West were not as extensive as suggested by his wife in her testimony against him.

"Now, why were you looking for this fellow?" Madigan asked, his voice rising a notch. "...You were going to hire him to do some foul deed for yourself, were you?"

"Absolutely not," the doctor responded.

Madigan asked Charalambous why he hadn't sought the help of people other than West. "What about your brother.... He's a karate expert?"

"He is, yes.... I wasn't that close to my brother."

311

"What about your mother? Say, 'Your favorite son here is in trouble, would you phone these girls?'"

"Well, I didn't think my mother would be very intimidating."

"Ohhh!" said Madigan, acting surprised. "Intimidating. You wanted muscle, did you?"

"No. No, I wanted—I wanted to have the form of somebody like Brian West, but with no substance as to, from the point of view, of a potential injury or anything like that.... My knowledge of Brian West is completely different than the way he's been portrayed in this court-room."

"He was a lamb, was he?" asked Madigan, sarcastically.

"He was like a big teddy bear around the karate club and, when you see him around children, that's the way he is."

"You were looking for a teddy bear, were you?" Madigan pressed, his rich Irish brogue rising and straining in disbelief.

"No, I'm just saying that's part of his disposition that I've seen."

Madigan asked if there weren't any "ordinary, decent people" who could have made a phone call for Charalambous to help him with his problem. "What about all these Greeks that you gambled with?" the prosecutor asked. "You had a whole mess of them that you gambled with, didn't you?"

"I don't know about a whole mess," Charalambous corrected, "but there were several."

Madigan asked if it were true that Charalambous wanted West to visit the Simmonds' residence because he was "ugly looking."

"He looks like a biker type person," Charalambous agreed. "...He has the appearance of someone that looks a bit of a ruffian."

Madigan again came up on the doctor with a surprise line of questioning, which began with the prosecutor asking Charalambous if his wife knew West particularly well. "She didn't date him or anything like that?" asked Madigan.

"No."

"She wasn't a friend of his family?"

"No."

"To your knowledge, she didn't have a pen pal relationship with him?"

"No."

"Wasn't in daily communication with him?"

"No."

312

"How would your wife—can you help us on this—know about the killing of Charles Kirton?"

"I have no idea."

"Do you think your son...would know about that and tell his mother?" It was another rhetorical question. The doctor's son was an infant not yet in school. Perhaps Madigan threw it in thinking it as absurd as some of the answers he was getting.

"No, I don't think so," Charalambous conceded.

"How would she know about the killing of Nareg?" the prosecutor continued.

"I don't believe that man was killed from what I recollect."

"Attempted murder of Nareg," said Madigan, correcting himself.

"I have no idea."

"Where would she get this illusion that Brian West let out contracts to kill?"

"I have no idea," said Charalambous. "She didn't get it from me."

"Didn't get it from you, eh?" Madigan said sarcastically. "So you thought you were bringing in a teddy bear, did you, a wolf in sheep's clothing or a sheep in wolf's clothing, which one?"

"Well what I wanted was someone that I could trust that could go over there and say something to either Sian or Katie Simmonds and I felt that Brian West was the right person."

"Now why would Brian West go over there, just for the love of you?"

"I wasn't—I wasn't sure that he would, but I thought that he probably would."

"Just for the love of you?" Madigan smiled.

"Yes."

"I see. And what was he supposed to tell these people?"

"Words to the effect, 'Don't lie about my friend or any of my friends.'"

"My friend?" Madigan sought to clarify. "The mysterious unknown man?"

"I think they would know."

"I see," said Madigan, drawing out his response. "He was to sidle up to them somewhere and whisper in their ear, 'Don't lie about my friend' and take off like a flash?"

"No, he was going to knock on the door actually."

"Why?"

313

"Because I think that anyone that had somebody like Brian West with his form knock on their door and say something like that to them—or say anything like that—it's like saying, 'Be careful of which way you're going because you're going in the wrong direction.'"

"How would they know what direction they were going when you weren't going to identify yourself?" Madigan asked, bemusedly. "It was going to be a mystery visit...."

"No, I don't think it would be a mystery to them at all."

"They would know instinctively," asked Madigan, "that you're the type of person who would send a ruffian like West over to them to make this comment?"

Said the doctor: "I assumed that they would know that they were lying about a certain person and that certain person was me."

Charalambous said he'd had difficulty contacting West because the latter had more than one residence, but West did return his call around Christmastime 1992. The doctor explained to West the problems he was having with the Simmonds sisters and West offered to help. "He kind of said, 'Well, I could talk to them for you, what do you want me to say?'"

"How would he know who the Simmonds were?" Madigan asked. The prosecutor wanted to confirm that West alone had no motive to kill Sian.

"He didn't know who they were.... I told him."

"How did you know where they were?" asked Madigan. The question seemed designed to expose yet more medical improprieties.

"Well," the doctor jumped in, "it was in their medical charts and I spent a lot of time with Katie Simmonds in consultation and treatment and I knew that she lived in the basement suite of the little house on 160 Street."

"You'd been there lots of times, hadn't you?" Madigan continued.

"No, I hadn't. I'd driven by, but I've never been there."

"What were you doing driving around that place?" asked the prosecutor.

"I was trying to get my—get up—get my nerve up to speak to them.... I might have driven by a couple of times."

Without being asked, the accused conceded that he had included the Simmonds residences in weekend drives with his family to look at property in Cloverdale and Langley. In between looking at real estate, he explained, he was trying to find the nerve to speak to either of the girls or their father.

"Why were you looking at their cars and memorizing their license plates?" asked Madigan.

"I wasn't memorizing their license plates," Charalambous said. "They have very striking vehicles.... I saw Sian's vehicle mostly at the same residence as Katie was."

Charalambous agreed with Madigan that he and his wife had once driven into the lane behind the 160 Street house. "We drove along that lane one day on one Sunday and we had to back out."

"Why didn't you phone them up and say, 'Look girls, I better talk to you'?"

"I already did that.... I thought it would be best to talk to them on kind of a...."

"Intimidating basis?"

"No. I was thinking of talking to them myself, personally."

"...Here you are, a medical man...and you won't speak to the father.... Instead you hire some thug who is supposed to do some mysterious thing for you. Is this what you are telling this court?"

"What I'm telling this court is that Brian West was not hired to do any mysterious thing. I asked him to go over and talk to Katie and Sian Simmonds."

"...You got in touch with this thug, Brian West?"

Charalambous wasn't about to concur. "I got in touch with Brian West."

"And you chose him because he looked like a thug?"

"That's correct.... At that point, I thought that it would be better if somebody like this—that looked like a thug—said those words to the girls.... They're probably going to complain again but, if they didn't know who it was, then they wouldn't be able to complain."

"But you see," said Madigan, tilting his head and smiling, "here you are, at this time anyway, a respectable professional man...."

"Yes," Charalambous agreed.

"...And you're going to send this fellow—who is a *designer thug* as it were—to go to these young ladies to communicate something to them on your behalf?"

The prosecutor's contemporary turn of phrase, coming as it did from an older man, elicited laughter in the public gallery. Even the

315

austere Justice McKinnon on his bench appeared unable to suppress a smile at Madigan's wit.

"That's correct," said Charalambous as the laughter subsided.

"Didn't you think that was an odd thing to do?" Madigan continued.

"In retrospect, I think it was wrong, yes."

Madigan now slipped in the first of several questions to see if the accused was as conscienceless as he suspected. "At the time, didn't you know it was wrong?" the prosecutor asked.

"I rationalized and justified it," replied Charalambous, "because I was—I felt I was in the right and they were in the wrong. They were lying. I was on the right side, they were on the wrong side. If I had to do it all over again I wouldn't do that."

"And your whole career was on the line?"

"No, it wasn't," Charalambous countered, disagreeing that a college suspension would have cost him his substantial income. "I believe there are provisions now—I'm not 100 percent certain—if you are suspended for a prolonged period of time, then you can have another doctor look after the practise."

Charalambous also disagreed with a suggestion from the prosecutor that he told West what times of day the Simmonds sisters would be home. "I described the girls to him," Charalambous said, "a tall one and a short one. The tall one probably drives the red jeep, she's a good-looking girl; and the short one probably drives the black jeep, and I gave him their address."

"Was he to report back to you about the success of this venture?"

"No."

"I see," said Madigan, employing the same incredulous tone as before. "It was a shot in the dark, as it were, was it....? You're saying you dropped into this fellow's house and said, 'Oh, by the way Brian, because you're an ugly brute I want you to convey some veiled threats to two of my ex-patients who are dragging me before the college, but don't bother telling me what happens, just go ahead and do it'.... Is that what you did?"

"He (West) wouldn't know what happened," Charalambous reasoned from the witness box. "I would probably know what happened before he did...." Charalambous speculated that West's proposed visit would either have prompted the girls to drop their action against him or resulted in yet another complaint to the college.

316

On further questioning by Madigan, the accused agreed that he might have driven by Sian's house after picking up his wife and daughter from kindergarten on the day of the murder, adding he couldn't remember for sure. He agreed it was a Wednesday, his regular day off work. "We might have driven through Surrey if we were going that afternoon to look at some subdivisions or something like that."

Charalambous denied that anyone had phoned his house that night to tell him about the murder. "I heard that—I think in my own evidence I said that I found out that night or the next morning.... I think I saw the house on the eleven o'clock news."

The doctor also disputed his wife's testimony that he had rushed into the bedroom to turn on a radio broadcast describing the murder. "Actually, the radio was already on in the bedroom when she was folding clothing or doing the ironing...."

"You spent the evening flipping channels?" Madigan interjected.

"I was watching television. That came later around eleven o'clock when I saw the little house."

"...And you knew it was Katie Simmonds' house?"

"Yes, I did."

"And you knew that you had given that address to this gorilla West?"

"That's correct."

"How did you feel when you saw that and realized what you had done?"

"Well I didn't know—I didn't know what happened, but I was...."

"You had a good idea that night that something had happened to Sian Simmonds?"

"To somebody at the house. I don't know if they named the person at that time.... I can't recall."

"But I'm sure they described a young girl being dead, didn't they?" asked Madigan. "...Did that twig a little bit on your conscience that maybe, just maybe, something had gone wrong?"

"It bothered me," Charalambous conceded. "I felt very uneasy."

Madigan speculated what the doctor would have done next. "You obviously immediately phoned Brian West to find out what his activities had been, did you?"

"I didn't have a phone number for him."

"Well you immediately put your running shoes on and ran down to Hailey Street to see what his activities had been to make sure?"

"At eleven o'clock?" asked Charalambous, blinking. "...No I did not."

"Well nighttime was one of your playtimes, wasn't it?" asked a surprised-looking Madigan.

"...There were some nights that I stayed home," Charalambous said. "There would be times—sometimes three or four weeks at a time that I would stay home in the evening and then I would go, on kind of a gambling binge like some people go on a drinking binge, and I would be out every night."

Madigan hammered away about West being a hired thug.

"I didn't say that," Charalambous corrected him. "You said that."

"All right," Madigan agreed, "I'm calling him a thug."

"You're saying 'hired' and I never said that.... I asked him."

"Yes," Madigan concurred. "Ever so nicely, I'm sure.... And now, you're looking at the news and, lo and behold, a young woman has been killed at that very location.... Didn't your conscience bother you on the evening of Wednesday, January 27, 1993?"

"I didn't know what happened."

"You might not have known what happened," Madigan said, suppressing irritation. "But didn't your conscience have a little twinge that maybe—just maybe—you had something to do with this?"

"Yes, that's correct."

"So what did you do about your conscience?"

"At that point I didn't do anything."

"Well," continued Madigan, "to be perfectly frank, you didn't do anything at any point, did you?"

Charalambous agreed he did nothing because he heard someone had been arrested for Sian's murder the following day. Audience members scoffed as he came up with his next line. "...Then I thought it was just a coincidence."

Was this the best he could do? This man with years of university?

The accused disputed his wife's testimony that he had told her the morning after the murder not to do anything outside her normal routine.

The doctor also denied that he had made a deliberate point of keeping Sian's obituary. "I usually bring the newspaper home from work," he explained. "My wife was reading through it. She said, 'Look at this' and I looked at it and I said, 'Oh, they cremated her—just put it with the other newspapers.'"

Charalambous agreed he had speculated to his wife that Katie

Simmonds probably wouldn't attend the college hearing in March. "I didn't feel she was going to come because she was lying...and the second reason (was) I felt that it would probably get postponed a few months because I didn't think she had finished grieving yet, that would take months and months and months, maybe never...."

Katie Simmonds, listening to this in the public gallery, drew in an audibly deep breath and wiped tears from her eyes.

Continuing his testimony, the accused offered his explanation for having visited Brian West on February 27, one month after the murder. "Everybody heard that Schlender had been caught and charged with the death of Sian Simmonds," he began. "I breathed a sigh of relief. I thought it was probably just coincidental, but then in early February my wife noticed a vehicle following her on three or four occasions...and we traced the vehicle through a lawyer and a private detective and it sounded like the vehicle was probably a police vehicle.

"...Then we became a little more attentive.... We discovered that there were eyes everywhere. When I went jogging around the school there would be the same jeep...and there was a little minivan parked half a block from our house. We'd go into the White Spot and you felt people's eyes on you, that they should have been eating their food and paying attention to each other, but you just had this sense that people were watching you. And that built up over the month of February to the point where I decided to go and ask West if he knew anything about this.

"...In addition to that...I'm not sure when this happened, but I also heard from various lawyers...that I was being investigated."

Madigan tilted his head inquisitively. "Why were you so, let's say, sensitive about parking in front of West's house?"

"Because I was being followed...and I wanted to talk to West...to find out if he had any knowledge...and the second part I didn't want anyone to follow me...to the house and discover his hydroponic marijuana growing operation...."

Madigan tilted his head again. "This is a very peculiar way of life for a medical doctor....?"

"It was unusual, yes."

"Why didn't you go...to your brother, say, 'Harry, there's a real problem here, here's what I did, very stupid of me, but now the girl is dead and I'm afraid that something may be involving me'?"

"I wasn't even hardly talking to my brother," Charalambous replied. "We had some differences of opinion and we weren't talking that much at that point in time."

Charalambous repeated that he wanted to ask West if he knew anything. "I wanted to ask him if he was being followed and when I had visited him there on the first occasion he told me—he called that a safe house. He says, 'This house is a house that I'm setting up for a certain purpose and nobody knows about this house.' So I didn't want to be followed."

Charalambous said he thought he lost whoever was tailing him by going around corners and cutting through cul-de-sacs.

"You're talking about the police?" asked Madigan.

"Yes, the police."

"And the police act for the public?"

"Yes, they're supposed to."

"Well why didn't you come clean to somebody and just get the whole deck cleaned off? Why sneak around at night?"

"Well I was panicked and I was scared and...."

"But you had done nothing?"

"That's correct. I had done nothing."

"How could you panic when you'd done nothing?"

"Well, when you get followed like that, the extent of the surveillance was just unbelievable. I mean, they were just everywhere."

Again, Madigan asked the accused why he hadn't gone to the police to tell them his story.

"I've had bad experiences with the police in the past," said Charalambous. "...I didn't trust them."

Charalambous told Madigan that he didn't want to lead police to his friend's house because West had a lot to lose, although "we were living in different worlds of course."

"But you had an enormous amount to lose, didn't you?" Madigan hammered.

"Yes."

"Not only your practise, but your wife, isn't that right? You had a wife and three little kids....?"

"Yes, that's true."

"Did you think he (West) was going to confess to killing Sian Simmonds....?"

"Well, somebody had already been arrested for that. I just wanted to know if there was any connection, actually."

320

"Did you think he was going to admit that to you?"

"I thought he would, yes."

"He'd say, 'Oh, on your behalf I killed her.' Is that what you expected him to say?"

"I didn't know what to expect at that point."

"Here you are sneaking up alleys to get into his house," said Madigan. "...Your conscience was getting a little more activated as time went on, was it?"

"This situation bothered me, yes," said Charalambous, adding he wanted to know if West knew Schlender.

"No matter what he told you, you were going to believe him, were you...even though he was growing marijuana in the house...so you knew he was back into crookery?"

"I anticipated he would tell me the truth," said Charalambous. "...I knew he was growing marijuana in the house.... He hadn't been growing marijuana in the past. This was just a new thing."

"He was into assaults in those days?"

"I'm sorry?"

"He was assaulting people?"

"On one occasion, a domestic dispute...."

"Call it what you want," said Madigan, more than a trace of impatience in his voice. "He beat up...his wife."

"That's right.... I believe there was alcohol and drugs involved and later on, after they went through the process and dealt with it, I think they became good friends again."

The court broke for a recess. Back in the witness box, Charalambous said he felt the Simmonds sisters' complaint would have been dropped "if the college...closely analyzed the medical records, interviewed the young women...and cross referenced everything...."

"Is the college your only conscience?" asked Madigan.

"I'm not sure what you mean by that," Charalambous replied.

"Surely you as an individual—forget the college for a moment—as an individual must have wanted to solve this allegation about your personal conduct....?"

"Well I didn't think of it that way," Charalambous said.

Madigan asked the accused why he hadn't spoken to Dr. Handley, the college registrar.

Charalambous said he couldn't do that because there were formal

321

charges against him. "I don't believe you can do that...that would be worse meddling than the meddling I was doing."

Madigan questioned the accused about Schlender's evidence that he had been sent to kill Sian Simmonds on behalf of West's unidentified karate instructor. "You do fit the bill, don't you, a long-time friend who was a karate instructor....?"

"I am Brian's long-time friend who is a karate instructor," Charalambous conceded. "But I don't know where that came from."

"Does he have another friend who is a long-time karate instructor and a long-time friend of his....?"

"Not as close as me, no."

Occasionally, Charalambous appeared to be confused as the prosecutor grilled him from different directions. "So do you know," Madigan asked, "why West would take this peculiar attitude if all you told him was to drive by?"

"Which peculiar attitude is that, Mr. Madigan?"

"To go to Schlender and say, 'Burn this place down'...."

"That can't be true," Charalambous replied.

35 Totem Pole

Madigan paused. Adjusting his gown at the shoulder, he reached dramatically into the box of exhibits to pull out a plastic bag containing the murder weapon. "You know where West would get this cannon?" he asked, holding the exhibit at eye level.

Charalambous, still seated in the witness box, shifted position and adjusted his glasses. "I don't think West ever had anything like that," he offered. "To my knowledge he did not."

The courtroom had gone deathly quiet. Then Madigan's voice once more broke the silence. "Do you know why on your instructions," asked the prosecutor, "he would go to a guy like Schlender and give him this thing?"

"I don't know that," said Charalambous, "and he did not do anything like that on any of my instructions.... When I saw him, he was going to go and speak to either Sian or Katie Simmonds himself personally."

The doctor denied having told his wife, after the hitman's arrest, that he knew people who could "take care" of Schlender once he was out of protective custody. "I didn't say that," Charalambous testified.

Madigan put down the gun. "You think Shelley made that one up out of her mind?" he asked.

"I'm not sure where Shelley is at right now," said the doctor.

The witness denied having met West in Stanley Park or ever having given him any money. He also denied having told his wife that West had changed his appearance after the murder to that of a clean shaven individual with red hair.

"How would your wife know that?" asked the prosecutor.

"I don't know," Charalambous answered. "...She was very close to the police at that time as you know."

"You think the police may have told her?"

"I didn't say that. I don't want to—I don't know what they told her."

"I see. How would she know about that same fellow—West, that lamb—putting out contracts and being well paid for them....? She said you told her."

"Well, I did not tell her."

"I see," said Madigan, getting ready for a line of key questions. "How would she know this Schlender had scratched Sian's vehicle?"

"I have no idea," said Charalambous. "I didn't tell her that."

"How would she know that Sian was mad?"

"I don't know."

"She kicked him in the groin. How would she (Shelley) know that?"

"I don't know that she did," Charalambous argued.

"She fought back very hard.... He had scratch marks. How would she know that?"

"I don't think he (Schlender) described that when he was here, actually," said Charalambous.

"The police tore up all the bushes at his house looking for a weapon....? Where would she get that from?"

"I have no idea but she—she didn't get it from me."

Madigan pressed on. "But you're the only one contacting West.... She wasn't visiting West.... She wasn't watering the plants in the hydroponic garden, was she?"

"No," said Charalambous, with a trace of bitterness. "I think she was busy doing other things.... She was going out with Scott Leslie, wasn't she?"

Charalambous agreed with the prosecutor he was unhappy that Shelley had left him after their final argument.

"You, a fifth-degree black belt in karate, had beaten...a twenty-two-year-old woman....?" asked Madigan.

"Yes," Charalambous admitted, "but it was mostly slapping.... I wasn't slapping her or hitting her nearly as hard as I could." Charalambous continued: "It was frustration and anger that had built up over that last month.... There was so much tension and frustration in the house.... Physically, we were getting along really, really well, and all of a sudden it was like I was living with a different person."

The doctor was preoccupied now, offering the court some gratuitous glimpses of his sex life. "She was very cold," he said, describing his wife. "She was distant. Even when we did have relations, as it was, it's as if she wasn't even there....

"I found out that she had started her affair with Scott Leslie and all the frustration built up to the point where that event (the beating) occurred. I don't deny it...."

"You weren't a charming companion yourself?" asked Madigan.

"...I had struck her about two or three times when she first moved in with me," Charalambous admitted, "but I never beat her like she is making out thirty or forty times or anything like that...."

Madigan fired still more questions at Charalambous about his meeting with West after he was followed by the police to the house on Hailey Street exactly one month after the murder. "So what did West tell you?" the prosecutor asked.

"...He told me that he did know David Schlender," Charalambous admitted.

"That must have shocked you."

"...It shocked me to a certain extent, yes."

"To a certain extent?" Madigan asked whimsically. "I mean, you weren't totally shocked."

"Well, I was shocked more by the next part."

"Ohhh," said Madigan. "Keep going."

"He told me he decided not to go over to Katie and Sian Simmonds' residence...and he asked David Schlender to do it...."

Sarcastically, Madigan returned to his previous theme about a mystery visit, wanting to know if Schlender was supposed to have gone to the house on 160 Street and said: "Well, I am Mystery Man, and do not lie about my friend, thank you and goodbye."

In as many words, Charalambous agreed.

"Isn't that ludicrous?" Madigan smiled.

"Why?" asked Charalambous. He was being challenged about the core of his defense. "I don't think it's ludicrous."

If it weren't ludicrous, Madigan explained, how were the Simmonds' sisters supposed to have known that the "friend" referred to by the mystery visitor was actually their family doctor.

"I felt that they would know," said the accused. "I didn't think they were lying about everybody in Surrey and Langley."

The accused said West confirmed that he had seen Schlender on the night of the murder. "Schlender had told him (West) that he went over there and to scare Sian's...." (The doctor realized he had made a slip and corrected himself, too late) "...well, to scare one of the girls and, when Sian saw the gun, she went at him, she panicked...he lost it and beat her."

Charalambous said he had suggested at the time that West should see a lawyer. "...Then we started talking about other things."

"What?" Madigan asked.

"Well, he was very excited about his hydroponic stuff...."

"You mean, after all this, you talked about *drugs*?" Madigan asked, his voice rising. "Are you telling this court that, after hearing that this bearded wonder had caused the death of one of your patients...."

"He changed the subject," Charalambous interjected. "...I hadn't recovered from the shock yet."

"Why didn't you go out from the pollution that was inside that room?" asked Madigan. After learning that West had hired a killer, said the prosecutor, the accused should have walked out.

"He never told me he had hired anybody," the doctor said. "Those are not my words, those are your words."

"All right," Madigan concurred, testily. "How did he get Schlender? Find him in a bag somewhere?"

"Schlender apparently owed him a favor and...lived in Surrey and West did not want anyone to find out where he lived...and find out about his hydroponic operations."

"No matter what direction you look at it, doctor," reasoned Madigan, "West got Schlender to go over and Schlender killed her."

"West asked Schlender to go over and speak to her," Charalambous countered.

Madigan again asked Charalambous why he hadn't done anything after hearing West's explanation.

"Brian told me...'What are *you* worried about? I'm not worried.' He says, 'I didn't do anything wrong and you certainly didn't do anything wrong.'"

"And you discussed hydroponic growing of marijuana.... New subject entirely...and the old one was forgotten?" said Madigan, waving some papers in his hand.

Charalambous again explained he hadn't come forward because he didn't think West had done anything wrong and he knew Schlender was in custody.

"Where is your civic duty if you don't have a conscience?" asked Madigan, sounding exasperated. "Where are any of these things that everyone should have?"

"I'm not sure what you're getting at," Charalambous said, meekly.

"Didn't it strike you, you had a little bit of a duty to notify somebody?" asked Madigan.

Charalambous said he was scared. "I don't understand what civic duty had to do with it.... The man had already been caught."

Madigan asked the doctor about the fact he'd renewed his passport approximately two months after the murder. "Why were you talking to your wife about Cyprus and an extradition treaty?"

"I never spoke to her with regard to that," Charalambous replied. "...No, not at all. I don't know where that came from either."

It was approximately 4:00 P.M. and, on that line of questioning, the court adjourned until the next morning.

The lawyers still had to give their final summations to the judge but Friday, November 4, 1994, was the tenth and last day of testimony. For the family, it had been a gruelling two weeks.

Charalambous was recalled to the witness stand. He was reminded that he was still under oath. Could Madigan shake him? A couple of times the previous day, Charalambous had looked uncomfortable. He had stroked his chin and nervously adjusted his glasses, as the prosecutor questioned him about the matter of the doctor's conscience and the theme of the supposed mystery visitor.

Charalambous agreed with opening questions that he already felt he was under investigation for Sian's murder when he went to West's house on February 27. By then, he repeated, he knew he was the object of extensive police surveillance.

"I mean, I felt that there were people following me everywhere," he explained. "Wherever I went, there would be somebody sitting beside me looking at me. When I went to the casino, there would be people there that were never at the casino before, sitting there playing roulette, and you knew that person just didn't fit into that particular picture. And so...."

"You sure it wasn't your guilty conscience," Madigan interrupted.

"No," said Charalambous.

Like a pit bull clenching his teeth, Madigan wouldn't let go, asking Charalambous why he felt he was a suspect in the death of Sian Simmonds. "So why would you on this particular day feel that the police were investigating you for her murder?"

"I felt uneasy that they were—they seemed to be wherever—and there was a patient of mine that was killed.... She did have a complaint against me, so I put two and two together and...."

"You got five, did you?" Madigan interjected. ".... You see, I keep telling you, at this time you are what appears to be a respectable medical practitioner in Surrey, not a denizen of the underworld.... If you had these suspicions...why didn't you go and air them out....?"

"Well, there's two reasons for that," Charalambous explained. "I don't trust the police that much, actually not at all...."

Madigan again looked incredulous. "You mean, as a respectable citizen, you don't trust the police?"

"No, I don't. And the second reason is...I was being followed everywhere and I wanted to find out more about what was going on."

"Why," asked Madigan, "didn't you go to the Ombudsman if you hated everybody else?"

"I...."

"Well?"

"Well, the way that I felt at that time was that I was being followed by the police. I felt very uncomfortable, very panicky, very scared."

"You had a lawyer, didn't you?" asked Madigan. "Why didn't you go to him and say there are these shadows following me?

"...I didn't feel that was the right course at that time."

"Because you had a guilty conscience, didn't you?" suggested Madigan, like an angler playing a fish at the end of his line.

"No, I didn't have a guilty conscience really. It's just really that I felt uncomfortable and uneasy."

The prosecutor asked Charalambous about his earlier statement that he had gone to West's house because he wanted to know if his friend was being followed too. "I mean, West did nothing, did he?" asked Madigan. "...So why would the shadows be after West?"

"Well," said Charalambous, starting his confused reply, "I didn't know. I was just—what I was doing is just kind of looking at all the—I was kind of guessing.... I wanted to know if he had any connection to David Schlender."

"Why would he?" asked Madigan.

"Well, I didn't think he did, but I was being—the amount of pressure that was exerted on me was over and above and beyond what you would expect for anything."

"Were you a friend of Schlender's?"

"No, I didn't know Schlender."

"What were you going to do by the way...if Sian Simmonds phoned the RCMP and said a *totem pole* has arrived at the door making this mysterious statement and I'm very frightened by this fellow? What would you have done?"

"If she had done that?"

"Yes."

"I have no idea."

Madigan continued to ridicule the cornerstone of the doctor's defense. "So you think they had this mysterious telepathy.... They were supposed to be able to read through this wooden statement and read Dr. Joe, is that the idea....? By some miracle the girls would say, 'That's Dr. Joe who is afraid to actually see us himself, he is warning us not to lie about him.'"

"I think that they would know," Charalambous persisted. At that time, he offered, he had only recently phoned Katie Simmonds to discuss the matter. "...What I was trying to do is, actually, just kind of shift their focus a little bit...and just maybe (they would) make a phone call (to the college) and say, 'Look, we don't want to proceed with this.' That's it."

Madigan asked the accused why he had driven numerous times by the Simmonds' residences if he were so sure that their complaint was unfounded. "For a winner, you are certainly behaving in a very indecisive and uncertain fashion, aren't you?"

"It may appear that way, yes."

"The reality is, doctor," said Madigan, closing in, "that with your very significant income and your very good practise—you had an awful lot to lose, didn't you?"

"No," said Charalambous. "I never looked at it from that point of view...."

Madigan suggested a college suspension concerned the doctor because it would leave him without money for his gambling addiction.

Charalambous admitted he no longer had any property to mortgage as he'd had when the college originally suspended him, but he did have some savings. "I had access to about $90,000 at any time," he said.

"Oh, how long would that last you?" asked Madigan. "A week?"

Charalambous ignored Madigan's sarcasm. "And we had the accounts receivable," the doctor continued. "You can just stop as well."

"Oh, you could stop gambling?"

"You could, yes."

"Had you ever stopped gambling before."

"I have, yes." Still calculating the odds, however, Charalambous thought there was only about a 25 percent chance that the complaint of Sian Simmonds would endanger what Madigan described as his "very lucrative" practise.

Charalambous admitted that the police surveillance caused him to worry that "My God, they think I'm involved in something." West, however, had told him he didn't feel people were following him.

"Why would you trust West...after that?" asked Madigan.

"I'm not—I'm not sure I follow your logic," said Charalambous. He had still felt uneasy, he testified, despite West's assurances.

"You didn't feel anything about Sian Simmonds, did you?" asked Madigan.

"No, that's not true," Charalambous replied.

"You just worried about your own practise, isn't that right?"

"No, that's—that's not true.... I thought it would have been better for them not to go through with the complaint because they were...doing something that was on the wrong side."

"What did you do..." asked Madigan, "to solve her killing?"

"Solve it? It was my impression they had a suspect already.... I didn't do anything."

"That's right," agreed Madigan. "Your only interest was protecting your big fat practise."

Charalambous admitted that he had expressed relief in a phone call to Gail Pikker after Katie Simmonds failed to show up for her college hearing. "She (Gail Pikker) was a friend of the family," he said. "She was very close to me and very close to my wife."

Madigan was almost finished with his cross-examination, but again he asked Charalambous why he hadn't come forward with the details that West had allegedly given him about the murder.

"The knowledge I had was that Brian West had asked David

330

Schlender to go over, knock on the door and speak to one of the girls," Charalambous said.

"And David Schlender was alleged to have killed her?"

"Yes, that's true."

"And you say that isn't any knowledge whatsoever that should be communicated to anybody?"

"No," said Charalambous. "I said that was not direct knowledge. I didn't have any direct knowledge."

"I see," said Madigan. "You don't have a law degree as well as a medical degree do you?"

"No, I don't," said Charalambous. "...I thought they (the police) were trying to implicate me, I felt I was under a microscope."

"You asked a fellow named West...you knew he had a record...and then you learned that he in turn had actually communicated with the man who was the killer of Sian Simmonds...and you never communicated that to anybody?"

"No, I did not."

"And you say you cared about the death of Sian Simmonds, did you?" asked Madigan.

"Yes, I did."

"Thank you," said Madigan abruptly. The prosecutor had finished his cross-examination. It was 10:53 A.M. As the court recessed for the morning break, some of the spectators were shaking their heads.

The defense called only one witness.

Chris Hinkson, the heavyset lawyer with the mustache, unflinchingly confirmed that he was hired by Charalambous in April 1992 when the College of Physicians and Surgeons asked the doctor to hand over medical files pertaining to the complaints of Sian and Katie Simmonds.

The doctor had signed a release so that the witness could testify to matters that otherwise would have been subject to lawyer/client confidentiality.

Hinkson recalled that Charalambous, in light of his prior history with the college, had not been naive about the possible outcome of a hearing. But the lawyer remembered having given the doctor his opinion that there was a 50 percent chance that the complaints would be dismissed. He had advised Charalambous, he recalled, that a suspension of six months to one year was probably the worst case scenario.

Hinkson also testified it had been "quite clear" to him that Katie

331

Simmonds, rather than Sian, had instigated the complaints and that Katie had seemed the more interested of the two sisters in pursuing the matter.

The evidence portion of the trial was over, but the prosecution and the defense needed time to draft their final arguments. Because of other commitments involving the lawyers and the judge, the trial would have to be adjourned for another eighteen days, until November 22.

"We're used to waiting," Chris Simmonds told reporters on the courthouse steps. "We've been waiting for twenty-two months but the next two weeks are going to be a tough time."

Before heading home, Katie Simmonds and her father expressed anger that the defense had tried to pit one sister against the other. "Sian was the one who brought up the complaints as soon as they happened," said her father. "Katie had already stopped seeing him (Charalambous) and I am the one that phoned the college, not the girls."

Chris Simmonds said he felt betrayed by the system. The college, he said, should have acted on the complaints much more quickly than it did. "We had no idea we were going to have to go through that for eighteen months."

The final arguments took place on November 22 as scheduled.

Richard Peck led off for the defense, filing binders full of case law, but verbally offering only a brief summary of the issues. The presentation seemed subdued and hurried, as though Peck couldn't wait to get it over with. Could he perhaps have been embarrassed by weaknesses in the case?

There was no argument, he said, about the fact that it was David Schlender who had killed Sian Simmonds, or theoretically that his client could be convicted of first-degree murder while the hitman had been convicted of murder in the second degree.

The question, argued Peck, boiled down to whether or not his client had participated in a planned and deliberate murder. If Charalambous had only wanted the victim to be threatened as he'd testified, the accused would have to be acquitted on both charges or at worst found guilty of manslaughter.

Peck argued that the case came down to the evidence of David Schlender and Shelley Charalambous, and he asked the judge to be "cautious" in accepting the testimony of either.

"The evidence of Schlender is tenuous in the extreme," said Peck. The hitman had consistently told the police that he had been sent only to threaten Sian Simmonds. Shelley Charalambous, the lawyer added, was prone to exaggeration and it was obvious from her testimony that she "bears the accused animosity."

The evidence, Peck concluded, was just as consistent with a plan to utter a threat as it was with a plot to cause death. Peck sat down, leaving it to Peter Wilson to review the two weeks of testimony.

Wilson spoke in the same ponderous tones as before. The defense, he said, was not disputing that the accused had been upset by the complaints to the college—or even that he had threatened, in front of his wife, to kill the Simmonds' sisters. "That he sent West to their residence is not an issue," added Wilson. "What he asked West to do is the nub of the case."

It was inconsistent with a murder plot, said Wilson, that Schlender had made no attempt to disguise his appearance at the scene. Schlender's first statements to the police had been favorable to his client but a "disturbing pattern" had emerged as the police questioning had continued.

The hitman, said Wilson, had appeared to panic when the police raised doubt that members of his family were in need of protection. It was only after prompting by the police, the lawyer suggested, that Schlender changed his story to say that he had been sent to kill Sian from the start. Schlender, the lawyer said, was obviously biased against the doctor as evidenced by his parting comment when he left the witness stand.

Wilson also sought to discredit the testimony of his client's wife. "She frequently took the opportunity of offering up gratuitous comments damning to Dr. Charalambous," said the lawyer. "Much of her evidence is a strained attempt to portray her husband as a monster."

The lawyer said it had been like "pulling teeth" to get Shelley to admit the extent of her relationship with Scott Leslie. "I suggest that Scott Leslie had a much bigger part in this affair than we would care to admit."

The fact that Charalambous had paid off her credit card even after she'd left him, the lawyer added, indicated that his client bore no animosity to his wife. Conversely, after his arrest, Shelley had allowed her husband's medical practise to disintegrate, purporting it had no

333

value even though eventually it had been purchased by another doctor for $60,000.

The prosecution was now ready with its summation. Sean Madigan asked the judge to look at all of the evidence, not just that of Schlender or the doctor's wife.

Charalambous masterminded the murder, said Madigan, because he thought it might save him from losing his substantial income. Of the three conspirators, the prosecutor added, the doctor alone had the motive to kill Sian Simmonds

"He needed that income," said Madigan. "He was addicted to gambling. Money flowed through his hands like water."

The doctor wasn't concerned at first, said Madigan, because the college had been moving "at a snail's pace." His view changed, however, when he was notified "like an echo from the past" that a hearing would take place. It was then that the doctor realized he would be ruined financially. He began plotting to "eliminate the prospect of any hearing" and started looking for his old friend Brian West. "The accused would want you to believe that actually, despite his ugly appearance, he's a very nice fellow."

Madigan ridiculed defense suggestions that Schlender had only gone to Sian's suite to threaten her. "Why would somebody carry a gun with a silencer?" he asked. "For fun? To look important? Or to kill?

"Why would West arm him? Why would West give him $3,500 to $5,000 just to scare a couple of girls?" Madigan described Schlender as a "confused and dangerous" man. "He's fine where he is now," said the prosecutor.

The lawyer referred to the evidence that West had been asked merely to warn the sisters not to testify against his friend. "There was going to be magic in the air," Madigan smiled. "They would know it was Dr. Joe. This is a professional man who even in his own words shows the mentality of a mercenary—a man without a conscience."

The prosecutor asked how it was that Shelley Charalambous could have known so many details about the murder and of Schlender's involvement in other crimes if she had not learned about them from her husband. "She must be related to William Shakespeare to get all this out," said Madigan. "She is a mystery writer."

The prosecutor referred to evidence that Charalambous had domineered his wife all through the marriage. "It would be safe to assume that nothing went on in that household without his approval," said

Madigan. "This woman with three kids with asthma was treated like a dog, or worse than a dog in that house. She left with a bag of pills for her kids and that's all. She had been soundly beaten and threatened with being shot."

It would be no wonder if Shelley were biased against her husband, said the prosecutor.

Madigan reviewed how Charalambous had "tiptoed through the tulips" to meet West one month after the murder. "What was his reaction when West told him that he knew Schlender? He advised West to see a lawyer...a professional man, his patient is dead, and that's his reaction?

"This is the same man who said, 'They were trying to kill me. That's what they deserved.'"

36   Judgment

These things do you swear. Let each person bow the head in sign
of acquiescence. And now, if you be true to this, your Oath, may
prosperity and good repute be ever yours, the opposite if you
shall prove yourselves forsworn.

It was the day everyone had been waiting for. Judgment day, Tuesday,
November 29, 1994, twenty-two months since Sian Simmonds' mur-
der, and the rain came down in sheets as spectators arrived early at the
New Westminster courthouse.

The lawyers had done their jobs and now all that remained was for
Justice McKinnon to render his verdict at 2:00 P.M.

Lining up before noon to be sure of their seats, many of the spectators trembled in anticipation as they pondered the outcome. Other than
trial participants and court officials, only family, reporters, and police
were assured of getting in. Apart from journalists representing the
media in Canada, the U.S. and Britain, there was a large contingent of
police officers that again included Corporal Gary Straughan and Staff
Sergeant Bob Briske.

But today it seemed—more than at any other time during the trial—
it was the emotions of three mothers that came most sharply into focus.

Susan Simmonds arrived with members of her family, hurrying to escape the inclement weather. "Good job you didn't forget your umbrella," someone said.

"It's Sian's," the victim's mother smiled, sadly, holding her daughter's umbrella as though it might protect her today against more than just the rain.

Praying for the opposite result, a solemn looking Betty Charalambous kept to herself near the front of the line. Would her son walk out of the courtroom with her, a free man?

And Jacqueline Jongkind prayed for a verdict that might trigger the long hoped for process of reconciliation with her daughter, with whom she hadn't really sat down for almost ten years.

The court convened on time. Charalambous, wearing a dark blue suit, was escorted to the prisoner's box, surrounded by five sheriffs, two of them armed, and one with bulging biceps. No one, it seemed, was taking any chances. A hush fell over the courtroom as Justice McKinnon took his place on the bench.

McKinnon began by defining the charges. Under the Criminal Code, he said, a person would be guilty of first degree murder if he carried out a planned and deliberate killing, or aided or abetted another person to do so. Guilt on the conspiracy charge would require a finding that Charalambous entered into an unlawful agreement with Brian West to cause Sian Simmonds' death.

The judge at the outset discounted the defense position that Charalambous had merely asked West to talk to the Simmonds sisters. "It seems to me beyond contention," said McKinnon, "that the accused is at least a party and co-conspirator to the unlawful act of threatening or intimidating."

There was no doubt, the judge added, that the accused started the chain of events that led to Sian Simmonds murder in her basement suite by David Schlender some time between 11:00 A.M. and 12 noon on January 27, 1993. The question was whether Schlender was sent there to threaten or to kill her.

"The problem with Schlender's evidence is that he is an unsavory person whose evidence must be treated with great caution," McKinnon continued. "...He admitted to so many lies it is difficult to know when he might be telling the truth.

"...Intelligence does not appear to be Schlender's long suit," said McKinnon, adding he would accept his testimony only where it was supported by other evidence. He noted the hitman finally incriminated

West only after police offered Schlender a "deal" for the protection of his family.

Spectators were still unsure which way the verdict would go.

"This case really comes down to the evidence of Shelley Charalambous," said the judge. "If there is support for Schlender it comes primarily from her.

"The determination as to whether there is a conspiracy, and whether the accused is a member of it, similarly depends on her testimony.

"The Special O evidence and all the other evidence presented by the Crown has little independent significance if Shelley Charalambous' evidence is not accepted....

"Conversely, if her evidence is accepted, then the other evidence takes on significant importance."

The judge kept the spectators guessing. The defense, he said, had rightfully pointed to what it considered inconsistencies in Shelley's testimony, and to examples of "extreme bias" and "exaggeration."

Only now was the judge about to make clear which way he was leaning. "There were examples of bias and exaggeration," he said. "The bias strikes me as a natural reaction to years of abuse admitted by the accused.

"...Shelley Charalambous commenced her association with the accused at age fifteen and it was he who molded her to his image of life.

"He conceded in his evidence what I characterize as a very strange view of life for someone of his stature in the community. He openly admitted distrust of police, he seemingly rejected the value of family, and he placed the acquisition of money above all else.

"He did not dispute her description of him as obsessive, compulsive and paranoid—at least about certain things. Although they had three children, he seems not to have spent much time with them, preferring to spend his free time, and the substantial income he earned, on gambling. He also admitted to physical assaults upon his wife, quibbling only about the extent of it."

McKinnon said he was mindful that the accused was not on trial for being a poor father or a poor role model, but it was understandable that his wife was biased and prone to exaggeration because of the way he had treated her. "Her characterization of him as a person capable of killing her and that he was someone she lived in fear of is not entirely without foundation.... I do not accept the defense characterization of her

338

as someone who is so biased and angry that she would deceive the court merely to obtain revenge upon the accused and/or obtain independence and financial gain."

McKinnon referred to defense suggestions that Katie Simmonds, rather than her sister, had been the instigator of the college complaint. "According to Shelley Charalambous," he noted, "the accused considered Sian Simmonds the instigator, which does not square with the evidence of the accused or his lawyer, Mr. Hinkson....The fact remains that Schlender was directed to Sian Simmonds and he went to some lengths to identify her. I accept that evidence which suggests to me that, whatever Mr. Hinkson might have concluded, the accused focused upon Sian Simmonds."

McKinnon discounted defense arguments that Charalambous hadn't viewed the college complaints as a dire threat to his continued practise. "It is apparent to me," said the judge, "that any thinking person in the accused's position would not engage in misconduct directed to thwarting the hearing.

"...Thus, on the accused's own view of events, he was engaged in unlawful conduct, which demonstrates...that he was deeply offended by the charges and desperate to ensure they did not proceed."

McKinnon returned to defense arguments that Schlender's actions had been more consistent with threatening than killing because he had shown his face at the murder scene. "That may have been due to alcohol and/or cocaine consumption or because he simply wasn't very intelligent," said the judge. "Whatever the reason for his casual approach, the facts remain that he was wearing gloves, he was armed with a loaded handgun equipped with a silencer and...none of that is consistent with uttering a veiled threat...."

The judge found that Charalambous, shortly before his arrest, had conducted himself in a manner suggesting imminent flight from the country. McKinnon rejected his claim that he had only been planning a holiday in Cyprus.

The judge also discounted the doctor's evidence that he had been planning to renovate his office about the time he was arrested. "He may well have been planning an office expansion at one time," said the judge, "but by May 1993, office expansion had to be the furthest thing from his mind."

McKinnon referred to the doctor's own performance on the witness stand. "His evidence was vague, inconsistent with the accepted evidence and tailored to suit his position. He often had no answer to questions posed to him on cross-examination, and when he did answer I found his many explanations incapable of belief."

McKinnon was ready to deliver his verdict.

"The activities of the accused both before and after the murder," said the judge, "the evidence of Shelley Charalambous concerning admissions made to her, the evidence of David Schlender, the evidence of Brian McCann, admit of no other conclusion than one of involvement in a scheme to kill. I am satisfied the Crown has proved beyond a reasonable doubt that the accused Josephakis Charalambous was both a party to first-degree murder and a member of a conspiracy to commit murder.

"I find the accused guilty on both Counts 1 and 2."

Charalambous still had to be sentenced but the friends and family of Sian Simmonds were unable to contain their relief. Everyone, except those sad few in the Charalambous camp, let out a huge sigh and the courtroom burst into applause.

Sitting behind the bullet proof glass with his back to the public gallery, Charalambous showed no emotion, but the normally mild mannered judge was angered by the outburst. "I do not want to hear any more of that," Justice McKinnon glowered at the spectators. "Everybody will have to leave this courtroom."

McKinnon continued his bluster, perhaps concerned things might get out of control when he passed sentence. "There will be no interference or disturbance in this courtroom," he said, calming down. "Do I make myself clear? All right. The accused will stand please."

Charalambous rose to his feet.

"Josephakis Charalambous," said the judge, "having been found guilty of first-degree murder, I sentence you to life imprisonment without eligibility for parole until you have served twenty-five years of your sentence."

Then the judge gave Charalambous a concurrent life sentence on the charge of murder conspiracy. The courtroom was hushed, the air once more thick with tension. McKinnon looked over toward the defense table. "Are there any submissions?" he asked.

"No submissions, My Lord," replied a subdued Richard Peck.

Before Charalambous could get through the door to the cells, Brian Simmonds, the uncle who had cleaned up his niece's blood the day after the murder, called out a parting insult.

Sian's uncle was seizing on the fact that American serial killer Jeffrey Dahmer had been murdered in prison with a sharpened broom handle only the day before. "Has anybody got a broomstick?" he shouted.

Charalambous may or may not have heard the remark. He looked dumbfounded. His lawyer had always got him out of trouble up until now. *This couldn't be happening.* "Get Peck!" Charalambous called out, asking to see his lawyer as he was led from the courtroom. Meanwhile, the doctor's mother, who had hoped to walk out of the courtroom arm-in-arm with her vindicated son, hurried away in the opposite direction without saying a word.

After it was all over, just what would Hippocrates, the father of modern medicine, have thought over two thousand years after his death of his fellow Greek physician? Many of the patients who had come to see Dr. Josephakis Charalambous for advice, some distraught and suicidal, concluded he had seen their vulnerabilities as an opportunity to exploit them. And the College of Physicians and Surgeons tragically had allowed him to stay in practise despite clear warnings that he had abused the trust that should never have been placed in him.

At one point during the trial, Charalambous had said: "I don't know where Shelley is at right now." Was he still trying his patient-is-catatonic routine? Sian Simmonds finally had stopped him, but still he maintained he had only wanted to warn her, not kill her. In the mind of the doctor, it was all such a miscarriage of justice. The verdict, however, said otherwise.

Chris, Susan and Katie Simmonds, and the others filed to the hallway outside, embracing friends and relatives. Off to the side from the TV cameras and crowd of reporters, Rick and Jacqueline Jongkind held hands as they shared a look signifying broad emotion and ecstasy. Their terrible ordeal, at long, long last, was over. Through it all, Rick Jongkind had stood by his wife.

Outside, demonstrators picketed the courthouse building with placards that said: "College of Physicians and Surgeons Fails to Protect the Public. They Protect their Own."

With tears in his eyes, Corporal Gary Straughan accepted hugs from members of the Simmonds family. It had been the most emotionally draining case he'd ever worked on. Now that it was over, reporters asked Straughan for his opinion about the role that had been played by medical authorities. "I'm not speaking for the RCMP but personally I

341

felt that the College of Physicians and Surgeons took an exorbitant amount of time to investigate the complaints," he said. The comment produced a later protest from the college but the policeman remained unapologetic. He had merely been expressing a personal opinion.

Straughan left the courthouse, joining members of the family for a well-earned celebratory drink at the Guildford Sheraton Hotel. During the seven-month investigation, he had assembled information that had taken up one complete filing cabinet drawer. Except to sleep, he had found himself rarely if ever home. "Our whole family pattern was thrown completely out of sync," he recalled. "I got up before they did and got home after they had gone to bed." Luckily for Straughan, his family gave him their support and understanding. Now that it was over, he would be able to resume the swimming, ice skating, and fishing trips that he and his nine-year-old daughter had come to cherish. He might also find time once again for skiing and the occasional game of golf.

At least two of the other police officers who had worked on the case with Straughan moved away from Surrey detachment. Deanna Kohlsmith was transferred to the criminal investigations unit at RCMP headquarters in Vancouver; and Don Rinn was promoted to staff sergeant and moved downtown. Constable Adam, whose house was almost burned down, was promoted to the rank of sergeant. But none of those who worked on the case would ever forget it.

It was almost two years since the murder but David Sella was still single, giving a simple if doubtful explanation as to why he didn't yet have a new girlfriend. "I don't have the time," he said.

And the others tried to pick up the pieces too. Barbara had not been surprised the day her father had phoned her in Los Angeles to tell her that Charalambous had been charged with murder, and she continued to live in California, never able to put the case completely out of her mind. Angela Street gave up her counseling, but continued to work as a dispatcher in the same RCMP detachment as her policeman husband; Edna Neighbour continued to work for another doctor as a medical receptionist, still as straightforward and sincere as ever.

Pat van Benten, Sian's aunt, had seen the red jeep on TV the day of the murder and had hoped in vain it had all been some kind of mistake. Now, often when she saw a tall, blonde girl in a shopping center she hoped the person would turn around and somehow it would be Sian.

Chris and Sue Simmonds, who had held each other through that first dreadful night, continued with Katie to try to pick up the pieces of their shattered family. Kate Davis, Sian's grandmother, was present at the victory celebration, now recovered after her bout in the courtroom. Irene Simmonds, the other grandmother for whom Sian had always had a special place, continued to live nearby.

Chuck and Dona Cadman congratulated Sian's parents on the verdict. Their son's killer had been sentenced to life in prison, but as a juvenile, even though he had been raised to adult court, he'd have to be declared eligible for parole some time between five and ten years.

Shelley Charalambous and her children remained in hiding, while her mother and sister began the difficult process of reestablishing the contact that had been lost between them for almost ten long years. Shawna, meanwhile, was beginning to feel "like a brand new person" and both she and her mother longed for their first real meeting with Shelley now that the trial was finally over.

Daryl Beere continued to work at the College of Physicians and Surgeons and the provincial government did enact requirements for him to be backed up by a special deputy registrar, responsible for sexual misconduct matters, as had been recommended by the college's own *Crossing the Boundaries* report. The government also required the college to create a sexual misconduct review committee, and enacted several new safeguards, including one requiring all college members to report suspected sexual misconduct by another physician.

At last, just before Christmas, the college acted to strike Charalambous from practise. The news was disseminated in a press release from college registrar Dr. Tom Handley. Without fanfare, the release stated: "On December 16, 1994, the council of the College of Physicians and Surgeons of B.C., acting pursuant to Section 47 of the Medical Practitioners Act, erased the name of Dr. Joseph Charalambous from the British Columbia Medical Register following his conviction of indictable offenses, namely murder and conspiracy to commit murder."

Denying that time investigating the complaint had been a factor, Handley said the reasons behind the murder were unprecedented anywhere in the world. He attributed the killing solely to the deranged mind of the accused.

It had been a sensational case, but the murders continued. In January, 1995 a pretty young woman named Melanie Carpenter disappeared from her workplace just a mile from Sian's house, and Fernand Auger, a paroled sex offender suspected of abducting her, was found dead in an abandoned garage in the neighboring province of Alberta. Though his suicide note made no mention of the victim, police announced two weeks later—on the second anniversary of Sian's death—that Melanie's stabbed body had been found by fishermen in the rugged Fraser Canyon.

The murder of Melanie Carpenter brought new public demands to keep violent offenders behind bars, and Melanie's father, Steve Carpenter—as Chris Simmonds and Chuck Cadman before him—became yet another voice for change.

Chris and Sue Simmonds continued their work for justice reform, attending a national conference in Hamilton, Ontario that came up with almost 150 specific recommendations dealing with crime prevention and criminal justice. The conference report was sent to federal and provincial officials across Canada and to the prime minister. "All of us shared a common commitment to see practical, workable improvements to our laws and policies towards a safer Canada," said Sian's father.

Members of the family continued to reach out but sometimes—on special occasions—they would take a white rose to the gravesite of their beloved daughter. Although Sian had been cremated, her ashes had been interred at the cemetery alongside the remains of the aunt she'd never known. There, both young women are remembered by a simple but sadly touching inscription:

Sian Davis: January 28, 1957 - March 26, 1973.
Sian Simmonds: January 28, 1973 - January 27, 1993.
All too loved to ever be forgotten. Together for ever.

37   The Light of Dawn

Shelley Charalambous had thought that a guilty verdict would leave her feeling ecstatic. When she received the news from a police-woman who visited with a bottle of champagne, however, the wine bubbled but all else seemed flat and anticlimactic.

Although the policewoman congratulated her on her performance as a witness, Shelley found that the verdict didn't change things as much as she had expected. The ten lost years could never be replaced and there always would be lasting scars from the damage in her family.

Above all, it didn't bring back Sian Simmonds.

Still, she was glad that it was over. It was something that had to be done. It was time now to build a future. And she had the children to keep her going.

Charges that Charalambous had sexually exploited a patient's daughter in exchange for prescription drugs were eventually stayed. Officially, it was stated that the young, teenage witness had lost her willingness to testify, but there was also the fact that prosecutors had already obtained a life sentence and that any additional time for a conviction would probably end up being served concurrently.

There were, however, still two more trials scheduled to take place in 1995 as *Fatal Prescription* went to press.

Brian Gerald West's trial for first-degree murder was scheduled to begin on October 11, while Charalambous was scheduled to be back in New Westminster on October 16 to face the charges of sexual assault involving three of his patients. Although the sex-for-drugs charges had been dropped, one of the patients still apparently was insisting that her case be heard.

Charalambous has appealed his murder/conspiracy conviction on various points of law. Currently, he is serving his life sentence in a federal penitentiary.

Shelley Charalambous has told her children the truth, and they are coping with the loss of their father with varying degrees of difficulty. His letters from prison to Shelley and the children, meanwhile, offer a window into his state of mind since his arrest and conviction. Presumably, they might afford psychologists a field day but, other than one brief explanation, the author will allow the letters to speak for themselves. The punctuations and style are those of "J. Charalambous M.D." The children's names have been changed to protect their privacy.

Oct. 3/93

Dearest Shelley Elizabeth Charalambous,

How are you doing? How are our children? The things I said to you that night were more than cruel and "if I could turn back time" I would. More than anything I want you and the children to be happy and well cared for; no matter how you might feel about me. The house was empty; so empty without you. I never thought that you would actually leave. I went to great lengths to find you and our kittens, to try to make up to you but you were unnecessarily "dwelling in dark imagenings (sic)." Did you think that I didn't want you anymore? Things happen sometimes and people do things sometimes that cannot be easily understood or explained, so they rationalize. You are not sixteen anymore, you are twenty-three and you must be much wiser now.

Anyway, I have to tell you that I never forgot that you gave up your brothers for me; I thought about it often and it troubled me. I want to see *our* children. I want to see our children. You know how I have *always* felt about you so why should I reiterate; "if I could reach the stars I would give them all to you." Shelley, I want to see our children...please. I shouldn't have to beg for that. Babe, you know that if it were up to them that all three children would *run* to see their father.

Let them. I'm asking you. You are not sixteen anymore. It's

346

important. Shelley, don't wait, don't let me down. You can't just bury your head in the sand.

I was thinking about your leg cramps the other day and it occurred to me that they are not caused by a lack of calcium but rather a transient decrease in serum sodium. The remedy would be for you to use a little more added salt in your diet. Have you ever known anyone that has suffered from post traumatic stress syndrome? It affects some people after earthquakes, plane crashes, storms and other tragedies such as family breakups and leaving home.

Be strong. "You know what has to be done. All you have to do is do it." Arrange it for me so that I can see our three kittens...please. I know you love me. I can feel it. I know what you are going through. It's not easy.

Much love, Joe

P.S. Stay cool. Think clearly. Be strong. Your name is Shelley E. Charalambous not Ingrid J. Jongkind. Read it again!

(Author's note: Ingrid is the name of a woman associated with the sex-for-drugs scandal. Here, the former doctor emphasizes his contempt by combining the name with that of Shelley's mother.)

If you ever have a problem envision it as a "speed bump rather than a roadblock" for otherwise you will feel overwhelmed and confused.

You once believed that love has a beginning but never ends for, if it does, it wasn't love in the first place but something else...dummy...let them come.

The following letter to his children arrived via the doctor's friend, Gail Pikker:

Oct. 7/93

Dear Gail,

I have some birthday messages for the children.

Your friend always, Joe.

Dear Allison*,

You are daddy's schoolgirl. You know that I love all my children...but how much?! My love for you, Rebecca* and George* is infinite in depth, height and breadth and transcends time, space and even death. I want you to love your mother, father, sister and brother like this for only if your affection can exist in at least these six dimensions will you be able to have a bond that will allow forgiveness

347

for any physical, emotional or material loss that you may suffer due to their inadvertent actions or deeds.

Forgiveness, empathy and communication are the keys to maintaining a family unit. "Love is the glue."

You will always be my punch bowl baby.

Love Dad.

Dear George,

You are the world's greatest bird hunter and I always enjoyed hunting with you. You must learn that there are three kinds of men in the world:

1. Men that observe others making mistakes and learn from this.

2. Men that make their own mistakes and learn from these.

3. Men that keep making the same mistakes over and over and never learn.

Most of us are in the second category but you must strive to be in the first for otherwise you will end up re-inventing the wheel, the pulley, the inclined plane, the lever, calculus and much more. Why reinvent them when you can build on others experience?!

You are a fabulous child and you will be a GREAT man,

Love Dad.

Dear Rebecca,

I am certain that you are the worlds most beautiful two year old. You remind me of a lion cub. I think of you constantly and wonder how you must be changing. Above all else I want you to have "class". "Class" for a lady is defined as "grace under pressure". Never be afraid of heights, or spiders, or boogy (sic) men or even death for there are many things that are worse. Whenever you feel "blue" remember that things are never as bad as you think they are and they are never as good as you think they are either. You must learn to stay cool, think clearly and be strong for otherwise you will feel overwhelmed and confused under pressure and you will lose any "class" that you may have. View any problems as speed bumps rather than roadblocks.

You gave me endless joy,

Love Dad.

Gail,

I'm getting some gifts for the children including Rebecca's earrings so that she will match with her mother and sister. I hope that they will be accepted.

Once again...your friend always,
Joe

Jan. 29/95
Dear Allison, George and Rebecca,

I am well and I hope that you are too. I was a little depressed for a while but I feel good now. I miss you and I want to see you. Allison, I was happy to hear that you are doing well in school, that you are in gymnastics and are going to Brownies (is that the chicken place or what?). It's almost time for you to start piano lessons isn't it. George, I'm glad that you are in Beavers and doing gymnastics. When you start school I want you to pay attention and learn as much as you can. Rebecca, are you still chubby? Did you like your Barbie doll? Was she bigger than you? I'm pleased that you are doing gymnastics too.

You must believe that our bonds are indelible. The forces that are pulling us together are much greater than the forces that are holding us apart and it is only a matter of time before we see each other again. Always remember that I did not forsake you and that you were and remain to be first and foremost in my mind. Blood is strong.

I want you to always stick up for each other. When you argue or fight do not blame each other but rather try to find out what went wrong and fix it. This is the Eastern approach. Be sweet, loving and sincere to each other. Remember to sit on the floor in a circle and hold hands.

At the end of each day you must take some time to tell each other and your mother what good things happened that day and what bad things happened. Also, talk about what tomorrow will bring. I'm happy when you are happy and I'm sad when you are sad. I hurt when you hurt.

As I said above, I'm fine, just a little bored. I exercise every day and I'm doing my best to stay healthy. I was eating too many chocolate bars for a while but I'm eating less now. The three of you should tell grandma Betty what you want for Easter. You should give your mother a hug and a kiss every day...I'm sure she needs it.

Love always, your father,
J. Charalambous M.D.

P.S. Happy birthday little Shelley. If you close your eyes and listen you will hear the laughter, they are laughing at you. When are you going to stop being silly? Ask yourself; where was I, where am I and where am I going? I observed your not so stellar performance. I was amused, it was comical, but most of all I was embarassed (sic) for you. At the end I could tell that you realized certain things too.

Overall when you were with me you were treated very well and in fact better than anybody you knew. You said so. Certain constraints come into play when a young woman becomes a wife and a mother. I think it was too much for you. Anyway the truth is that you fell for a line...you got sucked in but you were a willing victim. Sadly, you only thought of yourself. You were going for something that didn't even exist. If you take a plate of shit and you put perfume on it, at the end of the day you still have a plate of shit. You got sucked in and then you lost control—things snowballed on you. Worse than that you let your dark side take over...you reverted to what you knew from your childhood, from your formative years; the deceit, the lies, the infidelity, the cruelty, the moving from place to place, the duplicity, the destructive behavior. Who was it that once told you that, "apples don't fall far from the tree"?

What priority did you give the children? Very little...just dressed them up nicely and faked everything else. I'm not saying that you don't care but what do you really care about? Think and don't be stubborn. I mean to be instructive. Overall you are a good person and you know that I will always care about you...but what have you accomplished and where are you going?

My gift to you is this; listen to only one voice, my voice and you will know what to do. It's as if we are joined by a long elastic band that stretched to the limit but can never be severed. I'm not trying to control you, like I said, I'm being instructive...you don't have to listen just like you never had to stay with me if you didn't want to. Listen to me and stop being silly. Instead of listening to people that know less than you or don't care about you or both why don't you use this little test? Before taking a course of action ask yourself if the likely result will be good for our children or bad or have no effect. Put them first instead of yourself. You can even go back to some decisions you've made and do the test retrospectively. There is a lot of good in you and it will come out eventually. I am being genuine and sincere. I never meant to hurt you. Good luck.

March 5/95

Dear Allison, George and Rebecca

If you say that you miss me then I have to tell you that I miss you more. If you need me, then I need you more. If you love me, I love you more. My love for you is unrequited. Believe that fallen angels can fly again.

Remember that the choices you make will shape your lives forever. When you make friends love them for who and what they are for you are you and they are they and you are not the same. If you cannot accept them as they are and care for them then you cannot be true friends. Friends are like miracles they are few and far between. There are many things that I will say to you in the future but for now I must remain reticent. A few more aphorisms for thought. Beware of people that give you a little and take a lot. Stay close with each other and don't ever let anyone divide you and turn you against each other. If your (sic) sorry say your (sic) sorry. A few acorns fell on Chicken Little's head and he ran around yelling, "the sky is falling, the sky is falling."

I want to know how and what you are doing and especially if you are healthy. Take vitamins every day. You could write to me and send me pictures so I can see how you have changed. I want to know how tall you are and how much you weigh. The longer we are apart the closer we will be when we eventually get together. You have been in my heart since before you were born. Allison and Rebecca, do you want Bubble Angel Barbies? George, what do you want? Do you like Spawn?

Remember to sit on the floor in a circle and hold hands. Give your mother a hug and a kiss every day. I love all my children.

Your father,

J. Charalambous M.D.

Since her husband's trial, Shelley has been working in the food and beverage industry. Her lawyer has told her that her marriage was never legal and could be annulled, but that it would be preferable to end matters with a divorce.

When she moved in with the doctor in 1985, Shelley still had two years to go in high school. She is presently attending college to complete Grade 12 and is looking forward to a career as a counselor.

The police have advised Shelley that she must remain in the witness protection program indefinitely.

Meanwhile, Jacqueline's first efforts to get reacquainted with her daughter were awkward and stilted. Shelley had learned during their almost ten years apart to stifle her emotions. "It was the only way I could survive," she explained. Gradually, however, the walls between them began tumbling down.

The same went for the relationship between Shelley and her sister, but eventually that barrier started falling too. "You're my sister and I'll never leave you again," Shelley promised Shawna. "Ever, ever, ever." Shawna returned home excitedly. "The bond is back," she told her mother.

Both her mother and sister soon realized that Shelley had survived her ordeal better than they could have hoped. Coming from a loving family background had stood her in good stead. A model mother herself, Shelley was doing a superb job of minding the physical and mental health of both herself and her own children, and was working hard to build a future.

During one visit, the sisters were celebrating until the small hours of the next morning, when suddenly they decided to phone their mother. "Mom," blurted Shawna, as Jacqueline awoke to the phone, "listen to this...."

Shelley and Shawna had uncharacteristically each permitted themselves two or three glasses of wine. It was very late and they were somewhat off key, but tears sprang to Jacqueline's eyes as her daughters began strongly on the upbeat of an old, almost forgotten Helen Reddy hit from a long, long time ago. The Joel sisters wouldn't have won a Grammy for their performance that night but, as far as Jacqueline Jongkind was concerned, their rendition of "Delta Dawn" was the best she'd ever heard.

As she cradled the phone, it was music to Jacqueline's ears.